HINDUISM
in Great Britain

HINDUISM
in Great Britain

*The Perpetuation of Religion in
an Alien Cultural Milieu*

EDITED BY

RICHARD BURGHART

Tavistock Publications
London · New York

First published in 1987 by
Tavistock Publications Ltd
11 New Fetter Lane, London EC4P 4EE

Printed in Great Britain at the University Press, Cambridge

British Library Cataloguing in Publication Data

Hinduism in Great Britain: the perpetuation of religion in an alien
cultural milieu.
1. Hinduism———Great Britain———History
I. Burghart, Richard
294.5′0941   BL1168.G72
ISBN 0–422–60910–2

Contents

List of contributors

Rohit Barot is Lecturer in Sociology at the University of Bristol. His doctoral research was on the social organization of the Swaminarayan movement in Britain.

David Bowen is Senior Lecturer in Social and Religious Studies in the Department of Contemporary Studies at Bradford and Ilkley Community College. He has edited *Hinduism in England* and written *The Sathya Sai Baba Community in Bradford*.

Richard Burghart is Lecturer in Asian Anthropology at the School of Oriental and African Studies, University of London. He has edited, with Audrey Cantlie, *Indian Religion*.

Séan Carey was Research Officer in the Department of Social Policy at Bedford and Royal Holloway New College, University of London. His doctoral research was on the Ramakrishna Mission in Great Britain.

Robert Jackson is Senior Lecturer in Arts Education at the University of Warwick. He has edited *Perspectives on World Religions* and *Approaching World Religions* and is co-author, with Dermot Killingley, of *Approaches to Hinduism*.

Helen Kanitkar is Demonstrator and Bibliographer in the Department of Anthropology, School of Oriental and African

Studies, University of London. She edits the *Anthropological Bibliography of South Asia* and is author of *Hindus in Britain* and *The Adult Education Service and Immigrants in Britain*.

Kim Knott is Research Fellow for the Community Religions Project, Department of Theology and Religious Studies, University of Leeds. She has written *My Sweet Lord: the Hare Krishna Movement* and *Hinduism in Leeds*.

Merryle McDonald was formerly a community nursing sister in inner-city London. She is currently completing her doctoral research in social anthropology on child and maternal health among Gujaratis in the London Borough of Newham.

Werner Menski is Lecturer in Hindu and Modern South Asian Law at the School of Oriental and African Studies, University of London. His doctoral research was on role and ritual in the Hindu marriage.

Maureen Michaelson was formerly Lecturer in Anthropology at the University of Manchester. Her doctoral research was on caste, kinship, and marriage among Gujarati traders in Britain.

Donald Taylor is Senior Lecturer in Religious Studies at Middlesex Polytechnic. He is currently completing his doctoral research in social anthropology on Tamil temples and social organization in Britain. His first doctorate was in theology from the University of Oxford.

Acknowledgements

This volume began as a seminar convened at the School of Oriental and African Studies, London, during the autumn term of 1983. I am grateful to the Centre of South Asian Studies at the School for hosting the seminar and for providing secretarial assistance in preparing the papers for publication. Recognition and thanks are also due to Fiona Stewart who took on all the editorial chores during my absence from London in 1984–85. One of the papers included in this volume — 'The Indianization of the Hare Krishna Movement in Britain' — was previously published in a somewhat different version in *New Community* 10(3), 1983. I am grateful to the Editor of *New Community* for her permission to reproduce a modified version of the earlier article in the present volume.

Richard Burghart, 1986

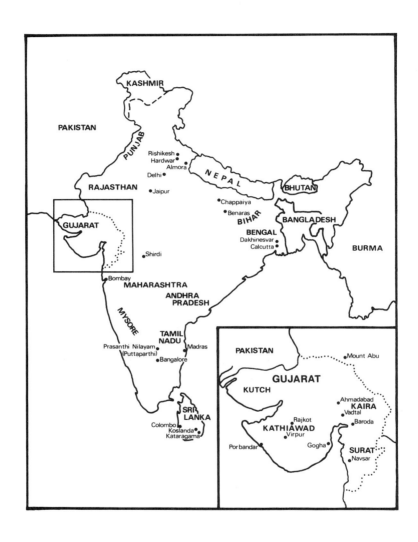

Introduction: The diffusion of Hinduism to Great Britain

Richard Burghart

In 1902 Madho Singh, Maharaja of Jaipur, was invited to London to attend the coronation of Edward VII. It was fitting that Madho Singh attend the ceremony, for Edward was Emperor of India and the Jaipur ruler owed him allegiance. Yet the Hindu king was filled with apprehension at the prospect of crossing the ocean and accepting British hospitality. To him, Great Britain was a remote, barbarous country, situated in the northwestern sector of the inauspicious 'Black Sea'. Madho Singh could not sustain his sacred person in such an alien environment. And such a journey would put his subjects at risk, for in the course of his coronation the people of Jaipur had been ritually constituted within the body of the king. Were Madho Singh to become personally defiled by his journey, his land and people would also become defiled. Thus Madho Singh faced a dilemma. He could travel to Great Britain, but only on condition that he did not leave India. He eventually found a way round his problem by chartering a ship, the S.S. Olympia, having the vessel cleansed throughout and ritually consecrated by the royal priest of Jaipur. Rice, dried fruit, vegetables, and water were brought on board, together with cows and fodder so that fresh milk could be supplied daily. Earth from the Sacred Land of the Hindus (*bhāratavarṣa*) and water from the Ganges were put in storage so that he could perform his daily ablutions and purify his alien surroundings. In this auspicious environment Madho Singh was safely conveyed to Britain.

In the jargon of the modern space age Madho Singh's ritually constituted vessel would be called a life-support system. This analogy is not inappropriate, for highly elaborate cosmological notions underlay Madho Singh's journey, the most central of which was that Great Britain — together with other European and North American countries — were 'islands' which lay outside the universe. This Hindu concept of universe appears strange to Western minds because it is exclusive in orientation. For Europeans, whatever exists is part of the universe; but for Madho Singh the universe was a materialization of Brahma. Impure and unruly beings are not part of Brahma's order; they are therefore not part of the universe. Persons with spiritual insight see the ritual universe as an auspicious sphere of light beyond which lie inauspicious areas of darkness inhabited by beings who are impure, uncivilized, ignorant, and dull. The centre of the Hindu universe is Brahma's abode and the periphery is formed by gods who defend the materialization in time and space of Brahma. Beyond the periphery lies the Black Sea, and the small island of Vilayat where live a race of barbarians who call themselves Englishmen. The English eat the flesh of Mother Cow, and have no 'social order' (that is to say, no caste). It should come as no surprise that Madho Singh had to take considerable precautions in attending the coronation of his Emperor.

In spite of the ritual danger of quitting the universe, Madho Singh was not the first Hindu to venture abroad. Indeed, Hindu migration to ritually unfit places had been going on for nearly 2,000 years before he set out from Bombay: such migration is as old as Hinduism itself. There are two patterns: either the migrants settled abroad, in which case they ritually consecrated the alien land so that it became part of the auspicious universe, or they did not settle abroad, in which case they still looked to India as their homeland. An example of the first pattern is the spread of Indic civilization across southeast Asia (Coedès 1968). The archaeological evidence shows that from the fifth century AD these places had been universalized by Brahmans. The evidence is too patchy to reveal how this religious diffusion took place. Some historians suggest that local rulers sent for Brahmans from India to consecrate their kingdoms; others claim that Hindu warriors from southern India conquered these territories; still others say that Hindu traders settled in mercantile outposts in foreign lands from where they spread their religion. Whatever the process of migration and religious diffusion may have been, the consequence of this settlement was the ritual consecration of these places. Alien tribal and lineage relations were construed in terms of caste; royal temples were built at the centre and along the periphery of the kingdoms; and Brahmans were called from India to perform temple and life-cycle rituals. Like Madho Singh's boat, these places became ritually fit universes of social relations, and the inhabitants began to consider their land as part of the Hindu universe. Not all Hindus overseas, however, seem to have followed this pattern. Before the early twentieth century Gujarati traders working on the east coast of Africa did not do so (Mangat 1969, Gregory 1971). These castes of traders travelled outside the Indian subcontinent for years at a time, but kept their families and ancestral deities in their natal villages in western India. Marriages were contracted there; life-cycle rituals were performed there; and at the end of their working lives they returned to Gujarat from where they dispatched their sons to succeed them in business overseas. These alien places did not become their country. While they lived abroad, India remained the ancestral home to which there was always the thought of return.

Seen in the light of nearly two millennia of migration by Hindu peoples, Madho Singh's journey was not a novel experience; yet one aspect of his voyage was new to the nineteenth century. Madho Singh had to leave the Hindu universe in order to pay homage to his Emperor. The colonialization of Africa, Asia, and the Americas by European powers, and the extension of the market economy during this period re-ordered politico-economic relations on a global scale. The people of the Indian subcontinent, who had previously seen their homeland as the centre of the world, now had to accommodate themselves to the fact that their country had become a peripheral region providing a base for the production of primary resources, a market for the sale of British manufactured goods, and a source of labour for other peripheral regions of the world. Tamils from southeastern India worked as indentured labourers in Sri Lanka, Burma, and Malaya. Biharis from north-central India worked on the plantations of Mauritius and Guiana. Punjabis from northwestern India took up jobs as craftsmen and construction workers in East Africa; and Gujaratis from western India travelled to eastern and southern Africa where they worked as petty traders and clerks in the colonial administration (Tinker 1974, 1977). The movement of Indian labourers around the periphery of western Europe's sphere of influence was part of the same phenomenon as Madho Singh's extraordinary journey to the nexus of those global relations. London was now India's imperial capital. India had been ruled before by alien and non-Hindu kings, but the centre of the universe had always remained on the Indian subcontinent. Never before had India been made so aware of its peripheral position in the world.

The decentring of the Hindu universe created considerable ambivalence for Hindus, starting a hundred years of intense debate on the relation between religion and politico-economic power. Ordinarily, the seat of imperial authority was situated beside the notional centre of the world — the shrine of the king's tutelary deity. In other words, the royal capital ought to coincide with the zenith of the ritual universe. London, however, was outside the ritual universe; and the British government chose not to construct their imperium in religious terms. There were various partial solutions to this dilemma. Some Indians, like Madho Singh, took London to be outside the ritual universe. This solution, however, divested Hinduism of much of its power; royal rituals became mere form without force and their enactment did not gain a new lease of life until the mid-twentieth century with the advent of tourism and the marketing of 'traditional India' to the western and Indian middle classes. Other Hindus ritualized the British Raj. For example, one

Indian panegyrist, Raja Baldeva Singh, reworked the saying 'the sun never sets on the British empire' in a thoroughly Hindu manner. 'Maharani Viktoriya' was cast in the form of the universal monarch whose reign extends in all 10 directions and who performs the work of the gods of the 10 directions. 'Because she brought gas lanterns and match sticks to India, she does the work of Agni, god of fire, who guards the southeast; because she brought justice to India and put an end to the law of the jungle, she does the work of Dharma Raja, god of justice, who guards the south'; and so on. Other Indians abandoned Hinduism and converted either individually or *en masse* to the Christian dharma of Empress Victoria. Finally, some religious leaders reinterpreted Hinduism in the light of Western values and found that their own faith was also a source of reason and justice capable of bringing about the uplift of Indian people. For such reformers the Hinduism of Madho Singh, with its ritual prohibitions and 'idolatry', was a superstitious corruption of the scientific truths of Vedism. Some of these leaders, such as Swami Dayanand who founded the Arya Samaj, remained in India where they sought to reform Hinduism and to reconvert Indian Christians. Others travelled to Europe and North America, without fear of the Black Sea, in order to speak to Westerners and Indians from the politico-economic centre of the world. Rammohun Roy and Dvarakanath Tagore of the Brahma Sabha (later Brahmo Samaj) undertook lecture tours of England as early as the 1830s and 1840s and Swami Vivekanand of the Ramakrishna Mission spoke in 1893 at the Parliament of World Religions organized by the Unitarian Church at Chicago. Similarly Swami Yoganand travelled to Boston to address the International Congress of Religious Liberals in 1920. For these religious leaders the fact that Great Britain or America was an alien cultural milieu was not as significant as the fact that the West was the imperial centre of the world. The message of these Hindu reformers took into account the material prosperity of the West, but it also asserted that India was still the home of those spiritual values that are the ultimate source of material benefit. The awakening of the West to Hindu spiritual values was, therefore, a way of reclaiming India's pre-eminence in the world, of re-centring the universe within the Indian subcontinent.

6 Hinduism in Great Britain

During the early twentieth century Hinduism was propagated in Great Britain either by modern Indian religious movements which had reinterpreted Hinduism in the light of Western values or by Western Orientalist movements, such as the Theosophical Society, which sought some rapprochement with Indian spiritualism. The aims and methods of these movements were diffused by lectures and pamphlets, the audiences were largely British, and the meetings took place in rented halls or in the homes of benefactors. Relatively few Indians then lived in Britain. Accurate census data are not available for this period, but an estimate for 1945 does not exceed 7,000 (Tinker 1977: 167). This figure includes Sikhs and Muslims as well as Hindus, so the actual number of Hindus would have been considerably less than 7,000. Of this number there was a large proportion of Bengalis and Punjabis and a lesser proportion of Gujaratis, Tamils, Maharashtrians, and Hindi speakers. Although it is likely that Hindu families reserved a place in their homes for the worship of deities, there is no evidence that a public temple for Hindus existed in Britain at this time. Apart from occasional tours by Hindu holy men, the only active Hindu religious presence was the Ramakrishna Mission led by the Bengali monk Swami Avyaktananda, who arrived in Britain in 1934. A mission centre was established in London the following year. Swami Avyaktananda travelled widely throughout Britain and Europe, preaching a personal interpretation of Vedanta which was informed by a marxist reading of the future course of world history (Carey 1980). Swami Avyaktananda's marxism eventually alarmed both his British benefactors and the central office of the mission at Calcutta, and led to his break with the Mission in 1948. Alleging that the Ramakrishna Mission had lost sight of the original message of Vivekananda, Swami Avyaktananda left London for Bath where he founded the Vedanta Society. Mission headquarters in India dispatched a replacement, Swami Ghananand, who brought the activities of the British society more firmly within the orbit of the Calcutta office. The London mission continued to attract devotees and benefactors, including a bequest from an Englishman which enabled the mission to buy a property and establish a monastic community in Britain. This community, founded in 1949 and located in Muswell Hill in north London, provided the first public place of worship for Hindus in Britain.

After the Second World War the availability of work for both professional people and unskilled labourers and an open system of immigration to Britain from Commonwealth countries contributed to an influx of migrants from India. Some were Indian students who had received training in medicine, law, accounting, and other professions and elected to establish their careers in Britain (Kanitkar 1972b). Most were Punjabis. There were also some Gujaratis, whose homelands in northwestern India had been divided in the British partition of India and Pakistan. The Punjabi migrants, who included Hindus, Muslims, and Sikhs, settled in manufacturing towns where they worked in transport and manufacturing industries. Their arrival in Britain took the form of chain migration: prospective migrants in India learned of employment opportunities and accommodation from relatives and former neighbours who were working in Britain (Desai 1963, Tambs-Lyche 1980b). Thus places of emigration were often highly localized in particular districts of the Punjab and Gujarat, and places of immigration in Britain were also highly localized (Winchester 1974). Certain towns or areas acquired a reputation for being Punjabi (e.g. Southall, west London, and the Leeds Road area of Bradford); or as Gujarati areas (e.g. Harrow and Hendon in northwest London). The original intention of many of these immigrants was to remain in Britain for a limited period of their working lives. Immigrants still considered themselves part of their joint family in India, regularly sending home remittances to support their kin. By the end of the 1950s there were approximately 70,000 Indians (not all of whom, of course, were Hindus) in Britain. Many were adult men making some contribution to the income of the family in India; thus the manufacturing towns of Britain became extensions of the Indian village economy.

The 1962 Commonwealth Immigration Act restricted the entry of Asians who did not hold British passports; in anticipation of this Act immigration increased fourfold in the two years preceding its enactment. Immigration controls were tightened even further in 1968, with the passage of another Common-wealth Immigration Act in which a grandparental clause was introduced as a condition of free entry. The effect of this was to disenfranchize East African Indians holding British passports of their right of entry, substituting instead a voucher system which limited the number of British passport holders who could be admitted in any one year. The voucher system proved to be an inadequate means of containing immigration, for at that time East African governments had begun to put into effect their policies of 'Africanization' or 'nationalization'. Administrative posts were given in preference to Africans, and self-employed Asians began to suffer from intimidation and interference in the management of their companies. Africanization reached its con-clusion in Uganda when, in 1972, General Idi Amin ordered all South Asians holding British passports to quit the country with-in three months, taking with them no more than £50. The majority of Indians came to Britain, where they were temporarily accommodated in refugee centres and eventually settled in localities with South Asian communities. Nearly all the refugees were Gujarati speaking. Their arrival in places such as Leicester, Bolton, Birmingham, Manchester, Coventry, and the boroughs of Harrow, Brent, Barnet, and Newham in London altered the distribution of Indians by ethnic group. Of approximately 307,000 Hindus living in Britain in 1977, 70 per cent were Gujarati in origin; 15 per cent Punjabi; and the remaining 15 per cent came from other regions of India, such as Bengal, Tamil Nadu, Maharashtra, Bihar and Uttar Pradesh, and from Sri Lanka (Knott 1982:16). With the curtailment of immigration to Britain, the Africanization of East Africa, and the regulation of travel to India by British citizens of Indian origin in 1984, the free movement of Hindus within the old imperial order came to an end. Indians in Britain may be related by ties of kinship, caste, regional culture, and faith to India, but for better or worse their prospects are increasingly bound up with the country in which they are settled.

The arrival of Hindu migrants and refugees contributed greatly to the establishment of Hindu religious institutions in Britain. Hitherto Hinduism had been propagated by sectarian leaders seeking British and Indian converts. Although religious leaders, such as the representatives of the Hare Krishnas, continued to arrive in Britain, by the 1960s there were large enough numbers of Hindu laymen living in any one city for them to begin to organize themselves for religious purposes. Bowen, in this volume, has documented this demographic shift in the city of Bradford, relating the arrival of Indian immigrants to the proliferation of caste, sectarian, and cultural associations. Some of the caste and cultural associations were the vehicles of local 'big men' who gained a personal reputation by organizing religious, charitable, and cultural 'functions' for the benefit of the community (Desai 1963, Tambs-Lyche 1980b). Other religious associations were more sectarian in orientation, starting as small congregations in the homes of lay devotees, and expanding to include like-minded devotees from outside the family. The arrival in Britain of Hindu women was a significant factor. Although Hinduism's privileged spokesmen are almost invariably Brahman and ascetic men, women take the more active role among the laity in the perpetuation of religious life. Before the mid-1960s the immigration of men was approximately double that of women. By the mid-1960s the sex ratio had evened out, and by the late 1960s women were arriving in considerably greater numbers than men (Tinker 1977:169). The demographic change from a male adult Hindu population to an almost normal distribution of sexes and age groups correlates with the formation of religious associations. Throughout the 1960s devotional groups began to meet in homes, serving in a sense as congregations without temples. During this period many temple trusts were formed in which Hindus pooled their resources with a view to the eventual purchase of a property and the foundation of a temple. In 1969 the first such Hindu temple, established by laymen, was consecrated in Leicester. Shortly thereafter registered temples were established in London, Coventry, Leeds, Bradford, and other cities and towns of Britain. There are now over a hundred Hindu temples in the United Kingdom, and the number is still increasing.

The fact that Hindu religious institutions have taken root in

Britain gives rise to numerous questions about the nature of Hinduism. How does a religion, which is often said to be a 'way of life', perpetuate itself in an alien cultural milieu? To what extent are Hindus in Britain affected by religious issues and disputes centred on South Asia? How does a religion that is so closely bound up with a people and their culture attract a substantial following among non-Indians? In what ways has Hinduism been reinterpreted in the light of Western values and institutions and how are these reinterpretations authenticated today? So framed, these questions are of interest to sociologists of religion, yet they are not very far removed from the pre-occupations of Hindus themselves who are also concerned, but for very different reasons, about the perpetuation of their way of life in Britain (see, for example, Pocock 1976 and V.P. Kanitkar 1979). Both the social and natural environment are seen as inhospitable; the problem of the transmission of Hinduism to subsequent generations is clearly recognized; and the 'natural home' of Hinduism is still thought to be the Indian subcontinent. In brief, both for Hindus themselves and for observers of Hinduism, the preservation of religious life in Britain raises complex issues about the relation between religion, culture, and territory in Hindu society.

The purpose of this volume is to consider some of these issues in the light of particular field studies carried out in Britain. Both Michaelson and McDonald focus on the Hindu family and argue for its centrality in the perpetuation of Hinduism. Michaelson considers the way in which the transcendental preoccupations of Hindus are expressed in possession cults and devotional congregations. Whereas the deities found in large public temples have been installed there by acts of public subscription, the deities who figure in possession cults are thought to have entered the home by acts of divine grace, not of human will, suggesting thereby the primacy of the family in any investigation of Hindu religiosity. By contrast, McDonald focuses on pragmatic Hinduism, in particular, the rituals and vows by which Gujarati women manage and celebrate pregnancy and childbirth. Here Brahman priests are unnecessary, for the rituals are organized and conducted by the women of the household, who in certain ritual contexts may even become icons of the Mother Goddess.

Foreknowledge of the position of Brahmans in Hindu society predisposes some scholars to define Hinduism in terms of the Brahmanical tradition, but this is not the sole normative Hindu tradition. In her comparison of local family traditions and Brahmanical procedures with reference to the life-cycle rituals of pregnancy and childbirth, McDonald notes some overlap in ritual form, but each tradition has its own concerns and its separate basis of authority. Family traditions are linked to pragmatic concerns and are legitimated with reference to ancestral authority; the Brahmanical tradition avows transcendental preoccupations and is legitimated with reference to the timeless Brahma. As might be expected, the rules of inheritance, arranged marriages, and migration chains which perpetuate Hindu families and lineages in Britain also serve to perpetuate domestic religious traditions. The Brahmanical tradition, however, has been less readily transplanted, for its presence depends upon specific regional and caste associations calling Brahmans from the Indian subcontinent and arranging for their maintenance in Britain. Menski, in his paper, focuses also on the relation between Brahmanical and local traditions, but to this equation he adds the British legal tradition. Dissatisfied with the civil marriage in which bride and groom make a contract *vis-à-vis* the state, Hindus regard the registry marriage as a 'formality' or possibly a betrothal, but not as the 'real' marriage, which remains the traditional Hindu one. This Hindu ritual is not a rigid code, but a mixture of Brahmanical and customary family forms negotiated by the priest and his clients at the time of the ceremony. By integrating the civil ceremony within a Hindu ritual scheme, Hindus in Britain have created a pluralistic legal situation. This pluralism, however, is devoid of legality from the point of view of the state.

Still salient in the British context are endogamous castes which notionally at least derive their identity from the performance of a traditional duty — be it the priesthood, commerce, or whatever. Formerly in south Asia the social organization of these duties created a complex division of labour such that each caste depended upon the other castes' fulfilment of their duties. Of this system of mutual interdependence only the ritual relation of Brahman priest and client remains in force in Britain. Castes have survived, but not the 'system'. In the perpetuation of the identity of such systemless castes a reputation for religious piety and charitable activities has become important. Such activities are organized by regional or national caste associations and may be based at a temple, which, as the fixed abode of a deity, gives the caste a ritual centre and makes its charitable activities the object of that deity's grace. The service to society and service to a deity are merged in a single institutional framework. Bowen has described how certain Gujarati castes in Bradford have organized themselves in this way: purchasing a property, establishing a temple, and making arrangements for a priest to carry out the daily service. Not all castes, however, manage their own temples. Some establish instead a close relationship with a sect and acquire a ritual identity as lay devotees and disciples. Such is the case of the Leva Kanbi Patels, a Gujarati caste described by Barot, who are followers of the Swaminarayan sect. Barot looks at how segmentation has occurred within the sect and considers the implications of such segmentation for the corporate nature of the caste in Britain. The fact that such conflicts antedate the arrival of the Leva Kanbi Patels in this country suggests that the caste members are able to reproduce their conditions of life in sufficient measure that pre-migrant patterns of conflict retain their meaning in what is otherwise an alien environment.

If the Brahmanical tradition is only tenuously established in the United Kingdom, then who are the official spokesmen for Hinduism? The advocacy role is played largely by ascetics. Since the early nineteenth century many modern Hindu sects have centred themselves on the Indian subcontinent, from where they have addressed the 'materialistic' West. These modern sects have taken to the global arena, for they see their world-wide activities as proof of the universality of the Hindu spiritual message. Taylor has contributed two papers on the formation of religious movements in Britain. In one he recounts events leading to the foundation of a Saivite ashram in rural Wales and describes the global context in which the founder of the monastic community sees his spiritual retreat. Taylor's other paper considers the different bases of authority in the Sathya Sai Baba movement. The movement grew rapidly in Britain, fed by accounts of the miraculous powers of Sathya Sai Baba. But as membership and donations increased, the necessity of a centralized administration imposed itself, even though, ideologically speaking, the administration was superfluous. Of what use is an annual report sent by the UK Council to the World Council headed by the Sathya Sai Baba when the sectarian founder, by virtue of his omniscience, is aware of the content of the report long before it is sent to India? In his two papers Carey focusses on the benefactors and followers of Hindu sects in Britain. In his study of ISKCON he looks at the sect in the aftermath of the 1960s. The Hare Krishnas had from the start gained considerable notoriety as a spiritual haven of pop stars, hippies, and disaffected youth; but as that generational ethos subsided, increasing support for the movement came in the 1970s from Indian Hindus in Britain who took to visiting their temples, providing thereby a lay community within which the sect could thrive. In his other paper Carey follows European recruits to the Ramakrishna Mission through the stages of their initiation, describing the meaning that a Hindu redemptive tradition has for its European converts.

The presence of Hindus in Britain has contributed in various ways to the redefinition of Hinduism. Jackson examines the content of religious education courses in county school curricula and notes the changing conception of Hinduism as a result of certain debates in the philosophy of education as well as the influence of immigrant Hindus. Knott looks at how Hindus themselves have reinterpreted their religious procedures. Her material comes from Leeds, where Gujarati and Punjabi Hindus pooled their resources and established a temple in which they could worship in common. Each regional group, however, preferred its own regionally specific procedures of worship. In order that the temple might thrive, attracting as large a community as possible, the two groups found themselves obliged to standardize their procedures of worship. The outcome was a kind of trans-ethnic Hinduism responsive to the constraints of the British environment; somewhat different from its constituent regional traditions yet still recognizably 'traditional', reflecting the perception by local Hindus of the continuity of their religious life in an alien cultural milieu. Do such changes and reinterpretations betoken the existence of what might be called 'British Hinduism'? The question cannot be so neatly put because the immediate forebears of Hindus in Britain today were previously subjects of the British Raj in south Asia. Hence the British context became salient long before Hindus actually arrived in Britain. In this more extensive context, though, certain changes do appear to have occurred. A commonplace statement of Hindu promotional literature as well as of the sociology of religion is that Hinduism is an 'ethnic religion'. Yet the historial material from the last several centuries and the evidence presented by the contributors to this volume suggests that it is only in an alien cultural milieu that Hinduism has become so. This, at least, is the conclusion to which I am led in the final chapter of this volume.

1

The evolution of Gujarati Hindu organizations in Bradford

David Bowen

Gujarati Hindu organizations in Bradford have developed through three phases, conditioned by the growth in numbers and diversity of the Gujarati population in the city since the 1940s. This development can be seen as evolutionary, responding both to internal cultural preferences and to external political and economic constraints. First came the establishment of unity among all the Gujaratis of Bradford; second, the organization of diverse religious fellowships and the formation of associations for the promotion of particular caste interests; and third, the re-establishment of unity among the Gujarati population by the creation of an all-embracing structure in which diverse interests are accommodated. Taken together, the phases entail a dialectic between homogeneity and heterogeneity, unity and diversity.

THE ESTABLISHMENT OF HOMOGENEITY

There were fewer than 300 Gujarati Hindus living in Bradford when their first community organization was founded on 15 August 1957. The minute book of the Bhartiya Mandal, or Indian Association, reveals that its original constitution was framed at that meeting and was later revised and embellished. The initiative for this development came from a group of about 15 men, who represented families belonging to several different castes. It was not, as has been found elsewhere (Tambs-Lyche 1980b), the accomplishment of one influential person seeking to establish a vehicle for personal social service and institutional control. It was a community effort which by the end of 1958 brought together members from approximately 125 households, mostly from the larger Gujarati castes of Bradford, such as the Prajapatis, Patidars, Kanbi Patels, and Mochis (see below). Less numerous castes were also represented, including one Brahman family. The roll of subscribers in the minute-book shows that there were no Punjabi or other non-Gujarati members in spite of the implication in the association's name that it was an all-embracing Indian organization. It is of interest to note, however, that at least three Gujarati Muslim households were represented, uniting with Gujarati Hindus on the basis of their regional culture.

The objective of the founders of the Bhartiya Mandal was the promotion of co-operation among Gujaratis so that members of this ethnic community might find mutual support in an alien environment. The association also set out to organize social, cultural, and religious events in which the identity of the participants might be affirmed. In 1959 it bought premises for this purpose in Sawrey Place, Bradford 5, a neighbourhood which had once been the centre of Polish, Ukrainian, and Russian migration to Bradford, and subsequently witnessed the first South Asian settlements in the city (Dahya 1974:84). The period between August 1957 and December 1959 was, therefore, a time of formative community activity among Gujaratis. Hindu festivals were celebrated. Gujarati language classes for children were held in the association's own premises. Variety programmes were organized at the small theatre in Bradford's Central Library, adjacent to the area of Gujarati settlement; and Indian film shows were sponsored, cinemas being hired for such occasions.[1]

In 1966 a second Hindu organization, the Hindu Swayamsevak Sangh (literally, the Hindu Self-help Union) was formed in

Bradford. The Swayamsevak Sangh is an all-Indian association with headquarters in different regions of the Indian subcontinent and in East Africa. Its British headquarters are at 56 Rokesley Avenue in London. The association is active among young people, especially males. In India its activities sometimes have strong political overtones, but amongst Gujaratis in East Africa and in the United Kingdom the political significance has been neutralized (Mackie 1979). The Bradford Swayamsevak Sangh's activities are directed towards character formation, with training in self-reliance and team effort. Self-discipline is also emphasized, and yoga is taught. Traditional Indian games are played, and other sports activities which require a minimum of manufactured equipment. Although local leaders endeavour to impart a sense of moral rectitude to the young, religious practice itself is not central to their activities in Bradford. Instead, the focus is on the values of Hindu civilization as they are upheld in conditions of migration. At first, many of its activities were held in private homes, rented buildings, or school halls hired from the local authority. The Sangh also acquired a substantial library of Indian books. By 1980 it was said to have approximately 350 members, varying in age and in degree of commitment; and in 1982 the Sangh's own headquarters, called Madhava Sadan, was officially opened at 52 Rugby Place, Bradford 7. In August 1984 a Sangh assembly, attracting young Hindus from all over the world, was held in Bradford. The three-day event was organized by the United Kingdom association and focused on the Indian cultural and moral heritage, on physical discipline in Indian sports, and on inner discipline in ethical achievement. On one of the days, which was open to the public, cultural exhibitions were set up and Indian martial arts and yoga techniques were demonstrated.

THE EMERGENCE OF DEVOTIONAL CONGREGATIONS

The initial impulse of the Bradford Gujaratis had been to form an organization which would fulfil a wide range of social and cultural needs, rather than to establish a temple. For the members of both the Bhartiya Mandal and the Hindu Swayamsevak

Sangh the celebration of festivals and other specifically religious events took place within the total web of community affairs. This is in marked contrast to the other South Asian religious groups in the city, the Muslims and Sikhs, who upon settlement rapidly made plans for the establishment of places of worship. In the case of the Muslims the importance of congregational prayer, especially on Fridays and with particular diligence during the month of Ramadan, was a powerful incentive to establish a place of collective worship. Amongst the Sikhs the central importance of congregational worship (*sangat*) impels them to gather together as a community in a way which is without parallel in ordinary Hindu practice. In Hinduism the importance of personal or family-based devotion diminishes the significance of congregational gatherings and hence limits the need for public temples. From the early days of Indian settlement in Bradford individual Hindus and Hindu households were content to worship in their homes. This Bradford chronology appears typical of other places of south Asian settlement in the United Kingdom, where Muslims built their mosques and Sikhs their gurudwaras well before Hindus began to establish registered public temples.

The formation of Hindu congregations was not simply a matter of cultural preference. Demographic factors were also important. It was not until the late 1960s that the Gujarati Hindu population increased notably in Bradford. Although detailed census data are not available, there were an estimated 21,000 immigrants from New Commonwealth countries living in Bradford in 1970 (Dahya 1974:90). It is not an implausible assumption that 3,000 of these immigrants were Hindu; and since local settlement patterns suggest a higher figure than the national 70 per cent for the proportion of Gujaratis in the Hindu population of Bradford, one might hazard a guess that approximately 2,300 Gujarati Hindus lived in Bradford in 1970. With this growth in numbers, concentrated for the most part in one area of the city, groups of kin and neighbours, friends and colleagues began to associate occasionally for religious purposes.

One informal group of like-minded kin and near neighbours began to organize themselves more formally for worship in

August 1967. A Gujarati householder, living in Bradford 7, turned the cellar of his small terraced home into a semi-public shrine where he, his family, and a cluster of devotees regularly worshipped Jalaram Bapa. Jalaram was a nineteenth-century Gujarati saint renowned for the miracles he worked and for his devotion to Lord Ram, a Hindu god worshipped in India as the seventh incarnation of Vishnu but often thought of by his devotees as a form of the Supreme Soul itself (Rajdev 1966; see also Michaelson below). The family who provided Jalaram with a shrine in Bradford are Prajapatis, a caste traditionally associated with pottery and, more recently, joinery. Although respect for Jalaram is evident in all sections of the Gujarati community in Bradford, the active membership of the Bradford Shri Jalaram Shakti Mandal is recruited for the most part from within the kin network of the Prajapati who runs the shrine. The group meets every Saturday evening to sing devotional hymns and offer prayers.

More than two years after the formation of the Shri Jalaram Shakti Mandal another devotional circle was formed among the Gujarati Hindus of Bradford. In February 1970, in a flat occupied by a family of Patels in Manchester Road, Bradford 5, a meeting of Sathya Sai Baba devotees took place. From this meeting a weekly congregation, or *satsaṅg*, was instituted. The weekly meetings are semi-formal, beginning with the singing of hymns and culminating in the celebration of *ārtī*, a brief act of worship in which light, incense, and flowers are ritually waved in front of the image of one's lord (see Knott, below). In this case *ārtī* is performed in honour of Sri Sathya Sai Baba, a charismatic Hindu leader and teacher who lives and works in the south Indian state of Andhra Pradesh (Laing and Mason 1982; Kasturi n.d.). Sathya Sai Baba is believed by his followers to be a manifestation or incarnation of god. He is also said to display remarkable paranormal powers. Wherever he travels, he attracts large crowds. The eminent journalist and commentator on Indian life, Kushwant Singh, once remarked: 'Next to Indira Gandhi, he is the biggest draw' (Mangalwadi 1977:147). His magnetism continues to attract an increasing number of devotees from all over the world (see Taylor, below).

The Patel family later moved to a house in Laisteridge Lane. The congregation was relocated in the new house, which is now often called the 'Sai Baba Temple' or the 'Sai Baba Centre'. In this case, the term temple (*mandir*) which can denote either a simple family shrine or a major place of worship, indicates much more than the former, but still does not have the elevated status of a building that has been formally consecrated with Brahmanical ritual and invested with marble images imported from India. In the case of the Sai Baba Temple the term is a title of respect, functionally and pragmatically acquired, and denoting the indisputable role that this house exercises for a section of the Gujarati community in Bradford. The designation 'Sai Centre' has come to be used frequently by those who enthusiastically promote the activities of the local congregation. The significance of this term in the national and international associations to which they are affiliated suggests that the local Sai Baba devotees comprise an organizational unit of quite complex structure.

The family in whose home the Sai Baba Centre is based are Mandhata Patels, but the congregation includes not only Mandhatas (sometimes called Kolis) but also Patidars (Leva Patels) and Prajapatis together with some Sikh and Hindu families of Punjabi origin. Approximately half the families once resided in East African territories. The fellowship is open to individuals of any ethnic background, and has even attracted a number of English affiliates. The membership of the group has fluctuated. From a low ebb in 1979 the fellowship has increased in size and activity from 1981. This was achieved largely by giving full rein to the young men of the congregation. At present (1984) it is normal to find approximately 70 people at the weekly devotional meeting, with many more attending special occasions and festivals. The group is quite aware of the importance of its syncretistic message in a religiously plural society (Bowen 1985).

The formation of the Shri Jalaram Shakti Mandal and the Sri Sathya Sai Centre are significant in the history of Gujarati Hindus in Bradford, marking the emergence of devotional fellowships whose activities were organized for religious purposes rather than as part of the cultural life of the overall

Gujarati community, which was the case with the Bhartiya Mandal and Swayamsevak Sangh. Although the worship of Jalaram and Sathya Sai Baba have some points in common, their implications for Gujarati ethnicity vary considerably. In the case of the Shri Jalaram Shakti Mandal, reverence for Jalaram is a well established tradition in Gujarati culture. His image is found in many Gujarati homes, in Gujarat as well as overseas in East Africa and Britain. Jalaram himself was a Gujarati of Lohana caste and his picture takes its place naturally in communal religious observances. Outside the Gujarati community, Jalaram is hardly known, and one can almost infer that a Jalaram devotee is a Gujarati. The same cannot be said of Sathya Sai Baba, who is a Telegu, not a Gujarati. But he does not symbolize Telegu ethnicity, for he claims to be a god. His following is India-wide and increasingly international. In spite of his claim of universal godhead, his cult appears strange to many Gujaratis. Furthermore Sathya Sai Baba is a contemporary guru. His spiritual credentials have not yet stood the test of time.

While attracting an increasingly wide following, Sathya Sai Baba also elicits bitter opposition and cynical rejection from more orthodox Hindus. Thus the formation of the Sathya Sai fellowship in Bradford in 1970 signalled the commitment of some Gujaratis to a form of religious practice that, if not actually heterodox from the perspective of received Gujarati piety, was not totally consistent with it. The religio-cultural activities that this group made available in the city were perceived by many Gujarati Hindus as tangential to their particular ethnic tradition, even if integrally related to the wider Hindu heritage.

THE FORMATION OF CASTE ASSOCIATIONS

At roughly the same time as these devotional groups were formed in Bradford, a number of caste associations were also founded. The first was of the smallest of the significant caste groups in the city, the Mochis. In 1968, 57 Mochi households formed the Kshatriya Sudharak Mandal, the Circle for the Uplift of Kshatriyas. The traditional occupation of Mochis in India was leather-working. Such work ordinarily carries the stigma of untouchability but not in this case because the Mochis crafted only prepared, dressed hides, unlike the even more inferior Chamars who tanned them (Pocock 1972:41). In Bradford some Mochis are cobblers; others sell leather goods, hand-crafted products and gifts; still others work in a variety of retail trades and business enterprises (Chavda 1983). Some of their surnames, like Parmar, Gohil, and Tailor, have become prominent in the city; other names, which are less well known, include Chauhan, Chavda, and Champaneria. The name adopted for their association, the Circle for the Uplift of Kshatriyas, alludes to their claim that Mochis were originally of much higher status than leather-workers, and that they were Kshatriya warriors, who in the social classification of varnas are inferior in rank only to Brahmans. The name of their caste association asserts their newly claimed dignity and reminds their fellow caste members of their collective aim in reforming Mochi identity. The association looks after Mochi interests in Bradford, organizes family gatherings, and runs a cricket club. Its menfolk are particularly active in the Hindu Swayamsevak Sangh.

One of the more common family names among Bradford Gujaratis is Patel. Historically the title of Patel was bestowed, both in the Mughal period and during the British Raj, on officials of various castes who were appointed to the office of headman in local administration. Thus the term Patel does not refer unequivocally to any single caste group. Some Mochi families have the name Patel, as do Kolis (see below) who usually refer to themselves by the honorific, Mandhata Patel. There are, however, two castes in Bradford with whom the term Patel has a close association, the Kanbi Patels, who originate from Surat District in southern Gujarat, and the Patidar Patels, who derive from Charoter, an area roughly coextensive with the administrative district of Kaira in central Gujarat (see Pocock 1972). Both groups were known as agriculturalists and landlords. In 1973 the Patidars of Bradford formed the Patel Samaj, or Patel Society. Although Patidars claim lordship over the land as part of their glorious ancestry, revenue collection and cultivation bear no relation to the contemporary preoccupations of

Bradford Patidars, most of whom are shop-keepers (as are Patidars elsewhere in Britain, see Tambs-Lyche 1980b). The Patel Samaj is not one of the more active caste associations of Bradford. It looks after Patidar interests in the city and organizes one annual event, the public celebration of Navaratri, the 'nine nights festival', which takes place in the autumn. Its members do, however, give considerable support to the Bhartiya Mandal.

The largest Gujarati caste in Bradford, the Prajapatis, formed their organization in March 1975. Prajapatis were traditionally potters, but in Britain they have diversified into carpentry, the building trade, and a variety of other occupations. The most common Prajapati names in Bradford are Mistry and Lad; less common names are Intwala and Prajapati. The impetus behind the formation of the Shree Prajapati Association lay in a country-wide movement of Prajapatis. The first local Prajapati organization in Britain was set up in Coventry in 1974, its inception stimulating the formation of similar associations in other parts of the Midlands and the south of England. The movement spread further, and very soon the initiative to form a national organization of Prajapati societies was taken at Ashton-under-Lyne, where a Gujarati settlement provides a base for caste activity in the Manchester and Oldham area. It was at Ashton in February 1975 that delegates from Prajapati communities in many parts of the northwest of England, the Midlands, Bradford, Luton, and London met to form the Shree Prajapati Association (UK). One month after the establishment of the national office, the Bradford branch was founded. There are now 13 local branches of the national body, each branch being an autonomous unit, but regularly associating with the others and periodically electing national officers. There is no central headquarters as such; the national secretariat is located at the branch from which the national secretary comes during his tenure of office. Annual events organized by the Shree Prajapati Association (UK), but in which the Bradford branch participates fully, include an annual ladies' conference, a sports day, and a variety show. The venue varies from year to year. The national association also publishes a periodical, *Prajapati Sandesh*.

The growth of the Shree Prajapati Association has been dynamic. In the spring of 1980 the Bradford branch acquired a substantial building, a former chapel with considerable potential for community use, in Thornton Lane, Bradford 5. The building is next to an area of dense Gujarati settlement. In addition to a large hall that serves either as a dining room or as a venue for traditional dancing at the annual Navaratri festival, there are many ancillary rooms. Thus from 1980 the association has been well equipped to promote the interests of the Prajapati families of Bradford and to provide a venue for caste-based activities. These include worship at the shrine which was set up upon acquisition of the building. Sporting events are arranged, such as badminton, five-a-side football, cricket, table tennis, darts, and pool and in some cases are played by well established teams. The Prajapatis see themselves, however, as performing a larger role in Bradford than merely promoting their own caste interests. Many of their activities are open to all visitors; and indeed, the leaders of the association are pleased that some Bengali and Punjabi Hindus are also attracted to the events which take place at Thornton Lane. Thus the Prajapatis have facilitated the development of Hindu cultural life within the main concentration of Gujarati settlement on the south side of the city centre (Bowen 1981b:53–4).

Service to the Hindu community as a whole and attempts to refrain from both caste- and sect-based divisiveness are important themes in the self-image of the Bradford Prajapatis.[2] In establishing a permanent temple at their caste headquarters, the Prajapatis sought to avoid all forms of sectarianism, including the veneration of such contemporary gurus as Sathya Sai Baba, by conducting worship according to received notions of Gujarati piety. In August 1983, when the time came to consecrate the Prajapati temple, the association decided to call it the 'Shree Hindu Temple' so that all Hindus might know that they are welcome to worship. Marble images of deities recognized by scriptural authority were brought from India and installed in the temple. Ram and Sita, together with Ram's younger brother Laksman, were given the central place in the temple; but Krishna and Radha, the universal architect Visvakarma, the divine mother Amba Mata, and Siva were also prominently placed. Images of Ganesh and Hanuman are also present. For its highest holy days the Shree Prajapati Association obtains the services of a visiting Brahman priest, but such occasions are rare. For the most part Prajapati laymen care for the sacred images, perform the *ārtī* ceremony and celebrate the annual cycle of festivals. In doing so, the caste sees itself as putting into practice the teachings of the Bhagavad Gita in which the essence of authentic service in the temple is purity of heart. That in turn is taken to mean sincerity and single-mindedness, plus the avoidance of certain sources of ritual pollution, such as the consumption of alcohol on days on which one performs ritual duties at the temple. With these criteria in mind the temple committee of the Prajapati Association draws up a rota of 12 volunteers who serve the ritual and devotional needs of the caste. Responsible lay leadership in religious matters is thus encouraged and dispersed within the caste. The local officers of the Shree Prajapati Association see this as a natural outgrowth of their settlement in Britain. It is said that until 1975 there were hardly any priests accessible to the Gujarati community. Local Hindus became accustomed to performing their own rites. Even when marriages were celebrated, members of the families concerned had to play the part of the priest. People did not like this, but they got used to it. Now families are likely to make sure that they obtain the services of a priest for a wedding, but otherwise the Prajapatis appear to flourish in almost every other way under a non-specialist religious leadership.

In addition to the Kshatriya Sudharak Mandal, the Patel Samaj, and the Shree Prajapati Association one might also mention the Mandhata Patels. Their honorific self-designation associates them with the name of a distinguished mythical king whose prowess is recorded in Hindu scriptural mythology, the Puranas. The Mandhata Patels originally came from an area of Surat district (Gujarat), just south of Navsari. Others sometimes refer to them as Kolis, a term widely used in western India for low caste, unskilled agricultural workers. The term has somewhat negative connotations and is so general in application that, of itself, it does not convey an accurate identity (Pocock 1972:

30,53,57,62). Although Mandhata Patels acknowledge the Koli designation, they prefer to use the honorific and more specific term 'Mandhata' to identify themselves. In Bradford there are only 33 families of this caste, the major areas of Mandhata settlement being in Leicester and London. The Bradford members of the caste are not formally organized into a local caste association; they are, however, connected with the United Kingdom association of Mandhata Patels.

It is clear that the establishment and perpetuation of any Hindu association, not least one which is caste based, must fulfil certain socio-cultural needs of its members. The increase in the Gujarati population throughout the 1970s provided the Gujarati community with sufficient resources and numbers to organize themselves into specific caste associations. Given the fact that many of the aspects of the traditional caste system in India, such as the customary occupational duty and the complex exchange of services, have not survived in the modern urban British context, one might ask why caste associations have formed at all in Bradford. A likely reason is that castes are still endogamous social units and that caste associations are built out of the networks within which marriages are arranged. The Bradford Gujaratis, however, do not explain the growth of caste associations in this way. Instead the rationale is seen emphatically in terms of the need to maintain the identity and the unity of the caste in an alien environment. The education of Gujarati youth in their cultural heritage, the provision of adequate and appropriate facilities for religious observances – these are seen as the subsidiary factors which moved them to establish caste associations.

THE RE-ESTABLISHMENT OF HOMOGENEITY

At the time of the inception of the Bhartiya Mandal in 1957 there was unity and harmony among Bradford Gujaratis which is reflected in the minutes of the occasion. Such an ethos is also apparent in Desai's glowing account of what he took to be the foundation of the first Gujarati cultural association in Bradford in 1959 (1963:88–91). Clearly that harmony became more difficult to maintain as the community increased in size throughout the 1970s. The extent of the demographic change can only be estimated. At the national level most of the Indian immigrants and refugees in the 1970s were Gujarati and most of these Gujaratis were Hindu (Smith 1976:12; Michaelson 1979:351). From an estimated Gujarati Hindu population of 2,300 in Bradford in 1970, numbers probably reached 6,000 by 1981. This calculation is based on an analysis of the 1981 census returns (Bowen 1985) and confirmed by statistical research on electoral registers (Ram 1984:66). As caste and sectarian diversity became manifest within the community, so the Bhartiya Mandal began to decline. This decline was not only a function of Gujarati resources being directed more particularly to the development of their caste associations and sectarian congregations; it was also due to the physical decline of the premises at Sawrey Place and uncertainty about the city council's plans for the fate of the neighbourhood. The building became increasingly unsafe in the late 1970s and had to be abandoned altogether in 1983, while awaiting repairs. In sum, throughout this period the Bhartiya Mandal had not been able to remain active enough to fulfil its unifying role.

In 1980, however, a new body known as the Bhartiya Associations of Bradford was formed, with the specific function of providing a structure which could bring together for common action the seven different Gujarati Hindu cultural, caste, and devotional organizations that had emerged in the city. They are listed below in their order of foundation.

Organization	*Year of foundation*
Bhartiya Mandal	1957
Hindu Swayamsevak Sangh	1966
Shri Jalaram Shakti Mandal	1967
Kshatriya Sudharak Mandal	1968
Sri Sathya Sai Centre	1970
Patel Samaj	1973
Shree Prajapati Association	1975

The initiative for the foundation of this organization was taken by M.B. Ladd, a quiet, self-effacing man who was the secretary of the Bhartiya Mandal, both chairman and president of the Bradford Shree Prajapati Association, and national secretary of the Shree Prajapati Association (UK). The first public venture of the Bhartiya Associations of Bradford took place on 28 July 1980 when a company of Indian dancers on tour in the United Kingdom presented an evening of classical dance.

In 1981 the Gujaratis initiated a move to bring about the wider unity of all Hindus, as well as Sikhs, in Bradford.[3] On 28 March no fewer than 19 Indian organizations were drawn together in the name of the expanding Bhartiya Associations of Bradford to mark the retirement of a respected community relations officer. The original seven Gujarati societies participated in the event as did two smaller groups, the Raja Yoga Centre and the Swaminarayan Mission. More importantly, the engagement of Punjabi and other non-Gujarati Hindus was secured through the involvement of the Hindu Cultural Society, a predominantly Punjabi association.[3] Two Sikh temples and the Guru Nanak Trust were also involved. This institutional involvement of the Sikhs and Hindus together in the articulation of Indian cultural unity was unique in the history of Bradford's South Asian minorities. In addition to these religious associations, six secular or non-sectarian Indian organizations also participated. They were the Indian Women's Association, the Indian Students' Association, the cultural agency known as 'Oriental Arts', the Indian Workers' Association, the Indian Youth Association, and Indian United Sports. It is clear that some of these societies have never been actively committed to the affairs of the Bhartiya Associations of Bradford. Thus it was an achievement to bring them together in March 1981 and to secure the tacit admission that the Indian population of Bradford had common interests which could be expressed effectively only if Indians were organized in a united manner.

An important factor in the mobilization of Bradford Indians at this time was that the leaders of different groups had become acutely aware of the way in which racial discrimination and the prospect of long-term unemployment had angered and discouraged their young people. This disaffection manifested itself dramatically in urban violence in various inner-city areas of Britain in the summer of 1981. Locally there were disturbances in Leeds and lesser ones in Bradford. The issue came to focus in Bradford on the case of a group of Hindus, Sikhs, and Muslims, aged between 18 and 24 years, who became known as 'The Bradford Twelve'. They saw themselves as harassed and victimized by the police. Criminal charges were eventually brought against them in a case that aroused national interest. The formation of the Bhartiya Associations of Bradford preceded these dramatic events by a year; and the enlargement of its constituency to include the Sikhs and other Indian groups preceded the riots by only a few months. There is no evidence that these developments were a conscious and co-ordinated response to the pressures of the time, but obviously the effectiveness of the Bhartiya Associations of Bradford in mobilizing the Indian community was a function of the threat which all Indians felt they were under in that period.

Following the success of the retirement party for the community relations officer, the Bhartiya Associations of Bradford planned a third public event the following year to mark India's Independence Day. Preparations were not made, however, at an early enough stage and the celebrations had to be postponed. After that the Bhartiya Associations entered a quiescent period. Although the leaders of several Hindu societies in Bradford remain enthusiastically in support of the Association and are poised to revive its activities, they also recognize that a suitable opportunity is unlikely to arise at the present time (1984). The recent disturbances in India, with considerable tension between the Sikhs and Hindus in the Punjab, have affected institutional relationships among British South Asians. It has not been a time when Hindu leaders have felt able to develop initiatives in community relations in Bradford.

In sum, this brief chronology of the formation of Hindu associations suggests that there has been a movement between unity and diversity in the organization of Gujarati Hindus. Ideologically Hindu sects espouse a universal message. The actual variety of the messages and, in consequence, the diversity

of sectarian movements create considerable segmentation in
Hindu society. Similarly the diversity of caste groups, each of
which sees itself as an autonomous, endogamous social body, is
a source of segmentation. Yet these differences are, in turn,
subsumed within the idea of Hindu society as a social organ-
ism (rather than as a sum of individuals) and they are transcended by a notion of Sanskritic civilization of which all Hindus,
irrespective of regional culture, are a part. These ideological
concepts of diversity and of unity, provide the evolutionary
framework in which segmentation is both articulated and absorbed. In this movement between unity and diversity one finds
among the Gujaratis of Bradford evidence of a characteristically
Hindu paradigm for the structure of a plural society in Britain.[4]

NOTES

1 Some of the above evidence runs counter to the testimony of Desai
  (1963:88–91) regarding the origins of Gujarati community
  organizations in Bradord, most notably in respect of the date given
  for the foundation of the Bhartiya Mandal. Desai asserts that it was
  founded in October 1959, but he must have been describing the
  spate of activity that preceded the purchase of the Mandal's
  premises in December of that year. Furthermore on the evidence of
  the Mandal's minute book, the role attributed by Desai to a former
  teacher designated 'T' cannot have been as innovative as he pro-
  poses, for the structure of the organization already existed. Desai's
  tribute to the extensive development of a scheme for lending
  Gujarati books, even to borrowers in other parts of the United
  Kingdom, confirms the cultural intentions of this organization.
2 Further evidence of the inclusive orientation of the Prajapatis has
  been suggested by Michaelson (personal communication). She
  notes that two family names found among Prajapatis, Suthar and
  Kumbhar, are more commonly associated with other artisan and
  service castes. Their use among Prajapatis may indicate that the
  Shree Prajapati Association includes a number of smaller castes
  which have become affiliated with it. This evidence provides a contrast to the reformist Circle for the Uplift of Kshatriyas which is
  more exclusive in orientation.
3 It must be mentioned that the first move for such an all-Hindu
  organization occurred on 30 June 1968 with the formation of the

Hindu Cultural Society of Bradford. Although two Gujaratis were amongst the ten people who initially sponsored the formation of the society, most of its support came from the Punjabi community and the organization is at present situated at Leeds Road, Bradford 3, an area which is known as a place of Punjabi settlement. The first registered Hindu temple in Bradford was established on the premises of the society at Leeds Road on 3 August 1974. The central images are of Krishna and Radha, but a picture of Guru Nanak hangs in a place of honour. The temple is hired on occasion by the Shri Jalaram Shakti Mandal, and recently a picture of Jalaram was attached to a side wall. It must be said, however, that in spite of the use of the premises by Gujaratis and in spite of the occasional attempts of the officers of the society to involve Gujaratis in their affairs, the languages spoken at the Hindu Cultural Society are Punjabi and Hindi, not Gujarati, and many Gujaratis think of the society as a Punjabi organization. For more details of this important local Hindu association, see Bowen 1981.

4 This paper, and the research on which it is based, could not have reached this stage of completion without the guidance and interest of Dr Ursula King of the Community Religions Project, Department of Theology and Religious Studies, University of Leeds.

2

Domestic Hinduism in a Gujarati trading caste

Maureen Michaelson

Although the study of Hindu temple rituals and temple-going is not without its importance, such a study for the Lohanas – Britain's second most populous Gujarati caste – would be largely uninformative and misleading. The Lohanas, like other Gujarati castes, are involved in an intensive weekly round of religious activities, but in the Lohana case these activities are organized by family and kin, the local caste associations, and various devotional congregations (*satsang*) in the neighbourhood. Formal temple attendance is sporadic, with some caste members never going at all, even though they might consider themselves to be 'very religious'. Instead, it is in their homes that people unite in meaningful religious activity. The aim of this paper is to describe certain domestic forms of Hinduism among the Lohanas and to assess their significance in the preservation of their religious life.

As long ago as 1963, Berger and Luckmann pointed out that focusing on institutionally specialized locations of religion in churches or similar bodies betrays 'a marked historical and cultural parochialism' (Berger and Luckmann 1963:423). This is especially true in trying to uncover the religious practices of

Hindus such as the Lohanas in Britain. Western concepts of religion expect religious activity to be largely institutionalized, conducted in consecrated buildings, and performed in the presence of officially ordained or sanctioned officers. Contrary to this, the Hindu home is designated as an abode of god and much religious activity takes place here. Second, whereas western concepts of religion expect theological and ritual orthodoxy amongst the followers of various sects and churches, and consistency of belief and practice, this is contrary to the spirit and practice of Hinduism. Hindus maintain that there are many ways to reach god, and the individual is free to choose any rite according to the time available, personal preferences, and the particular occasion. The material in this paper thus challenges western perceptions not only of the importance of formal religious institutions but of sectarian orthodoxy and theological strictness.

THE LOHANAS AND THEIR RELIGIOUS IDENTITY

The Lohanas are a caste (or more precisely a *gñātī*, or subcaste) of traditional traders and merchants from the Saurashtra peninsular of Gujarat, an area to which they still refer as Kathiawad (for detailed information on Gujarati castes in Britain see Michaelson 1979, 1983). Ninety per cent of the Lohanas in Britain come from villages and towns around two major cities in Saurashtra, Rajkot and Porbandar, or are the descendants of such people. The rest come from two other areas: the eastern Saurashtran port of Gogha, and Kutch. There are no Lohanas in Britain who emigrated directly from India without having had some personal links with the East African countries of Kenya, Tanzania, or Uganda, with Malawi in Central Africa, or to a lesser extent with South Africa.

Although Lohanas started migrating to East Africa at the turn of the century in order to trade, it was only after the 1950s that residence there for individuals became more permanent. Therefore, when assessing the nature and extent of the Lohanas' religious activity, it is instructive to note certain demographic and historical features about their migration to Britain. Since all the Lohanas originally arrived from East Africa as political refugees, their population consists of a normal age structure with four generations living in Britain. The presence of many knowledgeable and respected elders among the East Africans has much to do with the preservation both of the religious life and of caste distinctions between the numerous subcastes within the Gujarati population.

There is no simple correlation between age and place of birth. Not all the oldest people were born in India, while several members of the middle and younger generations were. During the period of residence in East Africa from the turn of the century to the 1970s, women frequently returned to India for childbirth. Countless children were sent home to India to be raised by kin still resident there, or for the whole or part of their schooling. Lohanas have always returned to India to celebrate life-cycle rituals, to propitiate ancestors and lineage deities, to go on pilgrimages, or to visit kin, and there has been a simultaneous stream of visitors from India to East Africa and Britain, including religious teachers and priests.

Therefore the Lohanas cannot simply be described or understood as a population of Hindus who have been removed from their land of origin for 70 years, and who therefore exhibit ossified and attenuated forms of their religion.

Approximately 30–35,000 Lohanas live in Britain. While they are settled in towns and cities all over the country, they have – like other Gujarati castes – tended to cluster in specific areas. The bulk of the caste's population has settled in Greater London and the southeast: caste leaders put this figure at 22,000. The major areas in terms of concentration of population and leadership within the caste are the northwest boroughs of Greater London (Harrow, Wealdstone, and Edgware) and Leicester in the Midlands, with a Lohana population of over 7,000. The descriptions in this paper relate primarily to the Lohanas of northwest London and Leicester, where the fieldwork on which this paper is based was conducted between 1974 and 1976.

The Lohanas refer to their religious identity in three related ways: they are Vaishnavite, part of the Sanatan Dharma, and followers of the devotional path. This identity is tailored to suit their status as a trading caste and to give meaning and sanctity to their trading way of life. Vaishnavites are those Hindus who have chosen Lord Vishnu as the most important of the Hindu deities. Following Pocock (1973:108), Vaishnavism does not mean the sole worship of Vishnu to the exclusion of other gods, but 'that cult which puts Vishnu firmly at the centre, and by Vaishnavism in Gujarat ... the Vaishnavism that chooses Krishna as the divine embodiment'. The predominance of Vaishnavism in Gujarat, with its doctrine of divine love expressed in fervour and song and its appeal to non-literary but wealthy merchant castes, is well attested in the literature (see Barot, below). The pursuit and acquisition of wealth is legitimated in Vaishnavism if this is done in the true spirit of service to god, to whom the wealth is dedicated. In this respect Vaishnavism is appropriate for traders for whom the pursuit of wealth is a caste duty (*dharma*).

A second way in which Lohanas describe their religious adherence is by saying that they are followers of Sanatan Dharma. This term, as used by the Lohanas, has four closely related meanings. The first relates to its strict original sense of the eternal religion, the perpetual, ancient, everlasting religion of all Hindus. The second sense refers to orthodox Brahmanic Hinduism, and is contrasted with the neo-Hindu developments of the nineteenth and twentieth centuries (see Morris 1968:55). The third sense means 'non-sectarian': any festival, rite, or life-cycle ritual conducted according to scriptural procedures is a Sanatan rite. Finally, any individual who is not a member of a sect is referred to as a Sanatan Hindu.

Despite the prevailing description of themselves as Sanatan Hindus, the devotional path (*bhakti mārga*) is a third essential component of the religious life of the Lohanas. Several Sanatan and other domestic rituals are accompanied by expressions of devotion. In addition, specifically convened gatherings in which hymns and chants are sung are one of the most popular forms of religious expression among the Lohanas. A description of these events is found below. The path of devotion has great appeal for the merchant and trading castes of Gujarat, since it holds open to householders a spiritual life on the condition that they relinquish the fruits of their actions by dedicating all their material efforts to the selfless service of the Divine. On the one hand, wealth is seen as a sign of god's grace as well as a sign that one has performed good deeds in previous incarnations. On the other hand, wealth enables one to dedicate one's profits to god. Here lies the importance to Lohanas of service (*sevā*) to the community. The most respected Lohanas are those who have used their wealth for charitable purposes: the building of schools, hospitals, temples, and caste buildings in India, East Africa, and now also in Britain. At all Lohana gatherings, whether they be weddings, devotional congregations (*satsaṅg*), or life-cycle rituals, donations for specified charitable and religious institutions are collected.

Although Lohanas see themselves as Vaishnavite, most Lohanas, unlike other Gujarati subcastes such as the Patels (see Barot, below), do not attribute importance to formal affiliation to any particular Vaishnavite sect. In fact, the great majority of Lohanas are not members of any particular sect. Both this majority and those who are members of sects remain in some respects eclectic in their devotion, worshipping both sectarian and non-sectarian deities. Overall, most Lohanas place considerable value on the solidarity of their family and kin in the religious celebration of auspicious occasions. Sectarian allegiance may be held, but this is not given primacy over family solidarity. Moreover, any Lohana family may have a religious ceremony conducted at its home by an official or priest of a sect, and according to the rites of that sect, without having to belong to it. In sum, while some Lohanas become members of a sect, many do not seek formal affiliation. They prefer to participate in religious programmes and devotional activities organized by individual members of diverse sects without actively seeking membership in any particular one.

The sect with the largest following among Lohanas is the Pushtimarg, or Path of Grace, founded by Vallabhacharya (see Bibliography; I shall refer to this sect by the Kathiawadi pronunciation, Pushtimarak). Several thousands of the Lohanas in

Britain count themselves as Pushtimarak. One cannot be a member without having been personally initiated by a quasi-divine leader, called Maharaj, or by a guru with the express permission of a Maharaj. Children born to members of the sect are not automatically members. Lohanas in Britain who are members have to wait for a guru to visit from India in order to have their children initiated into the sect. The place of the personal guru is of paramount importance in the sect in India, but this dimension is lacking in Britain. Similarly, although the sect has its own temples called 'mansions' (*haveli*) in India, in which only images of the Lord Sri Nathji are housed, there are no exclusive temples in Britain. Instead, polychrome pictures or statues of Sri Nathji are included at several Sanatan Hindu temples, as in the Shree Nathji Sanatan Hindu Mandir at Leytonstone in East London. Although some Pushtimaraks worship no other god but Krishna and adhere very strictly to certain food avoidances – causing some resentment from relatives and other Lohana caste mates from whom they therefore do not take food – the majority of Pushtimaraks do not observe the strict dietary taboos, and most join in the worship of other gods at non-sectarian religious gatherings. In addition, in several Pushtimarak households, images of other popular gods and especially of Jalaram (see p. 43–6) adorn doorways, lintels, walls, and household shrines. The absence of specific temples and gurus, and the highly eclectic religious practices of its sectarian members, means that the Pushtimarak sect is loosely organized in Britain.

Other Hindu sects of some importance to the Lohanas are the Swaminarayan and the Arya Samaj. Although the majority of Lohanas deny that members of their caste can be Swaminarayans (see Barot, below), saying that this is a 'Patel' or 'Kutchi' religion, many Lohanas do join in worship at Swaminarayan temples or religious gatherings. Several Lohana families have sought formal membership of a branch of the Swaminarayan sect which is, however, quite distinct from those branches of the sect whose members are predominantly from other Gujarati and Kutchi castes. In the last decade, recruitment to this sect from the Lohana community has been rising steadily. Although small, the branch is well organized and has a highly rigid and author-itarian structure (see Pocock 1976).

The absence of formal leadership or organizational structure among the Pushtimaraks in Britain means that the sect does not organize activities, gatherings, or celebrations for its members. The perpetuation of the sect, with its beliefs and specialized modes of worship, lies in the hands of individual members who pass on the lore to their children and organize informal *satsangs* among groups of friends and relatives. The Swaminarayans, on the other hand, arrange several activities outside the specifically religious, such as Kathiawadi folk dance classes and day trips to places of interest. They also have women's groups and youth organizations which function as social clubs. This structural difference between the two sects is reflected in the greater success of the Swaminarayans in recruiting new members in recent years.

Most Lohanas also deny that any member of their caste can be an Arya Samaji. The Arya Samaj sect has traditionally re-cruited members from the Indian urban and intellectual strata, and has been at the forefront of social change in India, demand-ing reforms such as inter-caste marriages, education for women, and the eradication of post-Vedic ritual from Hinduism. A very small minority of Lohanas, mostly members of the intellectual strata from Tanzania and Kenya, do claim to be Arya Samajis. Although some of these people do conduct all their ceremonies according to Arya Samaj ritual, they nevertheless join in the religious celebrations and rituals of others of their caste mates. In addition, several less sophisticated people who nominally claim to be Arya Samajis perform daily worship (*puja*) as well as other non-Vedic rituals customary within the caste. In contrast, several Lohanas who would otherwise vehemently deny that any members of their caste are Arya Samajis, themselves have Arya Samaj ceremonies for weddings and funerals on the grounds that these rituals are much quicker and therefore more con-venient in Britain.

Sects have little impact in organizing the religious life of Lohanas in Britain. The majority of Lohanas do not belong to any particular sect and identify themselves simply as Vaishnavas, or as followers of the Sanatan Dharma. Instead, it is the home and the domestic context which provides the main focus of religious life for the Lohanas.

DOMESTIC WORSHIP

All homes have a shrine (*mandir*), ranging from a simple shelf set aside in one room of the house, to whole rooms specifically dedicated as temples. It is also extremely common to find a shrine, consisting of a shelf and the paraphernalia of worship, discretely positioned in Lohana shops and offices. The more modest shrines contain pictures of the family's favourite deities, such as Krishna, Sri Nathji, Amba Mata (the most important goddess worshipped by the caste), Ganesh (the elephant-headed god), or Jalaram. The shrines may also contain photographs of the personal gurus of the individual family members, and any other items or souvenirs with a religious significance. The lineage deity (*kuldevi*), who is worshipped by the family at marriage and other times, is not represented by images in Britain as these cannot be removed from ancestral homes in India (for further details on family deities and ancestral martyrs, called *surapura*, see Michaelson 1983: 192,218,221–22).

The shrines of the followers of the Pushtimarga sect are far more elaborate, since a whole range of vessels, garments, and foodstuffs are required for the service (*sevā*) of Lord Krishna. These shrines are kept not in the open but in special cupboards or curtained quarters, so that Krishna may be left to sleep and play in private when he is not being ministered to.

In East Africa, it was quite common for the richest families to devote an entire room of their home as a shrine or temple. In private temples in Britain, that is, those in private homes which do not employ the services of a Brahman priest, there may even be very large images of deities imported from India. Private temples may be open to the public at agreed times or on specified days of the week. Several have come into existence as a result of divine intervention or miraculous occurrences. For example, in one London house, the goddess Amba Mata appeared nightly while the family was asleep, leaving a tell-tale track of red powder (*kankun*) footprints on the floor, and *kunkun* fingerprints on the pictures in the shrine in their living room. As a result, the family decided to devote this entire room for use as a temple. People come from far and wide to witness the miraculous prints of the goddess. The temple is also visited by newly married and childless women, who pray to the goddess for the birth of a child.

Domestic worship (*pūjā*) at the shrine may be conducted on a regular or an occasional basis. Most Lohana women and many men make perfunctory offerings to the deities on a daily basis. The more devout and leisured may spend half an hour or more in worship. Several individuals claim that they used to perform worship every morning in East Africa, but the lack of time in this country and the necessity to bathe beforehand prevents them from doing so. Some Pushtimaraks may spend up to two or three hours in daily worship, if they have the time. Their image of the child Krishna is treated like a living person who must be bathed, dressed, and fed daily (on the concept of worship for Pushtimaraks see Pocock 1973:114–17). Other occasional rituals take place at the domestic shrine, such as weekly fasts, which are undertaken as a sign of devotion to a particular deity. Similarly, religious vows, in which the devotee appeals to a deity for some act of grace and pledges in turn the performance of some act in recompense, may take place at the domestic shrine.

In addition to regular worship, occasional rituals and celebrations take place in the domestic setting. Most are conducted by Brahman priests and are attended by relatives and other caste mates, and they are usually followed by a meal. It is unusual to find guests of other castes invited to such occasions; they are primarily family events. Such rituals include thanksgiving ceremonies for the successful outcome of a religious vow, postmarital rites, anniversaries of deaths, and a host of other ceremonies such as house-warming rites (*vastu*) and scriptural readings (*kathā*). In addition to these voluntary ceremonies, Lohanas observe life-cycle rituals (*sanskāra*), such as the hair-parting ceremony in the seventh month of a woman's first pregnancy (*sīmant*), the name-taking ceremony (*chaththi*), and the tonsure, all of which take place in the presence of the deities at the domestic level (some of these rituals are described in detail by McDonald, below).

SATSAṄGS – DEVOTIONAL CONGREGATIONS

The most frequent and popular form of religious activity among the Lohanas are informal gatherings for the singing of devotional songs (*bhajan*). These gatherings are called *satsaṅg* (literally, 'in the company of truth'); they are held frequently and for a variety of purposes. Some individuals may attend different *satsaṅgs* every week, and on occasion, even more than one a week. They are generally held in the living rooms of private homes. The cramped conditions, where 30 or 40 people sit in close proximity on the floor in unified worship, adds to the special atmosphere. Both men and women attend *satsaṅgs*, though each *satsaṅg* group tends to be sexually segregated. They have far greater social importance for women than they do for men. For countless women these are the occasions when they can leave the drudgery of housework for an afternoon in order to pass the time with their friends and relatives in joyful singing; and in a warm, familiar atmosphere where gossip and news is exchanged.

There are two different types of *satsaṅgs*: Sanatan and sectarian. Sanatan *satsaṅgs* are held on regular days in the lunar calendar, the most important of which are the eleventh day of each half of the month, known as *agiyāras* (called *ekādaśī* in northern India); and the day of the full moon, which is the last day of the bright half of the month, known as *pūnam*. The worshippers on these occasions are members of the Lohana caste only; members of other castes are specifically excluded. While several of these *satsaṅgs* are also arranged on a neighbourhood basis and are held informally in people's homes, some are organized by the Ladies' Committees of the caste association. On important dates in the Hindu calendar, halls may be hired so that large numbers of the caste can gather together in worship. The worshippers do not contribute their own musical accompaniment; singing is accompanied by a single harmonium player. Even though the same Vaishnavite devotional songs are sung at both types of *satsaṅg*, the atmosphere which prevails at non-sectarian *satsaṅgs* is far more subdued. The Sanatan *satsaṅg* is the more common type. It attracts considerably larger groups of worshippers, including those who have sectarian affiliations. For some Lohana women's associations, *satsaṅgs* are combined with other activities: after the singing has ended, they might have a lecture by a guest speaker on a particular topic such as cooking or flower arranging. These occasions are important social events and provide a regular outing for both working and housebound people.

Sectarian *satsaṅgs* are joyful and energetic occasions, held separately by members of the Pushtimarga and Swaminarayan sects, and by followers of Jalaram. They include devotional songs specific to the major deities – Lord Krishna in the case of the Pushtis and Lord Swaminarayan in the case of the Swaminarayan sect. The songs are sung with fervour and the devotees accompany their singing with cymbals, tambourines, and wooden rattles. Sectarian members are not supposed to attend *satsaṅgs* held in honour of other deities. This rule is strictly adhered to by almost all Swaminarayans and also by the more observant Pushtimaraks. This causes great resentment on the part of their non-sectarian family members, who feel slighted when their relatives will not attend some of their religious celebrations.

At sectarian *satsaṅgs*, all devotees are marked on their foreheads with the distinguishing coloured paste of the sect (*tilak*). The general salutation (*namaskār*) between the assembled devotees on such occasions, and also when they meet at other times includes the formal recognition of them as fellow sectarians. When the *satsaṅg* ends, each devotee is marked with a further *tilak* of red powder (*kaṅkuṅ*) from the *ārtī* tray and given some sanctified food (*prasād*). They are also given little bags of *prasād* to take home to other members of their household who have not attended. While most sectarian *satsaṅgs* conclude when the singing has ended, the Swaminarayan sect then conducts a more formal part of the meeting where the written replies of gurus in India to their disciples in Britain are read out, a discussion is held, or the text of a sermon from one of the head gurus in India is read.

Sectarian *satsaṅgs* are frequently attended by individuals from other Gujarati Hindu castes. Devotional worship has always crossed caste boundaries, and in Leicester especially, sectarian *satsaṅgs* were also attended by a few individuals of other castes from the neighbourhood. However, the Lohanas were always in the majority at these occasions. Although people of all castes join in devotional and sectarian worship, the social ties created on these occasions are not extended into other aspects of the devotees' lives: the only time the devotees of different castes associate together is for such congregational worship.

SPIRIT POSSESSION AND THE CULT OF JALARAM

Among the Gujarati castes from East Africa the Lohanas are well known for their predisposition to become possessed. Most possessions occur at festivities connected with the goddess Amba Mata, such as at her special festival of the Nine Nights, called Navaratri. At these occasions both males and females, regardless of age, may become possessed. The possessions follow stylized patterns of bodily shaking, which differ for each sex. A possessed person at these occasions is believed to have diagnostic and predictive abilities. People of all castes like to attend religious functions where they suspect that a possession of this sort will occur. Possession may also take place at a *satsaṅg*, but here it is only women who appear to become possessed and the whole content and purpose of the performance is radically different. In this context, possession is a sign that the deity, who enters the devotee, approves of the proceedings and is, as it were, joining in the devotions to him- or herself. After the possession has ended, the assembled devotees lean forward to touch the person who has been possessed, to obtain a share of the god's grace.

One devotional context in which possession is known to occur are the *satsaṅgs* in worship of Jalaram, a Lohana merchant from Kathiawad who lived from 1799 to 1881 and who was renowned for his charity and his ability to work miracles. He at present occupies an interstitial and undefined place in the cosmology. He is not considered to be a deity, but is revered for his saintly qualities and devout actions. The belief in the efficacy of prayers to Jalaram was taken by his Lohana followers to East Africa, where his popularity spread to all sections of the Gujarati population, becoming a dominant focus of religious fervour not only among the Lohanas and other Hindus, but also amongst Jains and Muslims. Even some Punjabi Hindus and Sikhs came to believe in him. From East Africa the faith was transported back to India. People who had never previously heard of Jalabapa, as he is popularly known, began to revere him, including Jains and Muslims whose caste mates from East Africa had spread the message (see Zarwan 1977:23).

The ashram at Jalaram's birthplace in Virpur in central Kathiawad has become a centre of pilgrimage; and collections in support of it are raised at weddings and other social gatherings in Britain. The countless devotees of Jalaram are not, however, formally organized into a sect. There is no central authority or doctrine associated with the cult, and neither are there initiation rites, gurus, or preceptors acting as mediators between the devotee and Jalabapa. In fact, a large part of the popular appeal of Jalaram is in his immediacy: his ability to watch over, protect, and advise his devotees means that anyone who believes in him can approach him directly to get favours granted. In addition, since Jalabapa has an especially close relationship with Lord Ram himself, the latter cannot easily deny a request directed to him through Jalabapa.

One way in which worshippers express their devotion to Jalaram is by recounting stories of his saintly qualities, charitable deeds, and miracles. One such story, told to me by Lohana informants, concerns Jalaram's meeting with Lord Ram.

Jalaram was known not to eat anything unless he had first fed somebody in need. As he lived in a small place through which few travellers passed, he often went without food for several days. If a poor person came to the grocery shop where he worked, he would give them goods without taking any payment; but when the stock was checked, nothing was ever found to be missing. One day, Lord Ram dressed as an old man in a monk's robe and appeared before Jalaram. Jalaram invited him in for a meal. The old man complained that as he was so old and infirm, he needed someone to look after him. Jalabapa therefore sent his wife with the old man on his journey. She went willingly, as she had complete faith in her husband's actions. The pair of travellers eventually came to a river, and the old man gave Jalaram's wife his stick and bag to hold. He then disappeared. At the same time, a voice came to Jalabapa at his home, saying that it was Lord Ram himself who had come to see if he was as good as people said. He had proved that he was and could now fetch his wife. The stick and bag are still on display at the shrine in Virpur, but nobody is allowed to look inside the bag. The ashram continues to feed 'thousands' of pilgrims at a time, and the kitchen never runs out of food, no matter how many people are there. In Britain, the birthday of Jalaram (Jalaram Jayanti) is celebrated and several groups hold weekly *satsangs* in his honour.

One Jalaram *satsang* group meets regularly at the house of a Lohana family from Uganda. One night, many years ago, the father dreamed that Jalabapa would appear to him. The next night, there was a lightning storm, and on the white tiles in the kitchen there appeared a very clear image of Jalaram. Images of Krishna, a cow and a calf also appeared on the tiles, but in less clear detail. People flocked to this man's house in a small Ugandan village to make vows and to take sight (*darśan*) of the manifestation of Jalaram. When the Indians were expelled from Uganda, the family had the tiles carefully removed and framed, and brought them with their few possessions to Leicester. The tiles now have a place on the family's modest shrine, together with pictures of Krishna, Ganesh, and Kali Mata. Unfortunately, the images are now said to have faded; I was only able to see a few brown marks on the surface of the tiles.

At one *satsang* which I attended at this house, two possessions occurred. During the first a middle-aged woman began to shake and dance ecstatically and was said to have been possessed by Radha-Krishna, since the possession occurred during a song devoted to the divine couple. Then at the concluding ceremony of *ārtī* a woman, who normally cannot walk without the aid of a stick, stood up and clapped her hands vigorously for the duration of the *ārtī* hymn, which lasted for about seven minutes. The presence of Radha and Krishna at the *satsang* was the reason given for her renewed physical vitality.

Another *satsang* was held at the house of a barren Jain woman who wished to fall pregnant. Although this woman is a devout Sthanakwasi Jain, all the hymns sung were Vaishnavite devotional ones. At this *satsang*, as well, two women became possessed. One did an energetic folk dance with sticks (*rās*) which lasted for half an hour, and the second, an old woman, danced simultaneously, carrying in her arms a child of about six years old. The assembled devotees became very excited and shouted 'Mātāji bolo!' ('Speak, Mother Goddess'), for the grace of the goddess is believed to be able to make a woman fall pregnant. The events were apparently commonplace to the women at the *satsang*, and it was only myself who was struck by the fact that the possession by a Hindu goddess occurred at the house of a Jain and that the occasion was ostensibly a Jalaram *satsang*.

DOMESTIC HINDUISM AND THE PRESERVATION OF RELIGIOUS LIFE

Lohanas may sometimes be heard to assert that they are ignorant about their religion. When they say this, they are referring invariably to the philosophical aspect of their doctrines and to the scholarly or symbolic meanings of their rites and practices. This is a problem which has been brought into focus in this country, since they feel they should be able to explain their strange customs and to make them intelligible to interested outsiders. Previously, they simply carried out their rituals and ceremonies without considering whether they could explain their meaning or provenance. This knowledge was largely procedural or evaluative (e.g. does a particular ritual achieve its aim). The fact that such knowledge has not been 'lost' as a result of migration or exile is evident in accounts of contemporary lifecycle rituals which conform in detail to the descriptions in early ethnographies and administrative reports. For example, in her book published over 60 years ago, Sinclair-Stevenson described the rites of the Brahmans of Rajkot, one of the two towns mentioned above as being a major centre of Lohana emigration. In certain rituals, such as that performed in the seventh month of pregnancy (*sīmant*; see McDonald below), the only major difference between the Lohanas' present day practice and that described by Sinclair-Stevenson (1920:116–22) is in the time-scale: the ritual which previously took place over three days is now condensed into one.

Eight years ago, young children of my acquaintance were almost without exception uninformed and ignorant about several aspects of ritual and religion. Today, as teenagers or young adults, these same individuals have gained an impressive know-ledge of the procedural aspects of their religion. This has been learned informally, through the witnessing of the daily, weekly, monthly, and annual cycles of events over a number of years. At social and religious gatherings children of all ages, including the newborn, add to the general atmosphere of jollity, vitality, and noise. They remain at the celebration either awake or asleep until the early hours of the morning. In addition, the more 'westernized' people of my acquaintance, who previously shunned religious or family gatherings, have since the birth of their own children begun to take a more lively interest in religion generally, and to participate in the social and religious celebra-tions of their extended families.

Moreover, attendance at religious ceremonies of all kinds has, if anything, increased throughout the years that the Lohanas have been living in Britain. The reason that informants give for this is that in East Africa people met their kin and caste mates daily in the neighbourhood, in the pursuit of business, at the shops, at schools, and in the temples and caste buildings. In Britain, besides the greater distances between homes, Lohanas (especially in London) have much less free time because of the constraints of urban living, the nature of their working hours, and the loss of servants. In East Africa, most people claimed, every evening after work they would go home to bathe, and then go to the temple or to the caste building (*mahājanvāḍi*) where they would see friends and relatives. This daily temple-going has been replaced by the increased incidence of devotional worship (*satsaṅgs*) and other religio-cultural events. It is com-mon to find as many as 500 people gathered together for life-cycle celebrations; and there are innumerable private gatherings for worship in homes.

Thus while public worship in temples and formal sectarian membership are not of great importance, and while the Lohanas are the first to admit that they do not know much about 'religion', they are a highly religious people whose worship takes place for the most part in the presence of deities at the domestic shrine. Rituals in connection with the stages of life and the well-being of the family are observed; their procedures are recalled; and they serve important enough extra-religious functions (e.g. bringing the family together on social occasions) to make it likely they will continue. Normal socialization, rather than any specific educational or initiatory process, ensures that domestic Hinduism, at least, is not under threat.

Yet the evidence of Lohana religious life suggests that this argument might be taken one step further. To look for the preservation of religious life only in so-called religious institutions (e.g. church, temple, etc.) appears to be a bias from our own western cultural background. In fact, the distinction between the private institution of home and the public religious one of church does not apply in the Hindu context. There are several reasons for this. First, the home for Hindus is an auspicious, sacred context in which rituals (except for the inauspicious rituals of death) are conducted. By contrast, Christian life-cycle rituals (e.g. baptism, communion, marriage, etc.) take place in 'religious' institutions. Second, as we have noted, the Hindu home is the abode of a deity or of several deities, many of whom are seated in the domestic shrine. The household is an object of their grace; and daily offerings to the gods at the domestic shrine are made by members of the household. Thus in being an abode of the deity the home is like a temple.

There is, however, a further reason why it might be helpful to think of the Hindu home as a religious institution. In order to recount this it is first necessary to note a common distinction made by Hindus concerning the deities who reside in temples. Some deities are present in a temple by virtue of their having been put there by acts of men. That is, pious persons have purchased a statue or some other image of a deity and installed it in some shelter. A Brahman priest has then been called to establish the soul of the deity in that image so that it becomes the living presence of the deity. Other temples, however, are founded by the gods themselves. That is, some god or goddess, by an act of his or her divine will, becomes manifest at a place. Many temples at places of pilgrimage in South Asia are of this latter type. Temples established by divine will are more esteemed than those established by human will. In the present paper two cases have been cited of private homes being visited by a deity and subsequently becoming semi-public places of pilgrimage and worship. The first example concerned the goddess Amba Mata who daily visited the domestic shrine in her honour, which was subsequently turned into a place of pilgrimage for childless women; the second concerned the manifestation of Jalaram and Lord Krishna at the house in Uganda. In such instances, the distinction between private homes and public temples loses its analytical value.

Finally, the fact that all forms of domestic ritual, from worship at the family shrine to the holding of specific life-cycle rituals or occasional *satsangs*, may be held according to either sectarian or Sanatan procedures supports the claim of Lohanas that the form of worship is irrelevant. Worshipping only in formal public buildings or according to codified sectarian rules is contrary to the pragmatic and eclectic spirit of Lohanas, who stress that the Lord can be approached in countless ways. Lohanas find demands for sectarian orthodoxy and liturgical precision contrary and inimical to what they perceive as the expression of true religious feeling – the unhampered and uncircumscribed right to show devotion to god in a thousand different ways.

3

Rituals of motherhood among Gujarati women in East London

Merryle McDonald

In Britain Hinduism is seen as focusing upon otherworldly concerns – the fate of one's soul in this life and the next and the path to final emancipation from the cycle of rebirths. While this is undoubtedly a genuine preoccupation of some Hindus, the prominence given to this transcendental aspect masks the character of Hindu practices in the everyday lives of South Asians in Britain. Like people everywhere, Hindus are concerned with the health and well-being of their families and the achievement of personal aims in life. Rituals and worship serve a pragmatic as well as a transcendental purpose. In this paper I shall examine how this pragmatic aspect of Hinduism finds expression in the lives of Gujarati women living in East London. Rather than focus on a particular ritual, I shall take a series of events which concern all Hindu women, namely pregnancy and childbirth, and investigate the way in which Gujarati women have recourse to rituals in order to manage this crucial period of their lives.

TRANSCENDENTAL AND PRAGMATIC HINDUISM

The distinction between transcendental and pragmatic religion has become commonplace in the sociology of religion. A classic formulation (see Mandelbaum 1966) notes their difference in form and function. Transcendental religion has to do with the ultimate purpose of human life, the welfare of society, and the life-cycle rituals that integrate the individual with society. Pragmatic religion is concerned with personal welfare and individual gain. Each may appeal to different gods and have different ritual specialists. In the case of Hinduism, transcendental religion is conventionally said to be the preoccupation of Brahmans or of high caste people. The rituals are conducted by Brahmans and the gods are universal ones, such as Vishnu and Siva. Pragmatic Hinduism may be the concern of all Hindus, but its ritual practitioners are said to come from the lower castes, who worship gods and goddesses of local influence. Their ritual practices include ecstatic possession states.

In the most general sense, then, one can say that the transcendental 'complex', as Mandelbaum describes it, is informed by textual perogative and sacerdotal privilege, while the pragmatic, in the limiting sense with which he endows it seems to refer to the consultations of individual Hindus with a sub-priesthood empowered by deities of local influence. Mandelbaum's view implies that Hindus make a distinction between rituals undertaken for universal aims and those undertaken for personal aims (literally, the distinction is between rituals undertaken for the ritual act itself, *kratvartha*, and those undertaken for the sake of the ritual actor, *puruṣārtha*; see on this Das 1983:448–50). Yet when one looks at religion, in so far as it constitutes the very fabric of Hindu life, then the distinction loses some of its edge. Mandelbaum himself points out the potential overlap between these categories (1966:1176). They are, in effect, only separable analytically and are highly questionable when examined in the context of specific examples. This, at least, is the case with the material concerning rituals of pregnancy and childbirth.

In the Brahmanical literature, and hence from the point of view of the guardians of transcendental religion, pregnancy and childbirth rituals come within the rubric of 'rites of passage', a sequence of some 16 auspicious rituals (*saṁskāra*) which prepare the person over a period of rebirths for the ultimate goal of release from the cycle of rebirths and the union of the embodied soul with god. Inden and Nicholas (1977:37) observe that each ritual is like a rebirth, transforming the body into its new status and new sets of relationships, removing defects, and infusing it with beneficient qualities. According to Brahman priests, eight of the 16 rituals are associated with the pregnancy of the mother or the birth of the child. These are:

1   *Garbhādhāna*, a rite performed either before pregnancy or after conception to ensure the birth of a child.
2   *Puṅsavana*, performed in the third month of pregnancy to ensure the birth of a male child and to mark the cessation of intercourse.
3   *Śīghraprasavopāyo yantraśa*, prayers written on a piece of paper and worn on the woman's wrist for protection in pregnancy.
4   *Sīmantonnayana*, a rite performed in the seventh month for the safe delivery of the child.
5   *Janmajāta*, a rite performed just before the cord is cut.
6   *Anādiṣṭaprāyascitta*, prayers repenting the misdeeds of the parents to ensure that the child is born with no impure thoughts or deeds from the parents.
7   *Chaṭhṭhī*, the sixth day ceremony for the good fortune of the infant.
8   *Nāmakaraṇa*, the name-giving ceremony.

Among my female and male informants in East London, however, knowledge of the full sequence of these Brahmanical rites is minimal. In most cases the Sanskrit names have been replaced by Gujarati terms. Some of the rituals are omitted altogether; others are enacted according to family traditions which may go back generations. These variations, both in the rituals performed and in their content, are often specific to a patrilineage. Thus the rituals witnessed by a woman in her natal home may differ from those performed in her conjugal home. In the case of two sisters, marrying into different patrilineages, one might find herself performing the *sīmant* ritual in the seventh month of the first pregnancy while the other might not. Such variation in the practice of life-cycle rites also occurs in the South Asian context; the community's residence in Britain has not itself led to any attrition in the observance of the rituals. Rather, there are local and family traditions as well as Brahmanical ones and these may not coincide in practice. Even when they do, the reasons for carrying out the ritual may be quite different. The dominant theme that women express in their performance is not the Brahmanical notion of movement through stages of life in preparation for ultimate release from the cycle of rebirth, but the protection of the mother and child, ensuring their health and well-being throughout a period when they are vulnerable to illness, misfortune, and jealousy.

One could compare the list of life-cycle rituals to which my male Brahman informants subscribed with the rituals organized by women and actually used in the home. The first two Brahmanical life-cycle rituals, *garbhādhāna* and *puṅsavana*, are not practised; instead conception is solicited, especially in cases of subfertility or apparent infertility, by means of a vow made to a goddess. The third Brahmanical ritual, *śīghraprasavopāyo yantraśa*, has a roughly equivalent form in *pañcmāsī*, a protective ritual for the mother in the fifth month of pregnancy. The fourth Brahmanical ritual, *sīmantonnayana*, is a direct equivalent of *sīmant*, enacted during the seventh month of a woman's first pregnancy. The next two Brahmanical rituals, *janmajāta* and *anādiṣṭaprāyascitta*, are not performed, although there are domestic rituals surrounding childbirth, most of which have lapsed in the urban context with hospital births. The seventh and eighth Brahmanical rituals, *chaṭhṭhī and nāmakaraṇa*, do have local Gujarati equivalents but they are followed by an important Gujarati custom, the child's first outing to the temple, which does not figure in the Brahmanical list of rituals.

In sum, the aim of these life cycle rituals is, from the Brahmanical point of view, transcendental. Their enactment entails the recitation of Sanskrit mantras; and in most cases the calling of a Brahman priest to render the ritual efficacious. But in practice the rituals are organized by the women. A Brahman's service is only required for a 'name-giving' and in this case it is a Brahman astrologer, not a Brahman priest. The aim of the life-cycle rituals is to endow the mother with fertility and fortune, to protect her during her pregnancy, and to promote the fortune and well-being of the newly born child. Thus, functionally equivalent or formally similar rituals may be enacted in the Brahmanical and local Gujarati family traditions but in the former case the rituals are part of transcendental Hinduism, in the latter case pragmatic Hinduism. The distinction between transcendental and pragmatic religions is not an absolute one in form and function: there is slippage back and forth between the two depending upon how the ritual actors constitute the event.

RITUALS OF PREGNANCY

Gujarati rituals of pregnancy can best be understood against a backdrop of ethnophysiological knowledge. The procreation of children is thought to require substance from each parent, but there are various explanations as to how these substances are combined. The semen from the male is mixed within the womb with the woman's blood or with an egg to result in the formation of the foetus. While some women say that the foetus grows within the womb, there is also the idea that it develops in a sack, either inside or outside the womb, which extends from under the rib cage to the pubis. The placenta, variously located under the diaphragm or near the umbilicus, churns up the food the mother eats and a little of the juice from the food passes to the foetus via the cord to nourish it during the period of gestation. Each parent is dependent on the other for procreation, but ideas about the father's contribution in the transference of attributes or qualities (*guna*) to the child vary: some believe that both parents contribute to the process, but the majority feel strongly that the male role ends with impregnation, the qualities coming instead from the mind (*man*) of the mother and from the food that she provides for the child while it grows inside her. I have found little support for the idea which is to be found in the literature (e.g. Mayer 1960; Inden and Nicholas 1977) that the woman plays a passive role in conception, acting simply as a receptacle for the male seed and contributing none of her own characteristics to the child.

In addition to these ideas about the natural basis of conception (which are being increasingly informed by bio-medical notions picked up at antenatal clinics) there is also the idea that conception occurs by the grace of god. The absence of conception is a sign that the Mata – literally the Mother Goddess – has withheld her grace. In cases of suspected infertility or sub-fertility a woman might seek the help of the goddess as much as that of doctors. The appeal to a goddess for her grace usually takes the form of a vow. Such vows may, however, be taken for a variety of reasons, including the general protection and well-being of the family, the healing of an illness, or simply to achieve the 'goodness of god' by the demonstration of one's devotion to a deity.

Vows take one of two forms. The first, *māntā*, entails a promise to do something for the deity if the deity grants a request. A *māntā* is a strategy commonly used by women in cases of barrenness or suspected barrenness. One woman had been married for several years and had suffered three miscarriages. She consulted doctors and eventually it was discovered that she had a bifurcating uterus. She was advised to undergo an operation to rectify it and to enable her to have children. This she did, but at the same time she and her mother went to the temple and made a vow to the Mata, promising to redeem her pledge when she had successfully given birth. Part of the vow was a promise to journey to the shrine of the lineage goddess (*kuladevī*) in Gujarat and present a special scarf and some money to the goddess as well as to travel to a place of pilgrimage to the Mata at Mount Abu and donate the weight of the baby in sugar crystals to be distributed to the poor at the temple. The woman successfully gave birth to a baby boy, but it was more than 10 years before she and her mother were able to fulfil their pledge and journey to India. By this time she had to give the cost of the sugar crystals equivalent to what her son now weighed. If the wish of the *māntā* is granted by the deity, failure to carry out what has been promised can bring great calamity on the person concerned or on the family. If the wish is not fulfilled then the promise does not have to be carried out. It simply means that it was not one's fate for this to happen.

The second type of vow is called a *bādhā*. This form of vow entails giving up something, or making some act of self-sacrifice, until the grace of the deity is obtained. Usually a particular item of food is given up. Alternatively, food is given up for a day of the week which is associated with the deity. If a woman is unable to conceive, for example, she may make a *bādhā* to give up a variety of lentil (*mag*, also called moong) until she becomes pregnant. Or a woman might go on a general fast at a particular time of the Hindu year, such as on certain days in the month of Sravana (July-August) or on the eleventh day of the lunar fortnight (called *agiyāras*), or on a weekly or twice weekly basis. Each day of the week is set aside for a particular deity: Monday for Siva, Tuesday and Sunday for the Mata, Thursday for a favoured guru, usually Jalaram, Friday for Santosima, and Saturday for Hanuman. Saturday is not a day particularly favoured by women, and Wednesday, although sometimes said to be associated with Jalaram, is not usually connected with a deity. The woman chooses the day of a deity in whom she has great faith and fasts in the hope that a wish or vow will be fulfilled. The period of fasting ends with the fulfilment of the hope. At any gathering of Gujarati women, from young girls of 16 and 17 to the oldest women present, it is highly probable that at least some of the women will be observing a fast.

While ideas of foetal development are sometimes fragmentary, it is agreed that by the fifth month the foetus begins to take some shape, to start kicking and moving about. Until that time it is thought to be simply a mass of flesh or 'meat'. The individual soul is said to live within the heart of the foetus and while some say this is present from birth, others point out that the heart, and with it the soul, appears during the fifth month of pregnancy. If miscarriage occurs early in the pregnancy, a woman is considered impure until the blood flow has ceased, but if it occurs after the fifth month the period of pollution lengthens to 11 or 12 days, after which she bathes and washes her hair. If abortion is considered at all, and not all agree that it should ever be done, it is only permissible until the end of the fifth month, after which time it is said that one would be destroying the life of the child.

From this time, too, it is noticeable that more attention is given to the diet of the pregnant woman. A 'normal' diet is pursued during pregnancy with far fewer restrictions than in the postnatal period. However, there is some concern to balance the food intake in terms of the heating and cooling properties thought to be inherent in food. Excessively hot foods, such as red chillies, kidney beans, and a type of bitter gourd called *karelā*, are avoided. All of them give rise to a variety of digestive problems, including diarrhoea, which in pregnancy can be harmful to the foetus and in extreme cases lead to miscarriage. Excessively cold foods are thought to delay the arrival of the baby and may prolong the period of labour. Other restrictions, such as the avoidance of black-coloured foods which are felt to darken the child's skin, vary from one individual to another. Restrictions on the woman's activities may also increase from around the fifth month, with less of the heavy duties of the household such as hoovering and hanging out the washing. By this time too, the physical appearance of the pregnancy is marked and the woman is vulnerable to the effects of evil and the jealousy of others. *Pancmāsī* is performed to protect the woman from these influences throughout the remainder of her pregnancy.

Pancamāsī means literally the 'fifth month'. On an auspicious day in the fifth month, several items which are felt to be particularly effective in their protective properties are placed in a piece of black cloth and wrapped around the woman's wrist with thread by her husband's sister. Some of the oil which has been poured over the image of Hanuman at the household shrine each Saturday, and which over a period of time accumulates a blackish sediment, is mixed with some dust taken from the centre of the crossroads nearest to where the woman lives. To this is added a cowrie shell, some green moong, and an iron ring. This protective thread is cut off at birth. The cutting of the thread, with the cutting of the cord, physically separates the mother from the child, who now requires its own protective measures.

Sīmant, which takes place in the seventh month of the first pregnancy, is the most popular of the life-cycle rituals performed during pregnancy. It is commonly referred to as *kholo bharvo* or simply *kholo*, meaning lap, which also refers to the V-shaped corner of the sari from the leg to the breast in the distinctive way Gujarati women wear their saris. The ritual takes place in the seventh month because the threat of miscarriage is over and it is now safe publicly to celebrate the woman's pregnancy and the imminent birth. The foetus is by this time felt to be fully developed and awaiting birth. The whole theme of *sīmant* is the expression of happiness, joy, and fun, with relatives and friends joining in the celebration.

One of the days associated with the Mata, a Tuesday or a Sunday, is chosen for the ceremony. In the morning the house is cleaned and the woman bathes and puts on clean clothes. A shrine is set up, usually in the living room, with one or more pictures of the Mata in her various forms. Lakshmi, the goddess of wealth and fortune and Saraswati, the goddess of education and learning, are two of the images favoured. In front of each picture a stainless steel jug (*loṭā*) is placed with a coconut on top. For every jug placed at the shrine, seven women – representing the seven sisters of the Mata – are invited to take part in the ceremony. While seven is the usual number, five or nine are also acceptable, the important point being that the number is uneven. These women must all be *goyaṇī* women, that is unmarried women who are not menstruating and married women who are not menstruating and whose husbands are still alive. If a woman knows that her menses will fall during this time, she may eat particularly cold foods for several days to delay its onset. It is said that the *goyaṇī* women brought into the house will celebrate the pregnancy and assist the pregnant woman in her desire for an easy delivery. As a mark of respect to them – as sisters of the Mata – the pregnant woman sits on a low stool and washes with milk and water the big toe of each woman then places some red powder (*kaṅkuṅ*) and rice on their toe and forehead. In some families this takes place at the beginning of the ceremony, in others at the end. It may also entail a gift to the *goyaṇī* women, often a small stainless steel bowl. This situation is reversed during the ceremony proper when the women first offer *prasād* (food which is first offered to the deity) to the pregnant woman before taking it themselves.

After some prayers and singing in front of the shrine, the

woman retires to bathe and put on new clothes and, for the first time in her pregnancy, to wash her hair. A strip of material is laid on the floor, and as she is led back to the shrine a coin and a betel nut, items associated with good fortune, are placed in front of her foot at each step. A married woman who has successfully given birth and who has had no miscarriages or abortions stands in front of the woman at the shrine, for what is referred to as 'the passing ceremony'. In the V-shaped corner of her sari she has placed some rice, coconut, green moong, betel nut and a small amount of money wrapped in cloth. This is all passed backwards and forwards five times to the lap of the pregnant woman. These items are particularly auspicious and one is said to be transferring 'goodness and good wishes' to the woman. The husband's sister places a protective bangle, made predominantly from silver, on the woman's wrist, wishing her a safe and easy delivery. The woman and her husband then sit down facing each other and a small baby of five or six months is placed in their lap in turn. This symbolically enacts the birth of the child and is said to demonstrate that she too can have a happy, healthy child. The enactment of what is described as a 'joke' then follows when the husband's younger brother rubs a mixture of red powder and water into his hands and slaps his sister-in-law's face, leaving behind the red markings. She returns the 'joke' by repeating the action amid a great deal of chiding and laughing from the onlookers. Her husband's brother's actions are interpreted as saying 'look what has happened to you!', and her reciprocation being, 'well it will happen to your wife some day!'. At the end of the ceremony, a meal is served to the guests and if the guests are numerous a separate hall may be hired for this purpose.

In some families *sīmant* can extend over two days. On the second and final day a priest is called and special prayers are said for the woman in front of the shrine. The Mata is thanked for coming into the house and then bid farewell when the shrine is dismantled. In other families the ritual is simpler and shorter, with only five or seven women participating and the household shrine used as a focus for worship. Formerly, the ceremony was followed by the woman's return to her natal home where she would give birth to the child. This happens less now. Many women stay in their husband's home either from preference or because their parents are still in India or East Africa or living with their sons in this country.

Perhaps one reason why *sīmant* is so popular among Gujarati women is that it is the celebration of a woman's first pregnancy. As such it marks an important stage in the fulfilment of her role as a potential mother. A small group of women discussing this remarked that at *sīmant* the woman is 'like the Mata, she is about to become a mother for the first time'. During the ritual she is honoured as the Mata by the other women, who in turn represent the sisters of the Mata. At the end of the ceremony the pregnant woman receives a blessing from her mother-in-law, who is also Mata herself.

RITUALS OF CHILDBIRTH

No other rituals take place between the fifth month (or the seventh month in the case of a first pregnancy) and the birth. The two Brahmanical birth ceremonies – *janmajāta* and *anādiṣṭaprāyascitta* – are not observed in Britain and, according to my informants, rarely observed in India. Moreover, with all births now taking place in hospital, many of the physical problems associated with the pollution of birth, such as the disposal of the placenta, have been removed from the domestic arena. The mother, however, remains in a state of impurity throughout the postpartum. The blood passed after birth is *kacaro*, a term implying extreme filth and dirt. Until this has all passed from the body, anything from four to six weeks, the woman is impure, the degree of impurity decreasing with the passing weeks. Many of the dietary injunctions in the postnatal period are aimed at ridding the body of this filth. 'Hot' foods assist in the process and 24 hours after delivery the woman begins a diet of these foods which many observe for three or four weeks or more. Some women point out that unless all the dirty blood in the womb is expelled after birth, it may hamper the formation of another egg and so decrease the possibility of a further pregnancy. The same principle applies following a miscarriage, when hot foods are also eaten.

The colostrum is also considered filthy. Although attitudes are changing, I have found that most women who breastfeed (and not all do) are reluctant to put the child to the breast until the 'proper' milk arrives after two or three days, as colostrum is considered to be very harmful to the child. There are no clear ideas about how it arrives in the breast, but external heat may be applied in order to express it quickly and so begin breastfeeding.

About five or six hours after the baby is born, and before its first feeding, a mixture of jaggery and water or honey and water, called *galsūthī or galsudi*, is placed in its mouth. This is the first thing that should pass the child's lips and is said to bring sweetness and strength during its life. The mixture is made up and brought to the hospital by the husband or mother-in-law only after the news of the birth has been received, because until this time, there is always the possibility that something may go wrong. Some women say that the qualities of whoever gives this mixture are transferred to the child. One woman told of how her father's brother, whose marriage was childless, had placed some drops of the mixture in her mouth when she was born in East Africa. She was amazed, when she met him years later, how alike they were in temperament and character.

The *chaththī* ritual takes place on the sixth day after birth and is also referred to as *Vidhata*, the goddess of fate, or simply *chaththī karvī*, literally 'doing the sixth', when the child's fortune is invisibly written down by the goddess. Although some women are still in hospital on the sixth day, female relatives may organize the paraphernalia of the ritual and the ceremony is performed at the hospital bed. Because of the organization involved and the hospital environment, others choose to omit the ceremony altogether. The mother and child are bathed and dressed in new clothes. A wooden board or table of some kind is covered with a white or green cloth and lighted candles placed in front of it with some betel nut, red powder, green moong, and a small amount of money. Rice, sugar crystals, and salt are variations on these items, all of which are thought to be good omens for the child's future. The mother, or her husband's sister, takes the baby in her arms and turns it seven times to face the light of the candles, shielding its eyes with a piece of cloth or the end of her sari, as some say the light causes blindness or cross-eyes in the child. Prayers are said to the goddess for the future well-being of the baby and the board is left overnight in the woman's bedroom with a blank sheet of paper and a red pen. Around midnight, Vidhata is said to write down in the auspicious red ink the future life history of the child. The size of the ceremony varies, particularly if the sixth day falls on a weekday when the exigencies of urban life may limit guests to close relatives and local friends.

The use of astrology as a guide to naming is common among Gujaratis in East London. The essential pieces of information required are the exact day and time of birth. Beginning at six in the morning, each day is divided into one-and-a-half-hour periods, or *janmotrī*, the divisions of the day. These divisions when taken with the day of birth are more or less auspicious. Knowledge of the days and their divisions is common among the older women. Efforts may be made to 'fudge' an inauspicious time of birth, as it can be a bad omen for the child's future and for the family. An astrologer, often in India but sometimes locally, uses the information to determine the first letter of the name (*rāśī*).

The *nāmakaraṇa* ceremony takes place any time after the twelfth day, although some say it can occur earlier, depending on when the information arrives from the astrologer. This is given to the husband's sister who in theory always names the child, but in practice, and especially for the second and subsequent children, the parents often choose the name, sometimes in consultation with the husband's sister and the help of a book of names. Relatives and friends are invited to the ceremony. Some families take the opportunity to hold a large celebration of people who have not seen the mother and child since birth, while others confine it to 10 or 15 people. The mother and baby again bathe and put on new clothes. A large white cloth is spread on the floor and the baby, together with some green moong, betel nut, and money are placed on it. Four young children, belonging to older siblings, relatives, or friends, each take a corner of the cloth. They are all boys if the child is a boy, girls if it is a girl. With the cloth now in the shape of a hammock the children swing the baby up and down to the chant:

'Cradle and pipal tree and leaves of the same
Aunt has chosen (   ) as baby's name.'

At the appropriate moment the husband's sister says the child's chosen name (see also on this Sinclair Stevenson 1920:14). The children are given jaggery and coconut and food is served to the guests. The ceremony is called *nām pāḍun*, 'give the name', or *nām phoibā pāḍun*, *phoibā* being the child's father's sister. She also gives presents to the child and the mother and it is not uncommon for these to be sent from India or East Africa if the husband has other sisters not living in Britain. As well as a chosen name, the child takes the full name of the father. For women this will be replaced at marriage by the husband's name.

The occasion of the child's first outing is of great importance among Gujaratis and is widely observed. The period of pollution following childbirth is said to last for six weeks, during which time the woman should remain indoors and refrain from cooking or lighting candles at the household shrine. With each successive postnatal ritual, the degree of pollution appears to lessen as the mother is gradually reincorporated into the household and begins to resume her normal duties. The application of this rule, however, varies greatly in practice. Where a woman is not living in a joint household and does not have the assistance of her mother-in-law or other female relatives, it may be impossible to observe such a lengthy period of seclusion, especially if she has other young children to care for. Other women feel simply that once the blood flow after birth has ceased there is no need to apply the rule, although most continue to abstain from lighting candles at the household shrine. The first major visit to the health centre occurs in the fourth week after birth and, in my experience, Gujarati women are fairly punctilious in attending.

The first 'official' outing, however, usually takes place in the fifth or sixth week when the baby makes its first visit to the temple and the mother is released from the stigma of pollution. Mother and baby again put on new clothes, the child wearing the two loose gold bracelets called *pocī* given by its father's sister. At the Sri Nathji temple in Leytonstone it is possible to see numerous families on any day arriving first at the image of Ganesh to give thanks for a happy conclusion of the birth and then moving on to other images, including Ambaji Mata, to ask for their blessings for the child's future and to give the baby its first food consecrated by the deity (*prasād*).

The attainment of motherhood is one of the most important events in the life of a Gujarati woman. Motherhood refers not only to the physical process of pregnancy and childbirth, the nourishment of the infant in the womb, and the pain of birth, but also to the upbringing of the child, its continued nourishment, care, and well-being. The traditional period of seclusion after birth, when the mother remains constantly with the child for upwards of 30 days, is seen as a means of establishing and strengthening the ties of love and affection which exist between the two throughout life. 'Working mothers' and young women who fail to observe such seclusion are condemned by some older women for neglecting this crucial aspect of motherhood. In giving birth to a child, a woman affirms her own sense of personal worth and achievement and confirms her status as a married woman within the household, a status which may be minimal at first but which steadily increases as her children reach physical maturity. As a new member of her husband's household a bride may have little influence, particularly in her relationship with her mother-in-law who is the female head of family. The younger woman's position is considerably enhanced with the fulfilment of her maternal role and the growth of her children. This has been observed among other South Asian groups both in India (Hasan 1967) and in Britain (C. Ballard 1978). Women who fail in their attempts to give birth, or to conceive, are often thought to be the jealous agents responsible for the effects of the evil eye in healthy babies and young children.

During the Navratri festival which is held specifically for the Mata, as well as the large public celebrations that take place in the community, women may also hold a smaller ceremony in the home to honour the Mata. Failure periodically to invite the goddess into the home is thought to account for illness or distress which may have occurred in the family, or it may be used to explain why a woman's pregnancy was prolonged or difficult. To ask the Mata into the house is to ask for her protection and help, but to neglect to do so can be used as a retrospective explanation for domestic problems. An invitation to the Mata can be offered at any time and is often used as a fertility strategy: to request a child after one's marriage or to reassure a woman who is planning another child but who may be unsure, perhaps for economic reasons, of the wisdom of doing so. Such an invitation may also be offered if miscarriage has occurred or if the woman is experiencing difficulty in conceiving.

As in the *sīmant* ritual, seven women are invited for each stainless steel jug placed at the domestic shrine. Songs are sung in praise of the Mata and the women are fed at the end of the ceremony. Possession is a common feature of the rituals and the woman makes her request to the Mata through the *bhūī*, a devotee of the goddess who is possessed by her. Others present may also make requests in the same way. While such worship takes place in the home, a *bhūī* may establish a permanent shrine in her home and in one such house in Newham a room is given over to her shrine where women may go with a variety of problems to seek the help of the Mata through her devotee.

Whilst worship of the Mata concerns both men and women, it can be seen that Gujarati women bear a ritual resemblance to the goddess or to her sisters. A possessed woman has the Mata speak through her and at the *sīmant* ritual the young pregnant woman becomes an icon of the Mata and may be worshipped as such. She is bringing good fortune into the household with the imminent birth of a new member of the family. The great importance accorded to motherhood in Gujarati culture, and in India generally, is highlighted by the strategies employed by women who are unable to have children or have difficulty in conceiving. A sterile woman poses a threat to the well-being of the household and to other households in her propensity for producing the effects of the evil eye. Women worship the Mata, but the Mata manifests herself through them. The aims of the rituals are to ensure the health, well-being, and protection of both mother and child. Brahmans are not really necessary in this worship; nor is anything else apart from the presence of the goddess and the devotion of the women who seek her grace.

NOTE

This paper is based on 13 months of fieldwork in the east London borough of Newham. Research was funded by the Economic and Social Research Council. I am grateful also for the support of the Gujarati community and the Newham District Health Authority.

4

Caste and sect in the Swaminarayan movement

Rohit Barot

What effect does a sectarian movement, or rather a specific sect within a movement, have on the corporate nature of a particular caste group? Following Wach (1944:128) a sect is a 'group with special concepts, forms of worship and adherence to exclusive leadership exercised by an outstanding religious personality or by his physical or spiritual descendants.' The Sanskrit word which comes closest to the European understanding of sect is *sampradāya*, meaning 'an established doctrine transmitted from one teacher to another' (Monier Williams 1899:1175). In this analysis of the relationship between sect and caste in Britain the sect under discussion is that of Shree Swaminarayan Siddhanta Sajivan Mandal, and at issue is its effect within the corporate caste community of the Leva Kanbi Patels of Kutch, Gujarat.

The process of segmentation within the Swaminarayan movement and the formation of the Mandal has created a cleavage among the Leva Kanbi Patels in India, East Africa, and the United Kingdom. One question arising from this is how far they are likely to separate into two sect-based caste groups. But as I hope to show through an account of the Mandal leader's visit to Britain, the issue is not so clear-cut as to produce in the case of the Leva Kanbi Patels two mutually exclusive groups: the relationship between sect and caste here is not that of one reducible to the other.[1]

VAISHNAVISM, SAHJANAND SWAMI, AND THE GENESIS OF THE SWAMINARAYAN MOVEMENT

Vaishnavism in Gujarat is associated with the Pushtimarg sect of Vallabhacharya, eloquently written about by Barz (1976). Rejecting asceticism and renunciation, Pushtimarg lays emphasis on the affective relationship between the worshipper and his personal god rather than on the intellectual comprehension of the supreme through asceticism. While devotional worship cuts across caste boundaries and may appeal to all politico-economic classes in society, it is worth noting that it has developed fully and elaborately amongst the more prosperous Hindus in Gujarat and elsewhere. Pustimarg stands literally for the way of well-being which implies both spiritual and material welfare – a theme in keeping with the social background of mercantile communities in Gujarat. It is interesting that in his study of Hinduism Weber (1958:307) was sensitive to this class character when he observed that devotional worship as a movement appealed to 'a literary but wealthy middle class' as an alternative to intellectual pursuit of knowledge. Weber characterized the Vallabhacharyas as a 'merchant and banker sect'. He also noted (p. 315) that 'the richest trader caste, the Bania, was able to find a taste for service of god' in the sect and that an 'extraordinarily large number of them belonged to this somewhat socially exclusive sect'.

In the early part of the nineteenth century Pushtimarg passed through a crisis when its leaders were accused of moral and sexual corruption. As Briggs (1849:235–43), Monier Williams (1882:30), and others have suggested, the Swaminarayan movement grew as a puritanical reaction to the corruption affecting the Pushtimarg. The development of the Swaminarayan movement owed much to the ideology and organization of its charismatic founder Sahjanand Swami. A high-caste Brahman, he was born in 1780 in Chappaiya in Uttar Pradesh. As is usual in the Hindu tradition, he possessed miraculous powers from his childhood. He underwent severe ascetic practices in the Himalayas, returned to the plains, and is known to have travelled all over India, visiting the sacred complex of holy places and reaching Gujarat in 1800. In contrast to Pushtimarg, Sahjanand Swami preached a puritanical Vaishnavism. He introduced a clear dichotomy between lay householders and renouncers, also applying strict rules of separation between men and women, institutionalized through the creation of separate temples for them. The contact between renouncers and women was strictly prohibited. If a renouncer touched a woman, even accidentally, he was required to fast for a day. In his theological and philosophical position the Swami followed the Great Vaishnava teacher Ramanuja and accepted the doctrine of qualified monism as his fundamental precept.

From 1804 Sahjanand Swami appears to have developed a following in Ahmedabad and the surrounding areas of Gujarat. He recruited members from a wide social spectrum. Both sectarian and non-sectarian sources note that, unlike the Pushtimarg, he welcomed lower-caste participation in his growing organizational fold. Bhattacharya (1896:375) notes that the admission of lower castes did not diminish the esteem held for him by his followers: he was careful to exclude unclean untouchables, such as leatherworkers and latrine cleaners, in order to retain a measure of respectability among Hindus of the time. Throughout this period, the consolidation of British rule in India was altering the economic position of lower castes, while internal and external migration opened the way to prosperity, as it had done in the pre-colonial and post-colonial history of Gujarat. Members of the lower castes were undoubtedly attracted to the Swaminarayan movement in order to improve their ritual status.

Although religious groups were often hostile to him, Sahjanand Swami expanded his congregation. In 1810 he established a base in Vadtal which was to become an important primary focus for the movement. From there the movement enhanced its sectarian identity with the establishment of elaborate temples elsewhere in Gujarat. With its ideology and organization becoming distinctive, the devoted followers of Sahjanand Swami

declared him to be Swaminarayan, a divine embodiment of the
supreme conceived to be above the entire celestial hierarchy of
Hindus. This important theological development was consistent
with the sectarian view that Swaminarayan was capable of re-
leasing his followers from death and rebirth and conferring on
them the boon of absolute salvation (*ātyantika mokṣa*).

As an ascetic founder of his popular movement, Sahjanand
Swami had rejected the concept of householder as sect leader.
However, in dealing with succession he appears to have
accepted the hereditary principle rather than the appointment of a worthy renouncer to administer the property and
affairs of his primary organization: he appointed the lay householder sons of his two brothers to succeed him. In 1826 he
divided the jurisdiction of the movement into two parts to establish two administrative divisions or seats (*gādīs*). Ahmedabad
became the main centre for northern Gujarat and Vadtal for the
south. His elder brother's son became the head, called Acharya,
at the Ahmedabad seat and his younger brother's son occupied a
similar seat at Vadtal.

Although Sahjanand Swami distinguished secular, administrative affairs from belief and preaching, this separation – in so
far as it corresponded to a division between laity and renouncers
– was difficult to maintain in practice. As property and assets
accumulated from temple endowments, harmonious relations
between the administrative head, the lay members, and renouncers became more difficult. Though the renouncers must
traditionally be detached from handling money, they nevertheless began to express concern about financial management or
mismanagement in so far as it would influence the conditions
under which they worked. In addition, some renouncers began
to claim that one or several of them were the carriers of
Swaminarayan's divine charisma, and that they too were able to
grant or withhold absolute salvation. The movement became
fraught with differences of opinion on both organizational and
ideological grounds.

The conflict generated a process of segmentation which gave
rise to a number of semi-sectarian or sectarian organizations.[2]
The cult of Abji Bapa, the Shree Swaminarayan Siddhanta

Sajivan Mandal, and the Wadhwan seat established by a dissi-
dent known to have been excluded from hereditary succession,
developed at the Ahmedabad seat of the movement in northern
Gujarat. From the Vadtal seat in southern Gujarat arose Shree
Akashar Purshottam Sanstha, with the Yogi Divine Society as a
separate offshoot. Gunatit Samaj developed as a consequence of
a split within the Yogi Divine Society and was organized into the
Anoopam Mission for men and the Gunatit Jyot for women;
Guru Maharaj of north Gujarat branched off from Shree
Akshar Purshottam Sanstha; and the Swaminarayan Gurukul
movement constituted an autonomous body apart from the
Vadtal jurisdiction.

Most of these organizations, several of them separate and
autonomous sects within the movement, are now reproduced
among the Gujarati Hindus in Britain. The way they have been
transplanted in this country is perhaps better understood, although this will not be elaborated upon here, within the broader
class context where the movement and settlement of sect members is tied up with their transition from traditional division of
labour to market-based economies. Groups have moved from
near subsistence to relative degrees of economic self-sufficiency,
either as manual labourers or traders, merchants, and entre-
preneurs, and the changing class positions of individuals,
families, and communities add an important dimension to the
understanding of the ideological and organizational features of
the sects within the Swaminarayan movement as a whole (see
Barot 1980).

THE CREATION OF SHREE SWAMINARAYAN
SIDDHANTA SAJIVAN MANDAL

The conflict over the management of temple property and assets
created opposition between the Ahmedabad-based household
leader of the sect and some renouncers, which in turn eventually
led to the formation of the Mandal. This split within the movement divided the caste of Leva Kanbi Patels initially in Kutch
and East Africa and then in the United Kingdom.

The conflict appears to have developed as follows. At the turn of the present century the fourth Acharya, Shree Vasudevprasadji (1899–1937), became the hereditary head of the movement at Ahmedabad and assumed personal ownership of the movement's assets and property, investing temple income in unsound commercial ventures. Renouncers and lay members opposed this practice and a Leva Kanbi Patel from Kutch – a man known by the name of Abji Bapa – led the campaign to challenge the Acharya's claim to the property. In conjunction with a leading renouncer, Swami Ishwercharandasji, he established a body to oppose the hereditary head of the sect, calling it an Association of Truth Seekers (Satsanga Mahasabha). This confrontation between those who supported the head and those who supported Abji Bapa and his defiant association created a sharp cleavage within the movement. In turn, this divided most members of the Leva Kanbi Patel caste in Kutch between supporters of the head, who came to be known as belonging to the majority side (Moto Paksha), and supporters of Abji Bapa, known as the minority side (Nano Paksha): the words *moto* and *nano* referring to a numerical majority and minority and the word *paksa* to a particular side. Among the Leva Kanbi Patels the conflict entailed considerable hostility and violence. A leading man on the minority side was tied up in a sack and beaten to death. The friction created a deep division, estranging closest kin and affines from each other, especially after Abji Bapa's death.

Under Swami Ishwercharandasji's leadership the opposition began to develop a distinct character. This happened when the Swami recruited young Purshottambhai Patel of Charottar and renamed him as a renouncer, Swami Shree Muktajivandasji. Swami Muktajivandasji organized support for the minority opposed to the Ahmedabad Acharya. Although the opposition was successful in preventing the head from appropriating the sect's assets, the process of separation between the primary organization and the new opposition became marked when the opponents bought land in Maninagar near Ahmedabad to set up an organizational nucleus for a separate Swaminarayan sect. The organization based on this territorial locus was named Shree Swaminarayan Siddhanta Sajivan Mandal and from 1947

Swami Muktajivandasji became its first leader – although he was legitimated as the fourth renouncer to have spiritually descended from Sahjanand Swami. The Mandal developed rapidly among the Leva Kanbi Patels of Kutch and other Gujaratis. Separate Mandal temples began to appear in many Leva Kanbi Patel villages and in 1955 the Mandal constructed its own large temple, with oblong-shaped domes (*śīkharbandhī mandir*). This marked the Mandal's total separation from the Ahmedabad seat of the primary organization and its traditional head.

It was during this period that Swami Muktajivandasji is known to have supported the migration of poverty-stricken Leva Kanbi Patels to the countries of East Africa. Initially all the followers of Swaminarayan co-operated in the creation of one monolithic organization for all the Swaminarayan sects in East Africa. However, as the number of followers of a particular sect increased, the dividing line between sects became more important and undermined the body encompassing all the sects. Among the Leva Kanbi Patels the traditional division between Moto Paksha, still supporting the traditional head of the primary organization, and Nano Paksha surfaced in East Africa – the latter a separate Swaminarayan sect with its own distinctive beliefs and organization. This divide still constitutes a boundary of some significance among the Leva Kanbi Patels.

During the last 20 years Swaminarayan sects have appeared in Britain – and so has the traditional cleavage among the Leva Kanbi Patels. But this division not only reproduces the traditional opposition between the majority and the minority, it also provides a mode for the expression of issues which arise from the settlement of sect members in Britain.

SHREE SWAMINARAYAN SIDDHANTA SAJIVAN MANDAL IN BRITAIN

Most of the Mandal members living in Britain come from East Africa, especially from Kenya where they occupied a special niche in the construction industry. Decolonization brought radical changes in East Africa during the 1960s and non-citizen

Asians were gradually pushed out of the area (see Robinson 1986 for the account of their settlement in Britain since 1965 – it is too well-known to need further amplification here). The Mandal members began arriving in Britain in 1961 and their migration and settlement spans a period of some 20 years. The majority of the men in the Hendon settlement were in the construction industry. Those who settled in Bolton worked in the textile mills. Women usually worked in factories and mills in both locations. The evolution of the Mandal temple from a small shrine in one room to a large property worth more than £300,000 near Golders Green underground station shows that the sect has become fully consolidated here. As large numbers of Mandal and non-Mandal Leva Kanbi Patels settled in the UK, their presence eventually created conditions for the re-emergence of the cleavage based on differential sectarian affiliation. This happened in 1970 when the Mandal leader, Swami Muktajivandasji, visited the sect members for the first time – when I had just started fieldwork in Hendon. The incident in question is presented in three phases: the commencement, the confrontation, and the counter-action.

When Swami Muktajivandasji was due to arrive in Britain in 1970, the Leva Kanbi Patel opponents of the Mandal formed an informal, temporary group to oppose his visit to his followers. Their leader sent a petition to the Indian High Commission complaining that the sect leader's presence would convey a bad image of Indians living in Britain. The officials of the Indian High Commission said they had no powers to restrict the freedom of movement of an Indian citizen. Given the multiplex nature of the community, it is not particularly surprising that the Mandal leaders were aware of the opposition being organized and promptly identified the mischief being played by the Moto Paksha.

When Swami Muktajivandasji and his entourage arrived in Britain, the Mandal members organized a procession in which they wanted to have the Swami ride an elephant from Hyde Park Corner to Trafalgar Square. Eventually they settled for a car and Scottish pipe band, followed by a procession of Mandal men, women, and children. The Swami gave a speech from a specially constructed platform in Trafalgar Square and the young renouncers performed a folk dance. However, just as the leader was leaving the stage an egg was thrown from the crowd, narrowly missing the master. He was hurried away to a waiting car and the Mandal members immediately attributed the action to the Moto Paksha.

The second incident occurred on a stage in Brent Town Hall, when a spiritual play was being acted to emphasize obedience to the master as a precondition for salvation. Swami Muktajivandasji himself was on the stage, interjecting his commentaries as the actors moved from dramaturgical reality to the reality of devotion in which they would prostrate themselves before the spiritual master. While everybody was immersed in the play a young man in flared trousers and neck length hair walked up to the swami and said, 'I want to ask you some questions. Why are you conducting these useless activities?' Although the sect leader was heard to say that he was prepared to answer the young man's questions, the Mandal volunteers quickly grabbed him and escorted him out forcefully. The corridor outside suddenly echoed with his screams, followed by a silence during which the play was resumed. The opponents had arrived at the hall in full force with banners and placards which abused the sect leader. They accused him of appropriating a large amount of cash from his followers, engaging in illegal currency transactions, and not doing anything about economic development in Kutch. The accusations also ranged from allegations of criminality and malice to those indicating that young boys of the Mandal were forced into renunciation without any regard to their own wishes or those of their parents. A banner accused the Mandal of preventing Harijans (the low-caste untouchables) from entering the sect's temples in India. For the devoted Mandal members it was a deeply disturbing experience. Insulting behaviour towards their spiritual master amounted to a threat to their own wellbeing. It was decided that the Moto Paksha ringleader should be punished for his misdeeds.

The Mandal members chose an evening blacked out by the 1971 miners' strike to assault the Moto Paksha ringleader. They managed to abduct him from his house and, while driving around in a car, beat him up. Later they dumped him on the roadside, badly cut, bruised, and shaken. The police investigation led to the arrest of two Mandal brothers who were eventually tried at the Old Bailey for assault to cause grievous bodily harm to the ringleader. The trial brought out clearly the opposition between the two sides as an extension of the pre-migration polarity between the majority and minority sides. The barrister defending the two Mandal brothers made an opening statement to establish the fact that the conflict had its roots in the traditional opposition between Moto Paksha and Nano Paksha, explicitly using the vernacular word *pakṣa* to refer to the two factions. The evidence against the two brothers was overwhelming and they were sentenced to two years' imprisonment.

From the point of view of the Mandal members the conflict in Britain was merely an extension of the old conflict that had dominated their lives in Kutch for many years, often bringing painful disruption to them and their families. Though the sect members see the cleavage as a sign of lack of unity in the caste community, they also see their sectarian identity as sacred, especially in the person of the sect's leader – and therefore to be maintained and defended whatever the cost. In other words, the commitment to the sect and the kind of salvation to which it could lead overrides the considerations of the caste, a theme familiar to the Mandal members.

Although it is evident to an outside observer that *pakṣa* categories are applied to some non-traditional issues, sect members themselves are only marginally aware of this; for the generality of *pakṣa* means that it can be applied to a wide range of deviations. In Britain *pakṣa* is not a one-to-one reproduction of a Hindu category but a formulation influenced and modified by the experience of Mandal members: Hindu immigrants do not simply recreate their traditional universe here. The fact that *pakṣa* in this country and India are not identical units is reflected in what both the sect and non-sect members say about it. At least some sect members were perceptive enough to say, in a more detailed explanation of the events, that the Mandal's opponents did not belong to the Moto Paksha although their link to it was never fully denied and was emphasized at a more general level. Nevertheless, this partial denial of the link between the Mandal's opponents and the Moto Paksha recurred as a theme. In discussing the history of the Paksha divisions the description of the conflict between the two sides had a specific element in common. The discontinuities between the sides were expressed in the primacy of mutually exclusive affiliation of the actors either to the primary Swaminarayan organization or to the Mandal. When some Mandal members asserted that it was less valid to link their opponents to the primary organization, it seemed that a non-sectarian assessment of the conflict had not escaped their attention entirely.

As far as the opponents of the Mandal were concerned, their leader, who had been believed to be leading the Moto Paksha opposition to the Mandal in Britain, not only denied affiliation to any Swaminarayan sect, but generally denounced religious and sectarian practices as blindfolding the ignorant. Even though it cannot be assumed that his more secular outlook was a result of his experiences in Britain only, there was no doubt that they had played a part in influencing his opposition to the Mandal. From our long conversation together, it was apparent that the British tradition of protest and demonstration had had some effect on him and his supporters.

The disjunction of perception between the two sides is quite remarkable. The Mandal members recognize the conflict but do not recognize the differences for what they really are. By and large, with the exception of a small minority, most of them use words like atheist (*nāstik*), irreligious (*adharmī*), sinner (*pāpī*), and people in bad company (*kusaṅgī*) to describe their adversaries. The rationality of the non-sectarian perspective is often discomforting and is therefore dealt with with much feeling of unease. In designating members of the Mandal as 'ignorant peasants' and an embarrassment to other Indians in Britain, the leader of the opponents was expressing opinions and views not subsumable under the traditional Paksha opposition.

Since the Mandal members recognize Paksha, how do they apply the logic of separation and exclusion to the social bonds connecting them with non-Mandal Leva Kanbi Patels? For the Mandal members, Paksha has a real historical dimension, something more tangible than a distant folklore. It instantly symbolizes the conflict and its recurring experience in bitter estrangement. Though this conflict and cleavage have divided the caste group into two unequal halves, it does not as yet appear to have produced the kind of division which is complete, permanent, and irreversible, creating two separate groups from a single social entity. However, whenever the theme of separation comes up, it is not unusual for the Mandal members to express it in terms of the hierarchical ideology of caste relations they know so well. During this particular conflict in London, the idea of a separate Mandal-based caste group was mooted and an articulate sect member used the expressions 'those within the caste' (*sajātīya*) as opposed to 'those without' (*vijātīya*) to distinguish the Mandal from the Moto Paksha, as if they were two separate and unrelated social entities. Some diehards would assert that they would accept no food from their Moto Paksha relations and would insist on Mandal endogamy as far as it was possible to enforce – which was rarely. In general, the sect members imposed hard and impermeable boundaries only when an individual was known to have opposed the Mandal and its leader in public. In other situations the boundary tended to be much softer, allowing a fair degree of contact and interaction between those within and those without the Mandal.

CONCLUSION

The historical and ethnographic material on the Swaminarayan movement shows that the conflict between the Ahmedabad-based primary Swaminarayan organization and the secondary Mandal is the basis of cleavage among the Leva Kanbi Patels. Two dimensions are relevant to any discussion of the relationship between sect and caste. First there is the Indian Hindu part, which culturally and historically provides the identity of both sect and caste. Second, these entities have a British basis which is a consequence of the recent settlement of sect members in the UK, historically determined by colonial rule and the labour migration to East Africa and Britain.

Dumont's (1970:188) comments on sect and its relation to the caste system are relevant to the discussion here. He notes that 'in theory caste membership and sect membership operate at different levels'. In his somewhat cryptic explanation it is possible to discern that it is in relation to the individualistic part played by the renouncer that a sect is distinguishable from a caste. Dumont argues that the possibility of conflict between sect and caste is exceptional unless the sect makes itself exclusive *vis-à-vis* not only other sects but also caste values, forcing its members in the world to despise these values. However, he appears to be much less concerned with this conflict than with the view that sects come to resemble caste or, as he puts it, 'the sect degenerates into caste' (1970:188).

Although the comparative implications of this statement are less relevant here, it is sufficient to say that as far as the evolution of the Mandal is concerned, affiliation to the sect on the one hand and to the caste on the other among the Leva Kanbi Patels are two separate and distinctive phenomena not consistently related to each other. As both sect and caste appear to possess a distinctive autonomy of their own, they do not seem to be reducible one to the other. More precisely, a sect in this instance is not a caste – notwithstanding the overlap in personnel. As a sectarian organization, the Mandal is only partly coterminous with the caste of Leva Kanbi Patels. In a similar way, the caste only partly overlaps with the sect. Mandal members see their sectarian affiliation and caste membership as phenomenal entities of a different order and appreciate the incompatibility they create at the level of social relations. From time to time pressure for sectarian exclusiveness increases, but there is insufficient evidence to support the Dumontian thesis that the Mandal is in fact evolving into a separate, sect-based, endogamous caste group. Even if the Mandal members maintain the ideological consciousness of separation, in reality social relations cut across the sectarian boundaries.

Although it is indisputable that Hindus reproduce and retain traditional forms in Britain, it is worth noting that capitalism and the international division of labour have heavily influenced their lives, especially in providing a stimulus for migration and, in recent years, settlement in Britain and other European countries. Therefore, when they recreate their traditional organizations in Britain the transplantation of these forms has to be assessed in terms of their new experiences and aspirations – and not only in relation to their distant pre-migration status. In addition to the use of traditional categories in a new socio-economic context, the sect members are likely to become much more class conscious the longer they live in Britain. But even if class becomes a significant element in the consciousness of sect members, and there is some evidence that it is doing so, there is a greater likelihood that awareness of the sect and a distinct sense of belonging to a sectarian community with a caste basis will persist for some time to come.

NOTES

1 The fieldwork for this study was carried out in Hendon and Bolton between 1970 and 1972 and was written up as a Ph.D thesis entitled 'The Social Organization of a Swaminarayan Sect in Britain' (1980) University of London: SOAS. For their critical comments on this material I am thankful to Professor Adrian Mayer, Professor Michael Banton, and Dr Richard Burghart.

2 Although this outline notes separate organizational bodies within the Swaminarayan movement, it is better regarded as being provisional until more information and research can provide a proper and accurate picture of the full range of institutional bodies in this dynamic movement. There is likely to be lack of consensus between researchers on the pattern of differentiation within the movement. In his recent book on the Swaminarayan religion, Raymond B. Williams refers to Guru Maharaj of north Gujarat (1984:56–7), not found in my investigation. Raymond Williams's account does not refer to a seat at Wadhwan which a descendant of the Ahmedabad head is believed to have established.

5

The Indianization of the Hare Krishna movement in Britain

Séan Carey

The interest of Westerners in oriental religions, from Trans-cendental Meditation to Zen, is now well documented in the social science literature. But an intriguing question remains. What has been the effect of this occidental enthusiasm on the Asian communities from which these religions – both genuine and pseudo – have come? In this paper I shall take up this question with reference to the emergence and development of the relationship between one particular sect – the International Society for Krishna Consciousness (ISKCON), more familiarly known as the Hare Krishna movement – and its Indian followers in Britain. To that end I shall trace the history of ISKCON in the West, being careful to emphasize its traditional and ortho-dox components and then go on to examine the type of services that it provides for Hindus, the reasons why a number of young Indians have joined the movement as full-time members, and the very important differences that exist between ISKCON and other contemporary Hindu institutions. In order to take account of the views, motives and aspirations of the people concerned I have made extensive use of case histories.

THE HISTORY OF ISKCON

ISKCON was founded by His Divine Grace A.C. Bhaktivedanta Swami Prabhupada, a one-time pharmacist turned monk who, penniless at the age of 70, travelled by ship from Bombay to New York in 1965, surviving two heart attacks en route, to preach what he called 'Krishna Consciousness'.

Like other Indian gurus who had come to the West in the 1960s, Bhaktivedanta Swami's initial recruits were drawn from the hippies and flower-children on the East and West coasts. An active proselytizer, he appeared at the bizarrely named 'Mantra-Rock Dance' in the company of such counter-cultural luminaries as Allen Ginsberg, the Grateful Dead, and Jefferson Airplane. Later on he picked up a number of disillusioned college students who, fed up with what they considered to be the arid intellectualism of their academic mentors and the political impotence of their contemporaries involved in the anti-war and civil rights movements, found an ultimate solution in the message of ISKCON, which prophesied the collapse of the existing social order and the dawn of a new age of love, peace, and harmony. Overall it is true to say that ISKCON emerged in a particularly unstable period of American life and its converts came not from the ranks of the dispossessed but from those who enjoyed a high degree of 'affluence and privilege' (Daner 1976:7).

In the 1970s, however, the strictness of the ISKCON devotional praxis, the collapse of the counterculture, and the adverse publicity generated by certain anti-cult movements (which sought to 'deprogramme' recruits to new religious movements) ensured that ISKCON remained highly visible, even though it lacked a mass following. In 1972 there were some 4,500 full-time Western devotees; and that number has remained roughly constant, although there has been some recent growth in membership in continental Europe (Spain, France, and Italy) and in Latin America (Brazil and Argentina).

Bhaktivedanta Swami did not undertake his journey simply to save the 'materialistic' West from its follies and excesses. His plan was much more ambitious: he also wanted to save India. He believed that if he could make Western converts there was a chance that India would take note, cease its headlong rush towards modernity, and return to the path of religious righteousness. This strategy is now showing signs of partial success. ISKCON is a fast expanding organization on the Indian subcontinent; it now has some 23 centres there, with others in countries like Fiji, Kenya, South Africa, and Mauritius which have sizeable Hindu communities.

How has this expansion come about? The most important thing to be emphasized is that ISKCON is not some sort of Indian equivalent to new religious movements like Scientology, the Aetherius Society, or the Children of God. The term 'Krishna Consciousness' and the context may be new but the message is decidedly traditional. Bhaktivedanta Swami has re-produced a faithful and authentic version of the theistic religious movement associated with the sixteenth-century Hindu saint Sri Chaitanya, one of the most significant figures in the devotional movement which spread across north India between the four-teenth and seventeenth centuries and which still survives today in Uttar Pradesh, Orissa, Bengal, and Bihar. It was from this grassroots tradition that ISKCON emerged. It is important to note, however, that the modern Krishna movement was not solely a product of Bhaktivedanta Swami's religious enthusiasm and imagination. Indeed, to a very large extent he was merely following in the footsteps of the nineteenth-century Calcutta lawyer, Bhaktivinoda Thakur, and his son Bhaktisiddhanta Saraswati (Bhaktivedanta Swami's guru), who founded the Gaudiya Matha in Calcutta in 1918. The origins and develop-ment of this institution are still poorly understood but the in-dologist Thomas Hopkins makes an important point when he notes that the revitalization of the Chaitanya Vaishnavite trad-ition by these men provided a very important proselytizing platform for ISKCON's founder in the West and thus, by implication, among modern, urban Hindu constituencies. In the words of Hopkins:

'[Bhaktivedanta Swami] brought with him much more than his own abilities; he brought with him over a century of working through the problems of how the great Vaishnava path relates to the modern world and how that tradition can be related to a Western mentality: how it can be promoted within the West and how it can be propagated by the acquisition of new members. For instance, new members of the Krishna Consciousness organization go through a two-stage initiation. First they are given a religious name and beads to chant Hare Krishna on. The second initiation is the initiation into brahmanhood. But again this is not an American innovation. Bhaktisiddhanta Saraswati had done that in India, and it was simply carried over into this country by Bhaktivedanta Swami.'

(Hopkins 1981:28)

Another important point in accounting for ISKCON's success amongst Indians is that Vaishnavite devotionalism contains both 'parochial' and 'universal' elements (see Ramanujan 1973:40). Edward Dimock (1968:16) has neatly summarized some of these characteristics:

'Those who are familiar with Krishna's name through such texts as the Bhagavad Gita may be a little surprised to find him, in the greater part of the thought and literature of the Vaishnavas of Bengal as a lover rather than a warrior hero. Those who have heard of the so-called "Hindu trinity" (Brahma "the creator", Shiva "the destroyer" and Vishnu "the preserver") may be equally surprised to find that in the Bengali texts Krishna is himself the great god, not a mere incarnation of Vishnu the third member of this triad, as he is sometimes elsewhere in Indian religion.'

In the case of ISKCON other parochial elements include the energetic dance movements, familiar to anyone who has seen Hare Krishna devotees chanting in the streets. Yet, as Dimock notes, these parochial elements are not without their universal implications, for the Krishna devotees who dance in the street take Krishna to be not only their personal Lord but also the Lord of the Universe. I would suggest that this universalism, together with the revitalized proselytizing tradition of the Gaudiya Math, have been crucial in facilitating the rapid establishment of the link between ISKCON and Hindu communities throughout the world, although the specific details of this linkage will necessarily vary from one place to another.

THE SCENE IN BRITAIN

The first Hare Krishna temple in Britain was established in 1969, when a group of six devotees from ISKCON's San Francisco centre journeyed to London. As might be expected, they moved in the hip and trendy circles of the time. They even performed a programme of chanting and dancing at the notorious 'Alchemical Wedding', a sort of unstructured psychedelic happening at the Royal Albert Hall. Knowing of his interest in oriental religion, they also made contact with George Harrison of the Beatles, who produced a record with the 'Hare Krishna Mantra' on one side and 'Prayers to the Spiritual Master' on the other. It was a hit, and it was mainly because of this success that ISKCON grabbed the attention of the mass media. *The Sunday Times* even ran a front-page feature entitled 'Krishna Consciousness Startles in London!'.

But it is important to emphasize that even at this comparatively early stage in the formation of the movement in Britain, ISKCON devotees were anxious to reach the expatriate Indian community. They distributed consecrated food (*prasād*) three times a week at the London temple, canvassed Hindu commuters and businessmen, and also managed to be invited for dinner by the Indian High Commissioner. The movement also achieved publicity when, later in the same year, Bhaktivedanta Swami arrived at the London temple to install formally the images of Krishna and his consort, Radha, which had been imported from India.

Bhaktivedanta Swami was an incredibly energetic man, continually travelling from one country to another. The use of modern technology, especially the jet aircraft and the telephone system, allowed him to institutionalize a much tighter level of organizational control than that found in traditional Hindu sects, the leaders of which are not always in a position to discipline their members (Burghart 1984). Another constructive consequence of Bhaktivedanta Swami's surveillance and close contacts with his male disciples to whom he bestowed the sacred thread and Brahman status, was that he was able rapidly to introduce a remarkably high level of ritual worship in extremely pleasant, faction-free surroundings, something which, unfortunately, cannot be said of many of Britain's Hindu temples, while those few devotees who renounced the world and became monks (*sannyāsin*) offered both the model and the teachings for those anxious to pursue a deeper religious quest.

This juxtaposition of personnel which opened an ascetic path for a minority and provided temple facilities for the majority meant that ISKCON scored an immediate advantage over both the ordinary temples and other Swami-centred organizations like the Ramakrishna Mission and Bharat Sevashram Sangha which were very sedate, stressing an interiorized mysticism rather than the ecstatic, devotional, and congregational worship available at the ISKCON temple. In any case, these other organizations were not particularly evangelistic and tended to operate within well-defined regional allegiances: the Mission, as well as attracting a few Westerners, had a virtual monopoly on Bengali loyalties and the Sangha on Hindu migrants from Trinidad and Guyana.

One very important factor in the emergence of links between ISKCON and Hindus in Britain, however, was that the establishment of the London temple coincided with the influx of East African Asians in the late 1960s and early 1970s. Unlike many Hindus who are content to perform their religious observances at domestic shrines, these Gujarati and Punjabi Indians were temple-goers coming from a Vaishnavite backgrond. While some of them had distinctive sectarian allegiances, again based on regional patterns, like the Punjabi followers of the Arya Samaj and the Gujarati followers of the Swaminarayan movement, the vast majority were free-floating, eclectic in both doctrine and practice, and content therefore to use ISKCON facilities as they would any other Hindu temple or organization. They were welcomed with open arms by the Hare Krishnas who, while they might not have approved of their eclecticism, did not reject them outright because they felt that these people could eventually be persuaded to become devotees of Krishna.

A case study will illustrate this point. Krishan Murti is an Indian-born Punjabi who migrated to Kenya to seek employment. He left when the political situation for Asians deteriorated in East Africa and now lives with his family in Southall. He is a typical example of someone who was initially attracted by the universal elements of ISKCON and who now appreciates the more parochial aspects of the sect. He recalls how he first encountered ISKCON:

> 'When we came here in 1968 it was strange because we were used to going to the temple and we didn't know of any in London. We felt kind of empty. All we had was a little shrine in the house. We first heard of Hare Krishnas in the papers. The police were objecting to them chanting on the street and it was through that that we got to know where the London temple was. I can tell you we were surprised to find such a nice temple. We couldn't believe it. We were very impressed. We thought that the Hare Krishnas were very sincere, you know. In Nairobi those priests were very materialistic. They were always asking for money and only gave *prasād* if they knew you.'

At first he was a little surprised by the fact that the devotees were American and British, but he was not put off: 'In fact I felt ashamed that it was Westerners who were so enthusiastic. I felt that they were running towards God and we Asians were running away from him.' Later Krishan Murti met Bhaktivedanta Swami at the Rathayatra festival held in Trafalgar Square in 1974:

> 'Although I didn't speak to him I thought his face was just like a saint's. He wasn't like an ordinary man: he was something special. I'd met a lot of swamis in India and East Africa but I could see that he was a real preacher. He was very humble: he never said that he was God or anything like that. Just a devotee of Krishna. That experience encouraged me and I took my family along regularly to the temple after that.'

Bhaktivedanta Swami died in 1977 and most social scientists who had studied ISKCON expected it to be crippled immediately by schisms and power struggles (see, for example, Johnson 1976). But these never took place to any significant degree. Bhaktivedanta Swami had been careful to establish an efficient and well defined organizational structure consisting of a Governing Body Council (GBC), regional councils, temple presidents, and, perhaps most important of all, 11 gurus empowered to give initiation who thereby guaranteed the spiritual succession (*paramparā*). The charismatic power of the founder had been divided but not lost.

The effectiveness of this organization in dealing with clashes of interest and doctrinal variation was demonstrated in 1982. In that year the guru in charge of the United Kingdom (and Africa), a one-time sidekick of the psychedelic impresario Timothy Leary, was discovered to have reverted to his old ways and was advocating the use of what he referred to as the 'sacrament' (cannabis) and 'benediction' (LSD) as a faster route to Krishna Consciousness. For an organization that does not even permit tea and coffee this was clearly beyond the bounds of legitimate practical and ideological variation and the guru was summarily expelled from ISKCON by the GBC. In 1983 another guru was relieved of his duties by the GBC because of his public opposition to the direction in which his godbrothers were taking the movement. For a while it looked as if this might turn into a prolonged legal dispute over property rights but apparently the offending devotee has now returned to the fold though, significantly, stripped of his guru status. The overall result of these disputes has been that four senior Western devotees have been initiated as gurus and there has been some reorganization of responsibilities.

The guru who has taken charge of Great Britain is a lean American who goes by the name of His Divine Grace Srila Bhagavan Goswami Maharaja. An ex-medical student, he joined the movement in 1969, and was later appointed by Bhaktivedanta Swami to direct operations in France, Italy, and Israel. He also had overall responsibility for ISKCON's book distribution in Europe. In the short time of his leadership in Britain he has managed to revitalize the devotees' sensibilities

and restructure the overall organization in his expanded oper-
ational zone. As one senior devotee, drawing on an approved
vocabulary of significance, commented: 'He's pretty phenomenal. He hardly eats, needs very little sleep and he's expert at
inspiring the devotees. He really gets the best out of you – even
beyond your expectations. He's really captured Prabhupada's
mood that the whole world can be part of Krishna Consciousness.' In any event the new guru has a sound institutional base:
ISKCON has three main centres (in London, Letchmore Heath
near Watford, and Worcester) and three sub-centres in Britain,
and even though the number of full-time Western recruits has
remained relatively stable in the last few years, the growth of
interest among the movement's Indian followers has continued.
ISKCON has some 4,000 'life members' (the fee for membership has recently been increased from £201 to £333) and the
expansion rate is currently about 500 new members a year. Only
a few of these life-members are Westerners, with the bulk of
support, as I said earlier, coming from those Gujarati and
Punjabi Indians who had previously lived and worked in East
Africa. There are a smaller number of Bengali and Mauritian
Hindus and even a few Sikh and Jain life-members.

It must be stressed that only a very small number of these
Asians use the movement exclusively. Most are quite content to
participate in other religious organizations and institutions in
addition to their support for ISKCON. Probably the best index
of the type and scope of this association is provided by the
number of life-cycle rituals performed by the movement. In
1983, for example, ISKCON performed about 50 blessings for
newborn children, a dozen weddings (most of which were cross-
caste with a few done without parental consent, the unorthodoxy
of which made one senior Western devotee wryly comment that
they were fast becoming the Indian equivalent of Gretna Green),
and several memorial services. Needless to say, this level of
ritual activity is only a small proportion of the overall number of
rituals conducted by Hindu functionaries in Britain.

An institution that may well alter this pattern of participation
is the Indian Community Affairs programme (ICAP). Established in 1979, this has considerably expanded the facilities

available to its clientele. Hare Krishna devotees perform dramas
from sacred Vaishnava texts, like the Ramayana and Bhagavata
Purana, and hold classes for children every Sunday at their
temples. They have also established youth clubs in the London
boroughs of Southall, Wembley, Harrow, and Thornton Heath.
They distribute literature in all the main Hindu Asian settlements, perform door-to-door preaching, and hold devotional
meetings (*satsang*) in homes throughout the country.

Amongst the younger generation youth clubs have had the
greatest impact – I shall deal with this area in the next section.
For older folk it is the devotional meetings which have been the
most successful in spreading the word and making new contacts,
first because it is a familiar and important component of contemporary Hinduism (see Singer 1968), and second because it
exploits social networks based on kin and friendship ties in
the well defined areas of Indian urban settlement. The Murti
household is one of about 35 families in the London area which
hold devotional meetings every week. Krishan Murti explained
to me how this development came about:

> 'We started having *satsang* here when my wife passed away
> earlier this year. You see it is our tradition to have a service if
> that happens so I contacted the temple and the devotees came
> here every day for 13 days. We had some chanting and
> someone read from the Bhagavad Gita. It really helped me, it
> gave me peace of mind. So I thought it would be nice to have
> a *satsang* every month. It wasn't a new thing for us as we used
> to have them regularly in our house in Nairobi. When the
> devotees first came it was just my family and few friends but it
> has now got much bigger. We get 25 or 30 people every time.
> They like it very much. We hope we will attract even more
> people.'

ICAP's director and *satsang* leader is a former architecture
student from Northern Ireland, Martin Fleming, now called
Akhandadhidasa. A cheerful, energetic, and businesslike young
man, he sees nothing incongruous about Hindus learning 'their'
religion from a Westerner. In fact he likes preaching to Indians
because he feels they understand basic religious concepts

and he can build upon this knowledge to further the ISKCON point of view and demonstrate its relevance in the modern world:

'Our aim is to make everyone Krishna Conscious and it doesn't matter whether they're Western or Indian. But having said that, the preaching naturally differs between the two groups. When I give a lecture to Indians you can discuss things they already know something about. I mean, every Indian has heard about Krishna and the Bhagavad Gita. So when I'm telling them something about the Gita I try and relate it to the problems they experience living in this country. It's obvious that Mr Patel has a very different set of problems compared to Mr Smith.'

OTHER PROSELYTIZING PATTERNS: SUCCESSES
AND FAILURES

The stereotype of Hindu youth locked in a static, self-legitimating subculture that is generated by a firm and complete adherence to family and religious norms, values, and orientations is re-markably prevalent amongst social scientists in Britain (see Rex 1982). But this is an incredibly simplistic view of a very fluid and complex situation. Certainly my own observations in the London area lead me to conclude that many young Hindus lack an overall or even vaguely satisfactory conceptual map. Con-fusion rather than some notion of creative ethnic redefinition seems to be very much the contemporary pattern. An example from a separate study on the Ramakrishna Mission may serve to illustrate this point.

One day I was having a meal with a Bengali couple who were associated with the movement when their teenage daughter complained about the restrictions imposed on her behaviour: she could not understand why she was not allowed out more often and why, when she was allowed out, she had to come home much earlier than her western friends. It was a typical intergenerational conflict between parental concern over morals and adolescent demands for independence.

The conflict was expressed, though, in terms of ethnicity. The parents listened patiently, telling their daughter that all these things were for her own good and that one day she would appreciate these aspects of her culture. The young girl merely looked sceptical, and said that Indian society wasn't too marvellous and anyway all that was left of her parents' culture were shreds and patches of tradition – the food, her mother's sari, and the picture of the elephant-headed god Ganesha in the kitchen. Her parents were stuck for words, but their daughter had a point: she could not believe in the parents' religion because no one had explained why she should believe. The monks of the Ramakrishna Mission were not interested in talking to children and the girl's parents were not sufficiently well versed in the theology to do it for them. The tradition was not accessible: it was locked in a pious adult world which had little or no meaning for one who was precariously placed between two cultures.

A similar state of affairs did not exist, however, among Hindu youths whose parents had a close association with ISKCON. There is no doubt that the enthusiastic preaching of the devotees, backed up by pamphlets outlining the virtues of vegetarianism and the perils of drink, and good English language translations of classical texts, all go a long way to providing a set of moral directives and a sense of religious purpose. The youth clubs seem to be particularly significant in inspiring confidence. ISKCON devotees hold cookery classes, present dramas, and encourage everyone to join in the chanting of devotional hymns accompanied by the throbbing sounds of drums and electric guitars. For the socially aware young Hindu, these occasions are entertaining and exciting, and they provide a conscious mechanism for the preservation of this social identity. As one young Gujarati woman put it:

'I was always interested in religion, but coming to ISKCON has given me a real lift. A few of us started going to the youth club near my house and we used to chat and the devotees would show us how to do plays. It's good fun acting things out; much more interesting than listening to some priest reading it out like at the temple down the road. All of us girls do cooking too. It's very good for us. You see a lot of Asians are drifting away from their culture because even though they're still interested in religion, they haven't got the facilities to help them. Very often Asian families in Britain are pretty isolated with just the parents and the children – no extended family and the older people showing you what's what. See quite recently we had our grandmother over from India and it was only then that we saw how she used to get up and do puja and chanting on her beads early in the morning. So if we're deprived of all those nice things, then it is a good thing that we have alternatives like the youth club.'

With such a positive commitment to the cause I was intrigued to find out why my informant did not become a full-time devotee. Her answer was that while she was committed to ISKCON and her parents supported that commitment, she still looked forward to an arranged marriage and a conventional family life. She made it clear, however, that she would bring up her children according to the principles of Krishnas Consciousness. I think her account of why she did not want to join ISKCON has to be taken at face value. The availability and plausibility of a religious vocation does not mean that it will be taken up: individuals are the active subjects, not the passive objects in the conversion process. Yet my informant's comments do provide a clue that sectarian commitment and socialization may prove to be a powerful instrument in the process of identity management for future generations of Hindus in Britain.

Not everyone has these sorts of reservations. Of the 400 or so full-time members of ISKCON in Britain, some 43 came from Asian backgrounds. Most of them have joined in the last three years and my impression is that this number may increase considerably in the near future. Moreover while 40 per cent of the Westerners drop out in the first six months of membership, only one Indian recruit has so far left the movement. Not that the initial phase of sectarian socialization is necessarily all that smooth for Asians converts, but the end result seems to satisfy ISKCON's authorities. One temple president made this comparison between the two groups:

'I've trained up both Indian and Western boys and I find that Westerners are much easier in the beginning. Some of the Indians have to be put down a bit. You see one thing is that Indians are not that austere. An Indian home is very close and very warm and cosy which means that when the boys come here and you tell them to take a cold shower or pack their sleeping bags tidily they think 'why did I ever leave my mum?'. Westerners tend to accept the austerities a lot easier because most of them have been running around and into austerity of one sort or another before they joined. On the positive side, though, if you kick the Indian boys' egos a bit for the first six months they became first-class devotees.'

This comment prompts the obvious questions, who are these people who became 'first-class devotees' and why did they join ISKCON? Given the general type of support for the movement, it is hardly surprising that only a few of these converts were born in India: most come from East African backgrounds and nearly 70 per cent from the Patidar caste, which partly reflects, I suspect, the relative organizational diffuseness of this group compared, say, to the much tighter structure of the Lohana community, the other numerically important caste in Britain with an East African connection (see Michaelson 1979:35). The recruits are more or less equally divided between male and female and, with the exception of one married couple, all were single when they joined ISKCON. Apart from one man in his early 50s they are all young, recruited between the ages of 17 and 24. Nearly all performed well at school; roughly half went on to some form of higher education. A further point of interest, comparing Western and Asian recruits, is that while nearly all of the former had more 'racy', hedonistic elements in their backgrounds, only one Indian devotee admitted to taking drugs and to having any form of pre-marital sexual encounter (both of which, incidentally, he found profoundly unsatisfactory).

The case of Sunil Patel, now known as Lakshminathadasa, illustrates the conversion pattern of these young Asians. Born in Kenya, he was raised in a pious Gujarati household. The family did not belong to any particular sect but Lakshminatha's mother, like many Patidar women, performed a daily offering;

and on Sundays and festivals they all went to the temple. Their diet was strictly vegetarian. The family came to Britain in 1970 and started a small shop in Wembley. They kept up their religious pursuits, establishing a domestic shrine and visiting the Hindu temples in the area. Unlike some of the other Asian members who had come across ISKCON devotees in Nairobi, the first time Lakshminatha met them was in London in 1976 when he was returning home from college. They gave him a book and a magazine and he gave them a 50 pence donation. As he was not familiar with Chaitanyite Vaishnavism, the shaved heads and robes of the devotees seemed very strange at first, but a few weeks later a couple of devotees came to his house and were invited by his parents to return for *satsaṅg*. This they did and Lakshminatha was very impressed with the chanting of the Hare Krishna mantra; so much so that he purchased a rosary and performed a few rounds whenever he could find the time. He also visited the ISKCON temple in London. He said: 'It really blew my mind: it was so clean. Most Indian temples are a mess. They're dirty and there's no organization. The Brahmin priests are just there for the money.' For Lakshminatha, as indeed for all the Indian devotees to whom I talked, this initial exposure to the ritual and the temple environment, especially the warm and friendly community of the devotees, seems to have been very important. The Hare Krishna lifestyle had an excitement and intensity that the ordinary and all too familiar religious scene lacked. It was a total and serious way of life, which held out the promise of religious experience and ultimate liberation.

Lakshminatha readily admitted that he did not understand a great deal of the philosophy in the early days of his involvement, but that this soon changed as he asked questions and studied the literature. After finishing college he took a job studying heart disease in a London hospital. His experience there was a dramatic revelation of the transitoriness and tragedy of mortal existence that he had read about but not really understood.

'The thing that really got me was taking blood samples in the geriatric wards because there I got to see old age, disease, and death at first hand. It doesn't matter how important you are either. You take President Kennedy. He was so powerful but it only took one bullet and he was dead. I knew there was something higher and that we weren't just a bundle of chemicals. So although I was helping these people in hospital I came to understand that it wasn't real welfare work because it wasn't changing their consciousness. I felt I had to make a decision whether to join Hare Krishna or to stay in the world. I said to myself, everyone has to leave the world at some time or another so why not now?'

Life in an ISKCON temple is strict and ascetic. Devotees are required to dress in the approved robes and wear distinctive sectarian markings on their bodies; male devotees have to shave their heads except for a topknot and women have to wear their hair long with a centre parting (a side parting is considered to be the mark of a prostitute). In addition, devotees follow a strict lacto-vegetarian diet and avoid all intoxicants; sex is permitted only for married couples and solely for the procreation of children. At the Letchmore Heath temple, where most of the Indian devotees reside, single men and women have their own quarters; they sleep four or five to a room and everyone takes a cold shower even on the coldest winter day. This is often a massive shock to newcomers but most seem to settle down to the rigours of temple life relatively quickly. On the more positive side, it must be said that the highly structured routine provides a tremendous sense of emotional and intellectual security for members. As Lakshminatha commented:

'The first week I was there I was pretty fried up. I'd left a good job and a nice cosy room in my parents' house, given up all my possessions and traded them in for a sleeping bag and a hard bunk. But once I started to read a bit I got convinced that I'd made the right choice. The taste for spiritual life had come. Now I work in the print-shop. At the moment we're doing a book in Swahili and another in Ethiopian. Sometimes I work all night if there's a big job on and it doesn't bother me at all. In fact it makes me even more determined. I'm pretty satisfied really. I've found an inner happiness.'

Lakshminatha was lucky that his parents approved of his new vocation, but not all the devotees have been so fortunate. Several have been forced to flee their homes and bargain with their kin from the safety and protection of the ISKCON community, although most parents do eventually accept their offspring's new vocation. Here, it should be emphasized that Asian parental objections have nothing to do with the accusations of 'brainwashing' sometimes levelled at ISKCON by Westerners who speak in the name of secular individualism or from a Judaeo-Christian perspective. Indeed, it is fair to say that nearly all these Indian parents share at least some of the general features of their children's religious outlook: the real controversy concerns the degree of affiliation and commitment to the movement, particularly when it is set against other value-orientations like the importance of business, education, and the family.

The Chatterjees, a Brahmin family from Assam, came to Britain in 1969 so that the head of the household could advance his medical career. Like many Hindus, the family did not visit Hindu temples very regularly, but they gathered together every day to pray and make an offering of fruit, flowers, and incense at the domestic shrine. Moreover, whenever Dr Chatterjee returned to India on holiday he arranged for the sacrifice of a goat to the goddess Kali at one of the temples on the banks of the Ganges.

The family first met the Hare Krishna devotees through the door-to-door preaching programme and were very impressed with their sincerity. They started to visit the temple and this led to certain changes in lifestyle. They became vegetarian and Dr Chatterjee ended his goat sacrifices. The most important consequence, however, was that the son, Ramesh, became increasingly attracted to temple life. He looked forward to visits and had long and involved discussions with the devotees about the theology and philosophy of the movement. Observing these developments his parents became worried that Ramesh might join ISKCON, and it was, therefore, somewhat reluctantly that they allowed him to stay at the temple for a weekend. It obviously made a great impression. Ramesh told me that when he left he felt very sad: 'I liked the atmosphere very much. It was very lively. Home life seemed so dull after that.'

When the Chatterjees returned to live in India in 1979,

Ramesh was permitted to remain behind and finish his studies. Despite promises to the contrary, he continued to visit the ISKCON temple and even started a 'Vedic Society' at his college. A combination of youthful idealism, encouragement from the devotees, and the absence of any parental control contributed to Ramesh's decision to join ISKCON. The day he completed his final examinations he also packed his bags and entered the community. He wrote to his parents to inform them of his decision. There was uproar in the family (a situation not helped by the fact that he was the only son) and the father was immediately despatched to bring the boy home. But the story has a happy ending (at least for Ramesh). When Ramesh's father arrived at the Letchmore Heath temple, he had a change of heart and accepted his son's decision, even telling him that he should do his utmost to become a pure devotee of Krishna. For Ramesh and indeed for the other devotees the outcome was interpreted as a sign of the power of Krishna's intervention.

Yet not everyone is so easily won over to the ISKCON point of view. The Letchmore Heath temple was involved in a protracted dispute with the local, Tory-controlled Hertsmere Council, which claimed that the influx of thousands of Asians into the village on festival days like Divali and Janmashtami created an unnecessary inconvenience to the local population. It was only the threat of a costly legal battle that forced a compromise: in 1982 an agreement was reached whereby ISKCON is permitted to hold festivals for an unlimited number of people on six days each year.

But an altogether more serious problem is the attitude of religious leaders from other Hindu sects who take a different theological line from that of ISKCON. One Sannyasi, who worshipped not only Shiva but also Rama, Krishna, and Durga, told me that he had visited the London ISKCON temple on a number of occasions and very much liked the worship. He felt, nonetheless, that the exclusively Krishnacentric orientation of Bhaktivedanta Swami and his followers made them 'fanatics' and 'beyond all reason'. A representative of another sect made a similar protest. He said:

'Hare Krishna is totally illogical, totally wrong and totally against our scriptures. I don't know how they can preach the things they do. They are teaching people to live a holy life and become vegetarian and that is good, but when they preach that other paths are wrong, they are causing great harm. They preach a sectarian message. It is just like Christianity. They are just like the Methodists, Catholics and Protestants who teach that they are right and everyone else is wrong. That is not our Hindu way.'

It is true that ISKCON has injected a note of exclusivism into the contemporary Hindu scene but, far from being unorthodox, as my critical informant claimed, this exclusiveness was very much a part of traditional Hinduism. In the past argument, debate, and fierce sectarian rivalries were often the order of the day. Historically Hinduism has been more tolerant of religious differences than Islam or Christianity, but it was never as tolerant as my informants, following the lead of the nineteenth- and twentieth-century reformist sects like the Ramakrishna Mission and Divine Life Society, would lead people to believe. The reformist view is that theological and ritual differences are unimportant and what is crucial is pantheism and spiritual monism. This leads to the idea that all Hindu sects and, by extension, all world religions have the same ultimate goal. In reality, however, this is a distinctly modern view which formed in the meeting of Hindu and Western world-views.

ISKCON representing the Chaitanyite tradition of Vaishnavism, rejects this neo-universalistic ethic and does not attempt to patch up these differences with ecumenism. The debate will doubtless continue. Whether it becomes more acrimonious will depend, I suspect, on the competition for the social, economic, and political patronage upon which these sectarian organizations depend. ISKCON members, somewhat optimistically, but like true religious enthusiasts, are confident that they will triumph in the long run. Akhandadhidasa told me: 'At the moment in Britain we're just a spiritual outpost, but the time will come when Indians will recognize that we're the only genuine place.'

6

The Community of the Many Names of God: a Saivite ashram in rural Wales

Donald Taylor

The Community of the Many Names of God is situated at the end of a narrow track along the side of a valley a few miles outside the village of Llanpumsaint, some 12 miles north of Carmarthen, in Dyfed, Wales. The valley is known to the local people as Cwm Creigiau Fawr, the valley of the boulders, but the Community have renamed it Skanda Vale, after the Hindu god Skanda whose image occupies the central position in the Community temple.

Since it arrived here in 1973, the Community has become an important pilgrimage centre, attracting up to 15,000 Hindus and other visitors annually. The property comprises two farms, totalling about a hundred acres. The first farm is on the side of the valley. It includes a cottage converted into a temple, which is Skanda's abode, several chalets a short distance away that accommodate visitors, and a large cage housing a peacock, the vehicle upon which Skanda is said to ride. The second farm, purchased in 1980, is on top of the hill next to the first farm. It comprises a farmhouse in which the Guru lives, and a number of barns and outhouses in which are kept several animals, most notably Vallee, a young female elephant. The founder and head of the Community is Guru Subramanium. The other resident members include at present the Guru's designated successor, who is known by the title of Swami, and five members known as brothers. All, apart from the Guru, are English.

In this paper I will first, recount the Guru's story of the formation of the Community as a way of understanding the Community's relation to god; second, analyze the way in which the Community perceives its relationships with other religious faiths; and third, consider some of the pressures and constraints brought upon the Community by virtue of its position in contemporary British society.

THE FOUNDING OF THE COMMUNITY

There are many possible stories about the founding of the Community of the Many Names of God, but I shall rely exclusively upon the version of its founder, Guru Subramanium.[1] It gives a clear account of the events leading up to the establishment of the Community; and more importantly, shows that from the Guru's point of view the Community is an object of the grace of god.

Guru Subramanium was born P.R. de Silva at Koslanda, near Haputale in present-day Sri Lanka in 1929. His father was Dr D.B.J. de Silva, a Low Country Buddhist of the Goyigama caste. His mother was Miss M.E. Asserappa, a Tamil Hindu of the Vellala caste. His father belonged to the group of wealthy Low Country Sinhalese families who had taken advantage of the entrepreneurial opportunities introduced by British administrators during the nineteenth century. The sons of these wealthy families were mostly Western-educated, their education being paid for out of their own resources. Dr de Silva graduated from Edinburgh University and returned to Ceylon to take up a position in the administration in Colombo.

Guru Subramanium's mother was widely recognized as a very religious woman, who had her own shrine in a separate building in their compound in Colombo. Many people used to join her worship during the early morning and evening services. Many more used to come and see her about their problems, for she had the reputation of being a seer. The Guru gave me an example of what this meant. One day when he was about 10 years old he went with his mother to a house against which the owners suspected someone was working a charm. When she arrived at the house, she felt the vibrations that were causing the trouble. These vibrations led her to a room where there was a concrete floor. She pointed to a particular spot on the floor, and said, 'There. Dig down two feet and you will find what is causing the trouble'. This was done, and two feet below the surface of the concrete floor they found 'hair, clothing, human ash, bone fragments and an effigy of the person against whom the charm was to be worked'.

As a child the Guru felt he had gifts not unlike those of his mother. These became apparent when he was at school. He found that he could not agree with his teachers, especially those who taught the history of Ceylon. He would argue with them frequently, claiming that their description of historical events was wrong. They were merely repeating what was in the history books, whereas he knew that these events had taken place differently, because he could see what had happened. What they were saying was not the truth. For this sort of thing he was frequently punished by his teachers; and it brought upon him the anger of his father as well.

From the age of eight, the Guru became known at home and among his friends as Subra, short for Subramanium, because of his devotion to the Hindu deity, Subramanium, also known as Skanda.[2] As his devotion to Subramanium increased, the young Subra became filled with the desire to establish his worship in Europe and the West. When he was 18, he went to the Subramanium temple at Badulla near Kataragama to pray before the main image. Since the priest in charge was a friend of the family, he obtained permission to enter the inner sanctum and make his prayers there. Once before the image he made three requests: first that he should receive the authority of Lord Subramanium, second that Lord Subramanium should abide with him in whatever he did, and third that Subramanium should bless him in his endeavour to establish his devotion in the West.

He was about to leave when a three-hooded cobra appeared and asked him, 'What do you want?'. Subra repeated his requests and the cobra said, 'Because you have not asked for anything for yourself, you shall receive your requests; and whatever else you wish for, you will receive'. By this time the young Subra was taken aback, and wanted some confirmation of what he had seen and heard. On his way out he again met the priest, who asked him what he had asked for from the deity. Subra did not tell him, but asked him to find out himself from Lord Subramanium. The priest told him to go away and come back in two hours, during which time he would perform a ritual in order to find out. When Subra returned, the priest was carrying two betel leaves in which was wrapped a small replica of a spear (*vel*) about six inches long, the symbol of authority of Subramanium. He said, 'Take this. You have asked for Subramanium's authority; for his promise to abide with you; and for his blessing to do what you wish'. All this the young Subra took to be confirmation that Subramanium had granted the first request, namely for 'the authority of the Lord'.

The second request, that Subramanium should abide with him, still had to be fulfilled. Since the cobra had said that anything he asked for would be granted, he asked the priest to let him have an image of the Lord. But the priest refused and told him to return to Colombo. This he did, accompanied by his mother. The journey took five hours, and on his arrival back at their home he found that a lady had been waiting there five hours to give him a statue of the Lord Subramanium.

This last event prompted Subra and his mother as well as a few others to go on pilgrimage, this time to Vadahitekandha (which the Swami said means 'The hill where the Lord resides'), a place not far from the famous Sri Lankan pilgrimage centre of Kataragama. Vadahitekandha is a very steep hill, which at that time (1947) was covered by a jungle, with only an indication of a path winding its way to the top. It was a very difficult journey, but Subra and his party completed it, he carrying the statue on his head all the way. At the summit they were met by a holy man, who told Subra that he had been expecting him. The holy man then worshipped the image and anointed it, thus summoning the

Lord to reside in it. Once this was done, Subra and his party left for Colombo, taking with them the statue of Lord Subramanium. It is this statue that he brought to Great Britain and which is now in the temple at Skanda Vale. The Swami also added that it is now known as 'the miraculous image' because of 'the large number of vows offered by devotees and requests granted by the divine power residing in it'.

The third request, that Subramanium should bless him in his endeavour to establish his devotion in the West, took longer to fulfil. Soon after these events, the Guru travelled to England. It was after the last war and travelling was not easy, but the Guru wanted to see as much of Europe as possible. He therefore came to Britain in 1948 via the Suez Canal, stopping at Naples and travelling through Italy, France, and Germany. In a separate communication from the Swami I was informed that the journey to Britain was via 'Sweden, Denmark, Holland, Belgium, France, Austria, Czechoslovakia, Poland, etc.'.

Once in Britain, which he reached in 1948, the Guru obtained a number of jobs including one as a gardener for the Ceylon High Commission in London. He first of all lived in a flat in Sloane Square, where he set up a shrine to Subramanium, and began to perform daily rituals in devotion to him, gradually gathering a small band of devotees who would attend these rituals regularly. Then in 1961 he was provided with sufficient funds to buy the lease of a flat in Earls Court, where he remained for a further 12 years.

During the 25 years he was in London the Guru's devotion to Subramanium continued and intensified. He regularly performed rituals with the idol in which the presence of Subramanium had been summoned by the holy man of Vadahitekandha. As a result more and more Hindu devotees, drawn from the immigrant population of London, came to his flat. In time he gathered around him some British devotees, among them a Reverend James Keilor, who had been a minister of the Church of Scotland. According to the Swami he was much involved in 'promoting the worship of God in his universality'. This apparently was a broader vision of religion than the Kirk would allow, and eventually he left it to become the Moderator of the Free

Church Federation, with a congregation in Liverpool. Apart from these, there were also the devotees of Bhagavan Sri Sathya Sai Baba, most of whom were Sri Lankans and Gujaratis, who would attend the rituals and sing devotional hymns (*bhajan*). Quite a rapport was set up between the Guru and his followers and the devotees of Sai Baba (see Taylor, this volume).

In 1973 the flat in Earls Court was to be sold, and the owners asked the Guru to make arrangements to leave. He began to look for another property, but found none suitable for him and his followers. By now they had decided to form a trust, called 'The Community of the Many Names of God', which would perpetuate their devotion to Lord Subramanium, and a number of the Guru's English followers had already pledged themselves to be members of it.

The farm that the Community now owns was advertized in a magazine to which someone had drawn the Guru's attention. He visited the place and knew at once that this was what he had been looking for. He telephoned his solicitor who advised him not to make an offer, because he had neither money nor bank account. But he did make an offer, because he knew that somehow the money would be forthcoming. The offer was for £18,000. He went back to London and told the owners of his flat that he would leave if they gave him £10,000. They accepted. Then he raised £8,000 by means of a loan from reputable merchant bankers, secured by a life endowment policy taken out for the purpose. Thus he purchased the property, in spite of the fact that he had no money and that his solicitor had advised against it. On 12 June 1973 the Guru, together with a number of devotees, left Earls Court for Wales where they continued and increased their devotion to the Lord Subramanium, now within the framework of a charitable trust called The Community of the Many Names of God.

At first the close co-operation between the Guru and his followers and the devotees of the Sai Baba organization continued. Busloads of Sai Baba devotees (some Sri Lankans but mainly Gujaratis from the Midlands) used to come to sing their devotional hymns there. But gradually it was felt that the connection with the Sai Baba movement should be severed.

According to the Guru this was the result of mutual feelings, and was not due to any overt disagreement between the two groups. Indeed both the Guru and the Swami have visited Bhagavan Sri Sathya Sai Baba at Prasanthi Nilayam, the spiritual centre of the Sathya Sai Baba organization, not far from Bangalore in India. And Bhagavan Sri Sathya Sai Baba himself had 'repeatedly' approved the present arrangement and given the Community his blessing.

I asked the Guru how many people visited the pilgrimage centre and Temple during the course of a year. Neither he nor the Swami could give an accurate figure, but they suggested a total of about 15,000: 5,000 English, 5,000 non-Tamil Hindus, and 5,000 Tamil Hindus, mainly from Sri Lanka. In addition, the Swami said that most Swamis and Gurus on tour from India and Sri Lanka come to visit the Community; as well as a number of Buddhists, including Japanese Buddhists from Milton Keynes, some from the London Buddhist Vihara, and a few from the Buddhist Forest Order at Chithurst in Sussex.

In addition to the Brothers who live on the property there are usually a few young people sent by probation officers who knew the Guru when he lived in Earls Court and who believe that the life of the Community is a help in the rehabilitation of drugs offenders. This work the Guru and the brothers are only too willing to do.

At first the cottage where the worship of the Lord Subramanium was carried out was called a shrine. But in 1981 the Sri Lankan High Commission recognized the shrine as a 'temple worthy of an elephant', in other words, as a place of spiritual significance. Later that year a young female elephant, named after Lord Subramanium's consort Vallee, was flown to Britain. Deer are also kept in a nearby compound, since they too are associated with Subramanium temples. Finally there is the caged peacock which is kept near the temple itself; the peacock being the 'vehicle' on which the Lord Subramanium is said to ride. The temple is thus well endowed with human devotees and animal vehicles of the deity.

The Guru's account of the founding of the Community requires no further explanation. I shall only reiterate that from the Guru's point of view the establishment of the Community is not the result of human decision, but the outcome of Lord Subramanium's grace in blessing Guru Subramanium's request to establish the devotion of his Lord in the West. Behind the narrative lies a sense of marvel. The three-hooded cobra at Badulla, the image given by the lady at Colombo, the holy man waiting to anoint the image at the top of Vadahitekandha, even the wondrous way in which the money was raised for the purchase of the property, all these were signs that the Community was an object of divine grace.

Furthermore, the miraculous nature of the events was confirmed empirically by Lord Subramanium working through other persons in granting the three boons. The first request for the authority of Lord Subramanium was confirmed in 1947 by the priest at Badulla who appeared with the spear wrapped in two betel leaves. The second request that Lord Subramanium abide with the young Subra was also confirmed in 1947 by the lady at Colombo who gave to Subra the image of Lord Subramanium. The third request that the worship of Lord Subramanium spread to the West was confirmed in 1981 by the recognition on the part of the Sri Lankan government that the shrine in Wales was a 'temple worthy of an elephant'.

THE RELIGIOUS MISSION OF THE COMMUNITY

When I first went to the Community, I thought that I was witnessing the development of a syncretism of Hinduism and other religions, particularly Christianity. There were a number of indications suggesting that syncretism might be taking place. The very use of the word Community as a self-designation was redolent of the usage in certain Christian religious orders. The members of the Community called themselves 'Brothers', as is the practice in many Christian communities. The way in which the Brothers were accepted into the Community seemed very like the way novices are accepted into a Christian religious community. In the present Community an aspirant goes through a testing period, during which time he does not wear the recognized apparel of the Community, and takes his meals with the guests and other devotees. Once the period of testing is over he goes through a ritual which incorporates him into the Community at which time he takes his vows of chastity, poverty, and obedience, the same vows that are taken by Christian novices on being accepted into a Christian religious order.

In the temple there were statues of deities and saints other than Hindu ones. There was a picture of Guru Nanak and a statue of the Buddha, as well as statues of Jesus, Mary, and St Francis of Assisi. During the early morning worship The Lord's Prayer as found in the Bible was recited in English, the only difference being that 'hallowed be thy names' was substituted for 'hallowed be thy name'. The annual cycle of festivals, though mainly Hindu, included a celebration of Holy Communion at Easter and Christmas, the form of the service having been handed down by the Reverend James Keilor.

All these Christian, Sikh, and Buddhist aspects were obscured, however, by the Hindu structure of the place. Three different Hindu patterns of behaviour were salient. First were the rules of the Community (which the members themselves called an ashram). These rules relate mainly to diet. The Community is strictly vegetarian: no meat of any kind is tolerated on any part of the premises – this includes meat baby food, meat sandwiches, and even meat flavouring in crisps – and devotees are asked to refrain from eating meat prior to their arrival at the ashram. No smoking or drinking is allowed anywhere on the premises. Special rules apply also to entry to the temple. No leather object is allowed there, and that includes shoes, handbags, wallets, and belts. Similarly the Hindu rules of ritual purity apply to temple entry; men who are ritually impure through the birth or death of a relative cannot enter, nor can menstruating women.

A second Hindu aspect were the rituals performed in the temple. Worship (*pūjā*) is Hindu in form, comprising the ritual display of the flame (see Knott, below), and the singing of devotional hymns. Services are performed daily at 5 am and 9 pm on weekdays and food is offered to the deity at 1 pm. On Sundays the worship is led at 11.30 am by the Guru who at this time also anoints the deity. Indians words are used to refer to these ritual enactments. The devotees recite *mantra* (sacred verses); they sing *bhajan* (devotional hymns); and the Guru performs *abiṣekam* (anointment of the deity).

The third and possibly most important Hindu aspect of the Community is the presence of the Guru. Although Guru Subramanium does not claim to have set himself up as a 'guru', still he is respected as such by his followers; and he does see himself as a spiritual leader, if not the spiritual leader of the Sri Lankans in Britain. Like a Hindu Guru, he is said to have knowledge and wisdom. But this is no ordinary knowledge; it is intuitive. In my interviews with him he claimed that he had not acquired this knowledge from books, for it cannot be found in books. For instance, when someone comes to him with problems, he already knows what they are before the person tells him. When the person begins to explain the reason for the visit, the Guru stops him and tells him instead his problems. He knows these things, he says, because he can sense their vibrations and see the aura surrounding them. From these vibrations he knows what is wrong. Furthermore he not only knows what *is* wrong, but what *was* wrong. He knows of incidents in their pasts. He tells them he has heard what they have been saying; or if there have been any angry scenes at home, whether they have been shouting or swearing at one another. The Swami added to the Guru's remarks by saying that the Guru was 'the silent witness' in every devotee's home, and so becomes a member of the family. The Guru, however, was more anxious to point out that any devotee can come to him, and by his intuitive knowledge he can show them the way ahead.

The Guru said that often devotees would bring him photographs of the whole family, and he would diagnose the problem of each one, for even from photographs he could discern their vibrations. He has access to the inner motives of each person who comes to him, and can eventually bring peace and harmony into that person's life, and to the lives of those around him.

Guru Subramanium has earned himself a reputation by the way he has handled these problems, and as a result many devotees come to see him in order to be healed of their sickness. The presuppositions behind the healing are Hindu. He under-

stands illness to be a consequence of karma. Sometimes a
person comes to him whose karma is so strong that he can do
very little other than absorb a little of it himself. In such cases it
is important that the person feels the karmic effects of his
previous actions, so achieving a better rebirth. However, no
matter how intense the karma, that person can eventually realize
the divine in him or herself. Many women come because they
are barren, or wish to have a son. The special way the Guru has
of dealing with these cases is to lay a relic of Padre Pio on the
devotee and to recite some sacred verses.[3] The Swami claims
that a number of women have been cured of their barrenness by
this means.

Not all the sick come to Wales to be cured: sometimes the
Guru is transported spiritually to the bedside of the sick person.
He is then on the spiritual plane in one place, on the physical
plane in another. Such spiritual journeys form part of Hindu
spiritual lore about holy men, and are commonly attributed to
Sathya Sai Baba (see Taylor, this volume).

Guru Subramanium's identity as a Guru also extends to his
relationship with his followers. When I suggested that the
Brothers were his disciples, I was told that they preferred to be
called his followers. One of these he has designated as his
successor, now called the Swami. Both the Swami and the
Brothers are English, and come from middle-class backgrounds.
Some have university degrees. In spite of the Guru's reluctance
to use the word disciple, the relationship between the Guru and
his followers is similar to that found between a Guru and his
disciples in other Hindu ashrams. The Guru must be heeded,
especially when he teaches them how to read the scriptures,
pronounce sacred verses, or sing devotional hymns. His instruc-
tions are to be obeyed, willingly, because he knows what is best
for them.

Although the Community is recognizably Hindu and its
Hindu character preponderates over the presence of Christian,
Sikh, Muslim, and Jewish elements, the Community also sees
itself in certain respects as transcending 'Hinduism'. It is because of this transcendent relationship that I subsequently came
to see that the inter-faith relationships at the Community were

not an instance of syncretism. This transcendence may be illustrated by a statement in the Community's small broadsheet, 'Visiting Skanda Vale – a guide to all devotees', which reads: 'The Community of the Many Names of God is delighted to welcome anyone wishing to worship the Lord in the Temple at Skanda Vale. God's family is one family, and we do not recognize divisions based on differences in religion, race or background.' The Community is therefore above the level of oppositions which are to be found between different religions, including Hinduism itself. A similar transcendence is claimed by followers of the Vedantic school of philosophy, who see Vedanta standing at a level above the opposition between Hinduism and other religions. At this level Vedantic philosophy is the Truth that subsumes religious opposition. In the case of the Community, it is at this higher level that the Guru and his followers see themselves. From their point of view the opposition between Hinduism and other religions is reconciled in the true religion of the Community. The oppositions between the Many Names of God and the One Name of God, between Subramanium and the devotee, are subsumed in true devotion, where all oppositions are believed to be dissolved.[4]

That Lord Subramanium is regarded in the Community as the highest deity in whom all others are included, either as symbols of his reality or as other names of the one true name, is signified in the layout of the deities in the temple itself. The shrine of the temple is painted black; and various images, some sculptured in wood, others in the form of a picture, are placed around the room. On a shelf about waist high which runs along the back of the room and in alcoves and niches along the wall, images of deities and saints are placed, grouped according to their religion. The Hindu deities take up most of the space, but other sections are devoted to Buddhist, Muslim, Jewish, and Sikh religious objects. A small section is also set apart for the Sai Baba incarnations, Shirdi Sai Baba and Sathya Sai Baba. In the centre of the room, however, in the place of central importance equivalent to the holy of holies is the image of Lord Subramanium flanked on his left by his South Indian consort, Theivayanai and on his right by his Sri Lankan consort, Vallee.

The layout of the deities in this inner room illustrates the central position of Subramanium and the peripheral position of other Hindu deities, such as Siva, Vishnu and his avatars Krishna and Rama, and the monkey god Hanuman. All these radiate from Subramanium, who is the central source of all.

Figure 6.1 *Emblem of the Community of the Many Names of God*

A similar message is to be found in the symbol of the Community. A diagram of the emblem (see *Figure 6.1*) shows the central place given to the spear (*vel*) or authority of Subramanium, around which the symbols of the other religions are arranged. The fact that the emblem is identical to that of the Sathya Sai Baba movement (*Figure 6.2*), with the exception that the latter has a lotus-shaped column and flame instead of the spear at the centre, indicates the close connections that once existed between the two movements. But even here one might see this as the ultimate displacing of the authority of the Sathya Sai Baba movement by the authority of Lord Subramanium.

Figure 6.2 *Emblem of the Sathya Sai Baba Movement*

From the Community's point of view, the temple is the centre of the world, the source of Subramanium's power and authority. And this power and authority are beginning to be felt even in Wales. It is felt particularly strongly in the valley, or the vale, where Subramanium's spear (*vel*) has been planted. Subramanium in fact takes over Cwm Creigiau Fawr; for his devotees the valley has become Skanda Vale, or sometimes called Skanda *vel* (authority). The play on the two words vale and *vel* is deliberate.

I would suggest, therefore, that this view of the Community in its relations with other faiths is part of the ideology of modern Hinduism. According to this ideology, put forward by the Hindu Vedantist Vivekananda in the nineteenth century, Hinduism is the most ancient of all religions, and is the source of all religion and truth. At this level Hinduism as Truth is above even Hinduism as practised in its various manifestations. In the case of the

Community the situation is much the same: Subramanium as the One source of Truth is above all religions, even Hinduism. Thus Hindu deities take their place with the others around the centre of all, Lord Subramanium.

LEGAL AND POLITICAL CONSTRAINTS UPON THE COMMUNITY

There are a number of constraints upon the Community arising from the fact that it is situated in contemporary British society. In Britain the state allows a whole range of social groupings which go to make what is called civil society, and within which are to be found the family, political institutions, and religious institutions all of which are allowed to exist as long as they keep within the law. It is by means of the law that the state controls them. In England and Wales the law which directly affects the Community is that of Equity, and within Equity it is perhaps the Charities Act 1960 which is the most important. For the purposes of the Act, charity means any institution, corporate or not, which is established for charitable purposes and is subject to the control of the High Court. To have a charitable purpose it must satisfy certain tests: either it must fall within the list of purposes enumerated in the preamble to the ancient Charitable Uses Act of 1601, or it must be for public benefit, that is to say both beneficial and available for a sufficient section of the community.

The Community is concerned to be seen as a charity, and therefore it must be seen to exist for religious purposes, to be of public benefit and to be available to a large section of society. But it has to be careful, for it owns a farm and could be seen as a unit of production, hence a source of tax for the Inland Revenue. The situation is somewhat different from that of a temple which the Commissioners can easily see to be a charity, dependent as it is upon donations for its upkeep. Indeed, in many cases there is no need to form a charity, for once somewhere has been registered as a place of religious worship then the activities there are assumed to be for charitable purposes. But because of the farm, the Community must be explicit about the charitable nature of its activities. Not only does it have a Temple which is recognized as such by the Sri Lankan Government, but it also carries out service to the public at large. I have already mentioned how the Community takes in young offenders who are being helped to give up drugs. In addition to this the Community distributes food, especially fruit, which has been offered to the deity at major festivals, to elderly people living near the ashram. These activities are both regarded as services for the benefit of the public in general, and go towards the charitable image of the community required by the Charity Commissioners. But perhaps more important than that is the way this public service is interpreted in terms of the religious service (*sevā*) which the members of the Community, in the form of devoted servants, perform for Lord Subramanium. The notion of service to one's Lord is one of the central organizing ideas of the Community, informing the procedures of worship, the aim of one's daily actions, and the proper attitude which one brings to those actions. In this way the performance of public service is seen by the Community to be an outcome not of their obligations to civil society, but of their devotion to Lord Subramanium.

Another constraint upon the Community arises from the delicate situation which now exists between Tamils and Sinhalese since the outbreak of violence against the Tamils in Sri Lanka in July and August 1983. The Tamils in Britain have presented a united front in condemning the violence and in supporting their demand for a separate state in Sri Lanka. But behind this united front there are considerable differences of opinion about what the next step should be. There are those who feel that some sort of political solution might be possible, and are not anxious to press their demand for a separate state to the point of violence. There are others who find ample evidence in their dealings with the various Sinhalese-dominated political parties in the past to show that their demand for a separate state must be backed up with deeds and not words, even if this means violent deeds. These views and those of the various factions that fragment from them tend to polarize in the form of allegiance to different Tamil Hindu temples in London: one which tends to support the idea of a separate state, one which tends to accept a political solution, and one which remains ambivalent in the whole affair.[5]

Politically the Guru sees himself in a particularly important mediating position between Tamils and Sinhalese, since his own mother was Tamil and his father was Buddhist. Because he is opposed to all forms of violence, he favours the view that Sri Lanka should be a united nation in which the rights of minority groups are recognized and protected. But in favouring this position the Guru would appear to be placing himself and the Community in the company of those Sri Lankans in Britain who believe that they should be working towards that ideal. This means that he could be seen to be taking up the cause of one particular faction among the Tamil Hindus. Since he does not want this to happen, he treads carefully between the rival factions in the hope of not alienating anyone, and of effecting a reconciliation not only among Tamils, but also between Tamils and Sinhalese.

But this is no easy task, and has been made no easier by the extension of his charitable work to the peoples of Sri Lanka. For some time the Guru has been negotiating the formation of another venture, called the Wales-Sri Lanka Community Development Project. The purpose of this project is to set up an orphanage in Sri Lanka in which a number of crafts will be taught. The Community itself is very closely connected with this project, which now has backing from ministers and other important political figures in the current United National Party. This latter point is interpreted by some as proving that the Guru is in fact supporting a political solution for the Tamil-Sinhalese problem in Sri Lanka.

There are other consequences of this tacit support for a united Sri Lanka. First, the Community is recognized as an acceptable place for visits from Sri Lankan Theravada Buddhist monks. On the occasions when I have been at the Community there have been such monks paying visits. Second, the Community is recognized by the Sri Lankan High Commission in London. I have already mentioned that the Sri Lankan High Commission designated the temple as one worthy of an elephant. Thus the relationship between the Community and the Sri

Lankan High Commission is important. But the relationship works both ways. On the one hand, the Community must maintain itself as a religious institution, especially as a Tamil Hindu institution, for which it has the support of the Sri Lanka High Commission and government. On the other hand, the Sri Lanka government sees its support of a Tamil Hindu, as opposed to a Buddhist, religious institution as vital to its image in Britain and in the other nations of the world as a liberal democracy.

Having said all this, let me not finish by giving the impression that the Community is consciously political in any way. For the Guru and Brothers the Community is a spiritual centre, and this is confirmed by the many thousands of devotees who come on pilgrimage every year. Often conscious of being strangers in a strange land, they come to the temple to find spiritual strength and comfort in an atmosphere which they recognize and call their own. And it is this spiritual strength, the source of which they believe is the authority of Lord Subramanium, the one name above the many names of God, which they intend to foster and maintain for many years to come.

NOTES

Fieldwork in Britain during 1981–83 was sponsored by the Emslie Horniman Scholarship Fund, and I would like to express my gratitude to the Trustees for their support.

1 The Guru's story of the founding of the Community is the result of two lengthy interviews I had with him in August 1982 and May 1983. On both occasions the Guru spoke in the presence of his Swami, and the interviews were conducted in English. The Guru always showed me great kindness, as indeed did all the members of the Community. During the interviews I took notes and after the final interview I wrote a long account of the founding of the Community using, wherever possible, the Guru's own words. The Guru kindly made some corrections and additions to this preliminary draft. Thus the present narrative is as much as possible the Guru's approved version of the founding of the community.

2 Subrahmanya means 'having the quality of Brahman' and is one of the names given to the North Indian deity Skanda. During a long

process of development Skanda came to be regarded as one of the sons of Shiva. As this northern tradition began to coalesce with the southern Dravidian tradition so Skanda became identified with the Tamil deity, Murugan. In south India as well as in Sri Lanka, Skanda is known as both Murugan and Subramanium. In Sri Lanka, he is also known as Lord Kataragama, because of the temple dedicated to him at Kataragama. For a detailed discussion about the coalescence of the northern and southern Indian traditions, see Clothey (1978).

3 Padre Pio, who died in 1968, was a Catholic priest who carried out his ministry in Italy. During his lifetime he had stigmata that were especially evident in his hands, which he had to keep bandaged most of the time. As a result he gathered quite a following, but this was frowned upon by the Vatican. Attempts to have him canonized have so far been unsuccessful.

4 According to Burghart (1983) a similar view is held by the Brahmans with reference to the opposition between twice-born householders and houseless ascetics. Both are subsumed under the concept of the Brahman, which now stands at a higher, meta- level, and includes both terms. See also David (1977), where a similar approach is noted, to understand the opposition which exists between castes in Jaffna, Sri Lanka.

5 For a discussion about the relationship between the various Tamil Hindu temples in London, see D. Taylor, 'The social organization of the Sri Lankan Tamil Hindus in Britain'. Thesis in preparation: University of London (SOAS).

7
Charismatic authority in the Sathya Sai Baba movement

Donald Taylor

The Sathya Sai Baba movement claims to have 10 million devotees throughout the world, of whom 100,000 are said to be in Britain. On the one hand, these devotees are members of a highly structured organization centred in India, control of which is effected through a system of authority derived from the founder and administered through a number of trusts eventually to be applied to the lowest levels of membership. On the other hand, the founder of the movement, Sathya Sai Baba, claims to be the divine source of all authority; and hence empowered to act independently of institutional authority by performing miracles for the benefit of his devotees. This paper examines the relationship between institutional authority in the Sai movement and the gratuitious power of its founder and leader Sathya Sai Baba.

CHARISMATIC, LEGAL-RATIONAL, AND TRADITIONAL AUTHORITY

It is necessary at the outset to refer to a number of sociological concepts, derived from Weber, that clarify the notion of miraculous power and its relationship to authority. Weber distinguished between three types of authority: charismatic, legal-rational, and traditional (1968:215). Charismatic authority is that with which a person complies on the grounds that it is derived from a charismatic leader, who displays extraordinary, if not miraculous, powers. In accepting this authority, the followers satisfy their non-rational needs and goals, stemming from their emotional perception of their situation.

Charismatic authority contrasts with legal-rational authority with which a person complies on the so-called rational grounds that it is legitimated in terms of mutually accepted rules and legal norms. Compliance with legal-rational authority and the observance of organizational procedures is due either to the hope of future rewards or to the realization that a breach of the rules would affect the outcome of some future goal. The third type of authority is traditional, resting upon belief in the sanctity of immemorial traditions and the legitimacy of those exercising authority under them.

These three types of authority are ideal; that is to say they rarely occur empirically in their pure form, but are found in an interrelated form. For instance, an institution based upon legal-rational authority, such as an industrial organization, may have a charismatic leader at its head. Or to take another example, charismatic authority is usually unstable and may eventually be transformed into legal-rational authority, as happened with the institutional developments of the early Christian church.

In the case of the present-day Sathya Sai Baba movement one finds two different interrelationships between types of authority. First, Sathya Sai Baba's charismatic leadership is accepted on traditional grounds; and second, the movement is being organized on a legal-rational basis, which may be circumvented at any time by the charismatic leader. These two interrelationships are discussed separately below.

CHARISMATIC AND TRADITIONAL AUTHORITY IN THE SATHYA SAI BABA MOVEMENT

The Sai movement has from the start derived its authority from Sai Baba's ability to perform miracles (see Kasturi 1961–80).

The movement began in 1940 in Puttaparthi, a village in the state of Andhra Pradesh, when Sathya Sai Baba, then 14 years old and known as Sathyanarayana Raju, claimed to be the reincarnation of an Indo-Muslim saint called Sai Baba who had lived in Shirdi in Maharashtra State and who had died in 1918 (see Osborne 1975). Even before this, Sathya Sai Baba had been attributed with the charismatic power to perform a wide variety of miracles. Thus miracles and miraculous powers were firmly placed at the centre of the movement from its inception and during the ensuing years of its growth. Indeed, it is doubtful whether the movement would have grown so rapidly and extensively had it not been for the belief in miracles.

Sathya Sai Baba's charismatic authority was also, however, based on traditional grounds. The ability to perform miracles is part of the Hindu framework of belief about the world, and the acceptance of this framework is made on traditional grounds. Thus when Sathya Sai Baba claimed to work miracles and had this claim accepted, he was not departing from traditional Hindu beliefs or the grounds for their acceptance. Such a framework, which is characteristic of devotional Hinduism, entails a belief in a form of qualified monotheism in which the phenomenal world is thought to emanate from its divine source (regarded as a personal deity) and to go through a continuous process of degeneration and destruction, culminating in the reabsorption into the divine. The relationship between the divine and the phenomenal world is usually taken to be one of phenomenal distinction and dependence; that is to say, the phenomenal world is distinct from the divine but is also part of it. Given the right conditions, a man can realize the divine within himself and indeed within the whole phenomenal world itself.

In such a framework of belief incarnation (*avatār*) means the realization of the divine source, god, in human form. Within the Vaishnavite devotional tradition, the supreme god is taken to be Vishnu who is believed to have become incarnate nine times, with a tenth incarnation expected at some future date. In the Saivite devotional tradition incarnations of the supreme deity Siva are less common, but this does not mean that the deity is not believed to manifest himself in human form from time to time.

Although the doctrine of incarnation within these traditions can be confused (see Williams 1984), it is possible to distinguish between an incarnated deity in human form (*avatār*), a liberated soul (*ātman*), and a person with divine powers (*siddhi puruṣa*). According to my informants, incarnations are rare, for it is believed that there is only one incarnation for each particular age (*yuga*). Liberated souls, however, are those who have been released from earthly bonds and are free to be reincarnated with special powers. Gandhi was believed to be one, and was called the Mahatma, 'Great Soul'. Thus, though Gandhi was not regarded as a full incarnation he was regarded as at least a liberated soul, if not a partial incarnation. The Shirdi Sai Baba, too, was regarded by his devotees as a liberated soul. Finally a person with divine powers may become a guru or may simply have a charismatic presence, but he is not necessarily the reincarnation of a liberated soul as such (see also C.S.J. White 1972: 864–66 for a related set of distinctions, but one that differs somewhat from the accounts of my informants).

Fifteen marks distinguish a liberated soul or person with divine powers from ordinary men or women. These are the control over the five elements (earth, air, fire, water, and space); control over the five motor organs of the body; and control over the five sensory organs of the body. When a person shows that he has such control by making objects appear out of nowhere, by making the body levitate, by projecting visions, or bringing about auditions, then he is acknowledged to be either a liberated soul or someone with divine powers. But he would not be acknowledged to be an incarnation. To be acknowledged as such, a person has to exhibit a sixteenth mark, that of the triple powers of omniscience, omnipotence, and omnipresence.

When he claimed to be the reincarnation of the Shirdi Sai Baba, Sathya Sai Baba was believed by many of his devotees to be a liberated soul, or at least someone with divine powers. In 1963, however, he claimed to be the incarnation of the Hindu deity Siva in his androgynous aspect of Siva-Sakthi. In 1968 he made a further announcement that he was the universal god, so that devotions made to any form of godhead in the universe eventually came to him. All these claims, however, were made within the framework of Hindu belief. Even the assertion to be the incarnation of the universal god forms part of Hindu claims about itself (that it is the oldest religion, hence the source of authority for all other religions in the world). And these claims were accepted by his followers on traditional grounds legitimated by the sanctity of eternity.

These traditional assertions about the charismatic identity of Sathya Sai Baba made sense in terms of the development of the movement. For some followers the fact of the success of the movement, both in India and overseas, was evidence that their leader's power was greater than that of a liberated soul or a person with divine powers. They reasoned that he had to be an incarnation of the divine. Moreover, in order to further the movement it was necessary to develop legal-rational structures of organization, but such structures posed a threat to the movement in that its overall legitimacy stemmed from the charismatic authority of the founder. By claiming to be god, Sathya Sai Baba raised himself still higher, transcending the incipient organization of his movement.

CHARISMATIC AND LEGAL-RATIONAL AUTHORITY

Once Sathya Sai Baba claimed to be the reincarnation of the Shirdi Sai Baba, devotees of the latter came to the village of Puttaparthi to seek proof of it. It is said that he satisfied many (Schulman 1971: 52–3). Later, curious visitors were replaced by anxious pilgrims who came not for proof but for divine blessings. By 1947 his home proved to be too small, and a large complex of buildings outside the village was planned. It was completed by 1950 and Sathya Sai Baba moved into it, calling it Prasanthi Nilayam, the Abode of Highest Peace. This became the headquarters of the movement, and his permanent residence.

Sathya Sai Baba's fame spread throughout India, and the movement gathered momentum from the inflow of thousands of devotees, who had somehow to be organized. Accordingly the Sri Sai Central Trust was formed, controlled by a Council of Central Management. On this sit representatives from the various trusts and organizations that oversee the activities of the movement. The authority within the Trust to control the Sai organizations was invested in the World Council of Sri Sathya Sai Organizations. The Sri Sathya Sai Seva Organization comes under the control of the World Council, and is further sub-divided into three wings: the Centres Wing, the Women's Wing, and the Service Wing. Most devotees come within the Centres Wing which is responsible for more than 10,000 Centres of the movement (1980 figures). Each Centre has a small committee run by a president, who is responsible to a regional representative of the Seva Organization. Thus there is a well defined line of authority stemming from the Central Trust and linking the World Council of Sai Organizations, the Seva Organization, the Centre Committee, and the devotee. These administrative developments took place over a 30 year period from 1947 to the 1970s, by which time the movement had spread beyond India into lands of the Indian diaspora.

The movement began in Britain in 1966 when a South Indian Brahmin couple who had settled in Britain after years of service in Burma, began to make their devotion to him. They had read a review in an Indian journal of his official biography (Kasturi 1961–80) and were so impressed that they decided to worship him. As a result of their devotion, other Indian immigrants to Britain became devotees, and eventually the movement had to be properly organized. For this purpose Mr Indulal Shah, the head of the World Council of Sai Organizations, came to Britain in 1975 and set up the Sai Council of Great Britain with Mr Sitaram, the Brahmin devotee, as its first president (a fuller account of the early history of the movement in Britain may be found in D. Taylor 1986).

The Sai Council of Great Britain is a self-governing, autonomous body, but its activities are reported back to the World Council of Sai Organizations. Under the Sai Council of Great Britain come the Sai Centres, of which there are about 50 in Britain. In addition to the formal Centre there are hundreds of small informal groups, some of which aspire to formal recognition as Centres.

The Sai Council of Great Britain has a president and a six-member executive with one ex-officio member. The Council has the authority to recognize a group of devotees as a Centre. The requirements for such recognition are that the group comprise at least nine devotees who meet regularly and who are known to be good people. Once accepted as a Centre, the group elects its own committee and president. Such acceptance comes, however, only after careful scrutiny by the Council. The members of the informal group have to prove their worth by their attendance at meetings, the absence of dissension, and their active service to the community. If there is no evidence of community service, then an adverse report goes to Council.

The legal rational structure of the movement is still, however, secondary to the charisma of its founder Sathya Sai Baba. The case of the presidency of the Sai Council of Great Britain is an example. Mr Sitaram had been made first president of the Sai Council, set up by Indulal Shah in 1975. However, for personal reasons, Mr Sitaram stepped down from office in 1976. Sathya Sai Baba was displeased, and refused the appointment of a new president. This state of affairs continued until 1982 at which time he called for the names of candidates; and in that year a new president was appointed and Council constituted. Throughout the entire six-year period of administrative vacuum the devotees continued to meet in Sai Centres and, indeed, some were the recipients of the miraculous powers of Sai Baba in their own homes. Because of the devotees' compliance with Sai Baba's charismatic authority, the movement was perpetuated in Britain.

Although the Sai Council is in legal-rational terms an autonomous body, Council members believe themselves to be influenced by Sai Baba's miraculous powers of omniscience. All decisions of the Council are believed to be known by Sai Baba at the moment of their being taken, and thereby making a pure formality of the administrative procedure of sending reports back to the World Council of Sai Organizations in India. Members believe too that Sai Baba visits them in dreams and advises them how to vote or act, so that 'right' decisions are taken by the Council. Once again charismatic authority supplants the emerging legal-rational authority of the movement.

There is evidence, however, that this charismatic authority is in the process of being routinized. For example, in June 1985 at an audience given to a group of devotees from Great Britain, Sai Baba materialized a crystal '*lingam*' which he gave to the leader of the group. He instructed him to pour water over the '*lingam*' and to give the water to the sick, as this would 'do them good'. Every week at a certain Centre in London where the leader of the group is the president, the ritual is carried out by him. He is the only person allowed to touch the *lingam*. The water is distributed to the many sick people who come to the meeting, and gathered into containers to be distributed to those who cannot be present. Here the powers of Sathya Sai Baba are tacitly being routinized in ritual, and the person who performs the ritual is gradually being given the status of a ritual function-ary. This is one case that I know about from first hand; there are others that I have been told about.

In sum, the primacy of Sathya Sai Baba's charisma is assumed by almost everyone in the movement. He is regarded as the founder of each trust that is formed, as well as the governor of the whole movement. His divinity transcends the legal-rational organization of the movement. Yet his charismatic authority is open to routinization and this, in turn, suggests the eventual ascendency of legal rational authority.

DEVOTION AND SERVICE

The two main activities of the Sai movement are devotion and service. Devotional meetings are organized by each Sai centre, when devotional hymns (*bhajan*) directed to Sathya Sai Baba whose portrait is placed at the centre of the shrine, are sung for up to an hour and a half. To the right of the shrine is an empty chair signifying the presence of Sathya Sai Baba, and below it is a footstool on which is propped a photograph of Sai Baba's feet, the object of the devotion. A typical session also includes the recitation of the many names (usually 108) of Sai Baba, and it ends with the ceremonial offering of the flame (*arathi*) to the empty 'throne' and the portrait. By this means the substance of the 'light' of Sai Baba, so the devotees believe, is transferred to them through visual contact. The recitation of the divine names (*namasmarana*) and the special singing of divine songs (*nagar sankirtan*) are thought to draw the divine presence into the devotee which then dispels the threat of materialism and secularism that is ever-present in the vicinity. The activities of '*namasmarana*' and '*nagar sankirtan*' are thought to benefit the individual devotee as well as the neighbourhood of the centre.

The singing of such hymns is ubiquitous in all forms of devotional Hinduism regardless of cult or sect. Singer (1968) and Swallow (1982:152–57) have observed that the formation of *bhajan* groups was a response of the Hindu middle class to the tension between tradition and change in urban India. Such a functional explanation seems to apply to the British case. Migration of urban and middle-class Hindus to Britain peaked in the 1960s. After the Notting Hill riots in 1958 Hindus were unable to ignore the threatening and potentially violent nature of their social environment. Mr and Mrs Sitaram, who introduced the movement to Britain, belonged to this category of middle-class, high-caste Hindus to whom devotional group singing was well known. Following their arrival in Britain in 1963, they, like many other Hindus, responded to their alien environment by forming a small *bhajan* group, a source of mutual support and identity. When they subsequently decided to devote themselves to Sathya Sai Baba, they had little difficulty in persuading the other members of their *bhajan* group to do the same. Once devotion to Sathya Sai Baba had caught on in one *bhajan* group, it quickly spread to other groups. Thus the movement took root in Britain by means of a pre-existent network of *bhajan* groups that extended more or less to wherever Hindu immigrants were to be found.

Members of the Sathya Sai Baba movement, at various levels of organization, recognize the influence of devotional singing on group solidarity and its value in maintaining a network of relationships in a region. Hence considerable stress is placed within the movement on devotional singing; and members are expected to participate regularly in devotional activities at their Centre.

Another significant activity of the Sai movement is service

(*sevā*). The word can be taken to mean service either to god or to man. There is no distinction in value between the two. The promotion of service comes under the Service Wing or Seva Dal of the Sri Sathya Sai Seva Organization, and falls under four headings: 1. health and hygiene; 2. rural service activities; 3. famine, flood, and cyclone relief; 4. activities such as information bureau, vocational guidance, exhibitions, and libraries. All four branches of service are carried out on both a regular and a seasonal basis. Regular activities include: feeding the poor, classes for coaching underprivileged students, maintaining a first aid service, hospital visiting, and service to the handicapped. Seasonal activities include blood bank schemes, blood donations, medical camps, visits to remand homes, jails and reformatories. In 1980 over 10,000 trained men and women were engaged in activities of this sort.

This service is also seen as an extension of Sathya Sai Baba's ministry of healing. Stories of his beneficient miraculous powers include accounts of operations (Ganapati 1981:307), resurrections from the dead (p. 270–93), and healing of the dumb (p. 319), the lame (p. 312), and those with eye diseases (pp. 313,314,324). Many of the miraculous cures are said to be effected by means of holy ash (*vibhuti*) which he materializes out of nothing, but he has also been known to materialize medicines, pills, herbs, and even surgical instruments to perform these miracles (pp. 307–10). This concern to heal on the part of Sai Baba has been supplemented by more conventional forms of healing. In 1957 the Sai movement opened a hospital at Prasanthi Nilayam with beds for six male and six female patients. Today there are five Sai hospitals throughout India. The movement has also provided a number of mobile dispensaries for rural areas. But even in these hospitals, the miraculous methods of Sai Baba supersede Western medical practices. The doctors at Prasanthi Nilayam regard themselves as instruments of Sai Baba; and claims are made of successful operations that at one time would have been inconceivable even in hospitals of Western Europe or America (p. 325).

In Britain Sai devotees also carry out community service: visits to old people's homes, help with the medically handicapped, and visits to the sick in hospitals. Groups of 108 devotees have given blood; others are involved in the treatment of eye diseases in conjunction with the medical authorities.

Finally, a very important activity of the movement is its educational programme. In the Indian educational system, created by the British, religious traditions have had little influence on what was taught at university level. The Sai education programme intended to correct that by building colleges in as many states as possible and affiliating them to the university of the region, in order to be in a position to influence the university in its teachings of values and morals. A Sri Sathya Sai Arts and Science College for Women was established at Anantpur, followed by others at Bhopal, Hyderabad, and Jaipur. In 1969 the Sri Sathya Sai Arts, Science, and Commerce College was opened at Whitefields, near Bangalore, and another at Brindavan; 10 years later another college was opened at Prasanthi Nilayam. These colleges for both men and women form part of the Sri Sathya Sai Institute of Higher Learning, which has been accorded university status in India.

The Sai philosophy of education is based upon the five Hindu values of truth (*sathya*), right conduct (*dharma*), peace (*santhi*), love (*prema*), and non-violence (*ahimsa*). The aim of the educational programme is to inculcate these values into the pupil at every stage. The course is a supplementary one, running parallel with the school curriculum. The programme has come under the auspices of the Sri Sathya Sai Bal Vikas Trust, which has produced detailed courses for children of different age groups. Since its inception the Bal Vikas programme has been renamed Education in Human Values, and has been accepted by the Government of India for implementation in its primary schools.

In Britain the programme is being introduced through the Education in Human Values Society, founded by a member of the Sai Council of Great Britain. In 1984 the society organized an In-Service Teacher Training Course on Human Values in Multi-Ethnic Education in conjunction with the Inner London Education Authority, and a further conference in March 1985 (see D. Taylor 1984).

CHALLENGE TO AUTHORITY

Sathya Sai Baba's charismatic authority is vulnerable to challenge from both outside and within the movement. Outside the movement there are those who also claim to be holy men and who perform similar miracles. The production of a crystal '*lingam*' from within himself is performed by so many other holy men that Sai Baba announced in 1976 that he would discontinue the practice. Others of rationalist conviction, such as Dr Kovoor, denounced him as a 'fraudulent Godman whose miracles were nothing but plain magic' (Rajghatta 1985:48). To prove his point Dr Kovoor himself 'miraculously' produced a quantity of holy ash (*vibhuti*) which he distributed to eager recipients. He also challenged Sathya Sai Baba to allow his so-called miracles to be subjected to an investigation by a panel of like-minded rationalists, but Sai Baba refused, and lost a considerable amount of support in doing so.

Muted challenges from within the movement sometimes result in the withdrawal of membership. Dr Bhagavantham, formerly on the Council of Management of the Central Trust (also formerly scientific adviser to the Government of India), has recently left the movement; and another, Dr Gokak, formerly in charge of the education programme, has tried to demolish the myths that surround Sai Baba. Other Indian academics have also left; and it is claimed that 'many more devotees including most foreigners have already deserted the flock' (Rajghatta, 1985:48).

Other challenges within the movement are more subtle, and also result in some devotees exhibiting miraculous powers, such as producing holy ash and bringing about miraculous cures. So far these powers are claimed to be derived from Sathya Sai Baba. But it is not difficult to see that such activities are challenges to Sai Baba's authority. Unless they are met, the movement could disintegrate into numerous thaumaturgical sects centred upon charismatic individuals. One of the ways to meet this sort of challenge is to routinize charisma, thus transforming the structure of the movement to a legal-rational type.

Another way in which Sathya Sai Baba has met these challenges has been to secure his position at the Centre, by claiming to be the incarnation of the universal godhead, such that devotion to Christ, Allah, or whoever automatically comes to him. This sort of claim is not altogether unusual in Hinduism. It is interesting to note, however, that the Sai Baba advanced this claim in 1968, at a time when the movement was expanding into foreign countries, such as the United States, Australia, and Britain, and recruiting membership among emigrant ethnic Indians as much as western people. As the incarnation of the god of all gods the Sathya Sai Baba was thought to be the sole source of power. Today his devotees – whether they be Hindu, Christian, Buddhist, or Muslim – firmly believe this and are encouraged to continue within their own religious tradition, but seeing their devotions as being directed to him.

A further way in which Sai Baba has met a potential challenge to his authority is to thwart any discussion about his successor. In 1963 he announced that he was the second incarnation in a series of three. The first had occurred in the human form of the Shirdi Sai Baba who was the incarnation of Sakthi. The second, himself, was the incarnation of Siva-Sakthi; and the third would be the incarnation of Siva as someone called Prema Sai to be born in Mysore State eight years after his own death. By defusing the problem of succession, he also defused the problem of authority. All authority remains firmly in his hands as long as he lives. Anyone else who claims this authority in Sai Baba's lifetime will be recognized as a usurper or imposter.

However, concurrent with these assertions of omnipotence and omniscience, a legal-rational form of authority continues to develop with his approval. Omniscience is not thought to do away with the need for autonomous national Councils. Nor does his omniscience prevent factional disputes within Centres, and between Centres and informal *bhajan* groups aspiring to recognition. Decisions are taken locally by Centre committees and Centre presidents, even though these decisions are interpreted within the framework of miraculous belief.

Thus far Sathya Sai Baba has overcome most challenges to his authority. His devotees certainly behave as if they believe he is the incarnation of a deity and that he possesses miraculous powers. Their affirmations are made in what appears to be a sincere manner, in public, and they engage in non-sceptical dialogue about his miraculous powers. Such behaviour is especially evident at devotional meetings, when dialogue between devotees often turns to the topic of miracles. To engage in such a dialogue in a sincere and non-sceptical manner, implicitly affirming that the events being talked about are indeed miracles, is a form of behaviour that makes one a devotee.

This confirms that charismatic authority has primacy as far as devotee membership is concerned. The devotee has to do nothing to become a member of the movement. There is neither initiation ceremony, registration of names, nor entrance fee. All legal-rational procedures are dispensed with. All a member has to be is a devotee; and to be a devotee he or she must be seen to behave as a devotee by being willing, among other things, to engage in non-sceptical dialogue about Sai Baba's miracles, thereby acknowledging the primacy of his charismatic authority.

The primacy of charismatic authority should not be surprising, as charisma and thaumaturgical practices form the 'primal stuff of religion' (Wilson, 1975:70), which persists in modern religion and advanced complex society. Wallis (1976) also suggests that the transition from cult to sect (as the terms are used with reference to Western religious movements) involves an 'arrogation of authority' which is 'typically legitimated by a claim to a unique revelation which locates some source or sources of authority ... in the person of the revelator' (Wallis, 1976:17). There is some similarity here with the development of the Sathya Sai Baba movement, bearing in mind, of course, that the categories of Western sociology do not always fit the complexities of the Hindu religious context.

From the point of view of the devotee, the charisma of Sathya Sai Baba is the basis of his membership. The devotee's membership may be strengthened by receiving Sathya Sai Baba's grace in the present life, but because grace is given to whomsoever Sai Baba may choose, the devotee need not be the direct recipient of a miracle to have the benefits of devotion. He is willing to be the recipient of the general distribution among all devotees of Sathya Sai Baba's divine powers of salvation. So, as time goes on, we should not be surprised to find emerging within the movement an acceptance of Sai Baba's charismatic authority on the grounds of a general miracle, rather than on the grounds of specific miracles. And that general miracle would no doubt be the availability of salvation from the vicissitudes of this life for the benefit of all those who believe.

In their various ways, shifts, such as these, will no doubt take place in the charismatic structure of the movement. However, as long as the Sathya Sai Baba movement remains a religious movement, there is no doubt that acceptance of charismatic authority will have the edge on the incipient legal-rational structure of the movement.

NOTE

Fieldwork was carried out in Britain in 1983, 1984, and 1985, and was made possible by a grant from the Emslie Horniman Trust.

8

Initiation into monkhood in the Ramakrishna Mission

Séan Carey

The Ramakrishna Mission, like many other modern Hindu sects and meditation movements, contends that it is not a Hindu proselytizing body but a vehicle for spiritual transformation and development for individuals of any religion. This policy is based upon the notion that all religions are paths to the same goal, an attitude shared by many, both Hindu and Christian, who worship at the Ramakrishna Mission. But although the Mission lacks an aggressive policy of conversion, unlike such Hindu movements as the Divine Light Mission and the Hare Krishnas, still there are conversions if for no better reason than to perpetuate the sect. In the British context recruitment to the sect takes on an added interest. It raises intriguing questions about both the adaptation of the Hindu monastic system on foreign soil and the system of control and authority articulating the central concepts of mystical experience and knowledge in the Mission. In this paper I shall consider these questions with reference to the conversion of non–Indians to the Ramakrishna Mission, the probationary period undergone by candidate monks at the Mission centre, the ritual process by which the probationer becomes a novice, and the ritual of initiation into full monkhood within the monastic order.

THE CONVERSION EXPERIENCE

According to the Ramakrishna Order any long-term exposure to the ordinary world of householders leads to impressions and tendencies that are difficult, if not impossible, to eradicate, even after an individual has withdrawn from the original sources of impurity and contamination. Thus the Order rejects the classic Hindu ideal whereby the individual renounces his householder status and becomes a monk toward the end of his life, after discharging his family duties. Also rejected is the alternative ideal, whereby an individual renounces the world whenever he realizes the futility of worldly pleasure. At the same time, however, Vivekananda's original injunction that only 'Hindu boys' belonging to 'good families' should be allowed to join the Ramakrishna Order has been widened considerably and we are now told that 'absolutely no consideration of a candidate's social status' is heeded provided an individual is qualified 'spiritually and otherwise' (Gambhirananda 1957:136).

In general a candidate should not be younger than 18 or older than 30 in India, 36 in the West. An entrant must produce a medical certificate to show he is free from physical and mental abnormalities and has a clean bill of health.

In India, a candidate would be expected to have passed matriculation, but in Britain no formal academic qualifications are necessary because it is thought that the basic requirements are fulfilled by state education. A candidate is also expected to be acquainted with the Ramakrishna Mission literature and to have close contact with a monk of the Order, who acts as his guru or teacher, for some time prior to entry.

In Hinduism initiation into monkhood entails an act of world renunciation in which family ties may be broken or seen as unimportant. Although this may be the case for the Indian monks of the Order who distance themselves from their own families and preach non-attachment, the Mission is very keen on maintaining good relations with the parents of Western monastics. To that end, they are always invited along to discuss their son's proposed entry into the community and after this initial encounter the family are invited to have a meal at the centre from time to time, and monastics are expected to keep their parents informed on some of the details of their lives. In the early stages of the monastic journey, individuals are permitted to leave the community and return home for a few days but, over time, they are expected to distance themselves from the more intimate areas of family existence. There is no evidence to suggest that they ever totally cut themselves off from their kin. Indeed, the parents of the assistant swami are householder devotees in the Mission. This adaptation to British sensibilities has proved successful. Although most parents could not be described as wildly enthusiastic about their sons' monastic vocation, the Order has avoided public controversy over entry into their organization.

There were few residents at the Mission Centre at Bourne End, Buckinghamshire during my period of investigation. The basic community comprised only two monks (*sannyāsin*), one novice (*brahmacārin*), one probationer, and one pre-probationer. In addition there was a resident lay devotee who lived in the community but worked outside. There were also two individuals who had recently left the Centre and a small number of young men who had recently arrived to 'try out the life'. All the members of the community were Westerners except the swami-in-charge and the resident layman.

The Westerners were from affluent, well-educated backgrounds. Two had attended minor public schools, while the others went to grammar schools or their equivalents. None had been to university. Indeed all the members had come to the Mission before the age of 21. Two of the participants were British; the others were Dutch and German. Religion seemed to have formed a significant component of their childhood experience and their religious backgrounds were Quaker, Anglican, Lutheran, and Roman Catholic. But in all cases there was a disillusionment and a search beyond what they took to be the confines of conventional, institutionalized Christianity and its restrictive orthodoxies. One member commented that he was never able to accept the uniqueness of Jesus Christ and although he had no theological support for this idea, he felt that it would have been unreasonable for God to have manifested himself at only one time and place. Significantly he was also in search of a meditation technique with which he could commune with the divine in the here and now. Overall, the members did not seem to have experimented with other oriental movements before their contact with the Mission, although they were acquainted with Oriental-inspired, mystical literature. Nor did drugs and an involvement with the 'counter-culture' form an important influence in their past.

The monastics all reported that they had experienced a profound sense of dissatisfaction in their lives. Ordinary social arrangements were perceived as being trivial and superficial. One member had been involved in the early CND movement and had sat on the pavement with Bertrand Russell outside the headquarters of the Ministry of Defence in Whitehall. Eventually he grew tired of what he considered to be the egotism and posturing of radical, middle-class politics. Another member reported that he deliberately cultivated solitude and systematically isolated himself from his friends. On reflection he thought that he had been more than a little pretentious but claimed a certain legitimation for his behaviour because it at least gave him the opportunity to think his life through. One participant, in his account of joining the Order, focused very clearly on the problems he had faced in locating a real and authentic identity in modern society – a problem that was compounded, in his opinion, by his search in the sociological and psychological literature where he only found meaningless references to roles, statuses, and social influences.

In many ways alienated from their surroundings, these individuals were unable to solve their deepest problems and so having experienced a condition of powerlessness, they turned to an asymmetrical spiritual relationship involving dependence and subordination. As with other Western participants in oriental religious movements, the members of the Order were in search of an authoritative truth that was both dynamic and personally rewarding (see Cox 1979:96–7). Not surprisingly a monk of the Mission was a powerful mediator since in his own meaningful and positive alienation from ordinary society, particularly Western society, he embodied and signified a path that led to immortality and an ultimate identity – that of the Universal Self (*ātman*) – beyond the dualities of human existence. One monastic recalled his first encounter with Swami Ghanananda who was commonly regarded as a realized man. He said:

'One Sunday I went to a lecture at Muswell Hill. It was a small house and very unpretentious. There were about 40 people, mainly middle-aged, in the room. Then this robed figure came in. That was my first sight of the man who was to change my life. I didn't understand what he said – he was saying something about consciousness – but I knew when I left that I'd never met anyone like him. I used to go to the centre every Wednesday after that. They had a meditation room upstairs and people bowed to the picture [of Ramakrishna] which I couldn't understand. Anyway I asked the Swami how to meditate. I was fascinated by meditation and I also used to read Ramakrishna Mission literature concurrently with the New Testament. At the time I was living alone in a bedsit at Earls Court but one day I said to the Swami, "It's a very quiet place you've got here". So he said, "Why don't you come and live here". So I said, "Yes I would like that".'

Not all the members entered the Order after a 'conversion experience'. One monastic had become interested in Hinduism through his reading and had travelled to India in search of a teacher. There he made contact with the Mission, but was advised to return to Europe to follow his vocation. This he did, spending four years at the Mission centre near Paris. But feeling the need to expand his own mystical propensities, he left France – with the approval of the swami-in-charge – and spent four months on the periphery of an Indian reservation in Canada. While at first the Indians were afraid of him and thought he was mad, when they heard he was a 'monk' they offered him food and a hut. He refused at first, because he wanted to be alone, but after a while he accepted their offer because it was too cold living in his tent. He began to teach the Indian children on the reservation, and talked to the elders about their religious traditions. This reinforced his belief that all religions were paths to a sole ultimate truth, and his position as an outsider observing the communal life of Indians led him to recognize the importance of membership in a religious community for his own spiritual quest.

So if it is apparent that the young Europeans who came to the Mission were pursuing an individual inner truth, which was believed to transcend radically all social vehicles, the evidence suggests that they also placed a high significance on a charismatic personality and a supportive community. Both were crucial cognitive and affective mediating mechanisms on the path that led to that truth. Since the Ramakrishna Order has a stable organizational base, it is possible that many members find an extension of Christian values in which, even for the ascetic, the ideal of attaining salvation is attained within the 'community' of the Church. As we have seen, several participants joined the Mission not only because of their interest in Hinduism but also in order to expand their Christian sensibilities. In this juxtaposition of the individual and the community, Hinduism and Christianity, there is an intriguing matrix of spiritual power, social meaning, and personal quest.

THE PROBATIONARY PERIOD

The length of time during which an individual prepares for monkhood differs in India and the West. In India a person joins a Mission centre as a pre-probationer for a year, after which time he is recognized as a probationer. After a further four years, including two compulsory years at the Belur monastery, near Calcutta, the individual becomes a novice; then after another period of four years the candidate is eligible for monkhood and full membership of the Order. In the West, however, the process is much longer and varies from centre to centre. In Britain the pre-probationary period is often two or three years, during which time the swami-in-charge assesses the candidate's steadfastness of purpose. This extended period also gives the candidate adequate time to adjust to the disciplined life of the Centre. When the swami is convinced of his resolve, he gives the candidate probationer the initiation appropriate for laymen, and becomes the probationer's guru.

After several years as a probationer, the British devotee attends the training centre at the Belur monastery. This institution was established in 1956 after many tentative schemes in India and the West and it is now general policy, except in a few centres in the USA, to send probationers to the Mission's headquarters. At the end of this period, the probationer becomes a novice, returns to his previous centre in the West and after another four or five years is eligible to renounce the world and become a monk. Only very occasionally are monastics permitted to remain in India after training because it is felt that the adjustments required of a foreigner to adapt to life in India are too arduous.

The monastic path is an intensive form of socialization designed to break up an individual's past patterns of behaviour and reshape them into new configurations compatible with the spiritual goals of the Mission. To a great extent this process amounts to a loss of intentions and activities that in ordinary society would permit the constitution of a personality. In the monastic context, the territories of selfhood are invaded in order to move participants to qualitatively different areas of experience, directing them to a new self-perception and, as they believe, to their dissolution into the Universal Self. According to Bharati (1961:106–07) this is a subtle procedure and he notes Vivekananda's ingenious innovation in the original formation of the Ramakrishna Order. In traditional Hindu monasticism the initiate undertook to adhere to a strict regime as regards food, dress, and sleep. But in the Ramakrishna Order in India the monastic is treated exceptionally well and it is only after a while, and often imperceptibly, that privileges are withdrawn. Juniors normally abandon their privileges of their own accord. But this account tells only one side of the story; for as we shall see in the British context, the socialization process may give rise to considerable personal problems.

The manner in which an individual must detach himself from his family has already been mentioned. Another restriction is that entrants are obliged to dispose of their possessions. For most probationers this does not pose any real problem, since they have not accumulated any significant quantity of personal wealth. Candidates may keep a certain amount of personal clothing but luxury items like cars and record-players are forbidden because it is believed that they symbolize past habits and would lead to recollections of ordinary society. In time, then, when old articles have been discarded, all individual needs from shaving implements to food and clothing are supplied by the community. This process tends to create a sense of identity with and dependency on the Ramakrishna Order.

One of the hardest initial challenges is created by the specific prohibition against juniors working in areas in which they have had some prior expertise and experience. It is only after an individual has progressed along the monastic path that he is permitted to use his talents. For the most part, however, this requirement seems to be regarded as a necessary and legitimate discipline if the subject is successfully to transcend the confinements and deceptions of the ego.

Because of the focused status system in the Order, the example set by the monks, especially the swami-in-charge, to the junior members is important and the monks condense a range of meanings which provide a purpose and direction to the younger participants. The notion of hierarchy and movement framed in terms of mystical excellence serves to conceptualize and place an individual's problems in terms of the institutional set of meanings. Continuity rather than discontinuity is a preferred experience in the initial stages and this is one reason why Western youths are encouraged to stay in the West, rather than go to India, for their entire monastic training.

In spite of the prospect of spiritual rebirth in the monastery, the probationer cannot readily detach himself from the relationships and identities of his previous life. These personal problems may colour relationships within the monastery as he defines and redefines his spiritual goals. In one case it took a probationer some four years to bring his personal problems to some resolution. My informant's difficulties seem largely to have arisen from his realization that the Mission's ideal of religious harmony and universalism had very definite implications for his practical behaviour. Indeed, he felt that the Mission's cultural tradition intruded upon and, to a very great extent, conflicted with his own cultural sensibilities, which were Chinese. After a period of turmoil he came to the conclusion that if he was ever to understand the Mission, which he considered was rooted in Hinduism, he had to understand his own culture. This included the Confucian notion of filial piety. As he was a senior male member of his natal family, he felt a heavy responsibility towards the happiness of his parents which was incompatible with the way of a Hindu monk. He eventually decided to leave the Order and to try to apply some of the spiritual insights he had gained in the monastery to his ordinary experience in the world. After all, as he told me, if all paths led to the truth then Confucianism was as good as any other route. He became involved in a social priority school in the East End of London and took an active part in family affairs, helping his parents with their restaurant business. He still visited the centre occasionally and told me:

> 'I'm trying to be a true Vedantist and see if it's possible to function in society. To a certain extent I think I've achieved my aims. I can lead a full life outside the Centre ... and also go back to it occasionally. Some people who have left cannot return. They resolved the problems of the community by opting out. But I'm quite happy being a member of the Mission. It's difficult to meditate outside, but with true Vedanta it's not essential for everybody.'

Even with those junior monastics who remained in the Order there was considerable evidence that the Mission's cultural tradition was perceived as problematic. One probationer was seriously perplexed about the validity of his vocation since he still retained a deep sympathy for Christian values, and was put off by the Hindu cult trappings of the Order which seemed to displace them. Having joined the Mission to expand his vision, he had now encountered new restrictions. This sense of unease was further amplified by the fact that he was due to leave for the Belur monastery training school:

> 'My emotional lift has always come from Western monasticism and the intellectual justification from the East. But

unless that jump is made soon I can see there's going to be trouble. I'm not particularly fond of the devotional aspects of Hinduism. It seems curiously extrovert to me and its expression is disorganized. I suppose I'm a puritan at heart. But for me Ramakrishna is God incarnate. I occasionally see him in dreams but I don't like to think about it too much as it's ego-boasting and there's a good chance that it's a delusion. For a Westerner in the Order, it's very difficult but I take consolation from the fact that even a mediocre monk can get through nowadays.'

The Ramakrishna Order expects individuals to meet problems on their journey, and such difficulties are seen as opportunities for progress and movement. Whatever the outer conditions and contradictions may be, an individual is meant to realize that it is all illusion (*māyā*) and that he should search for a deeper meaning in an inner movement towards the reality of the Universal Self. Any monastic may ask for a transfer to another centre if he feels that he has been treated unfairly or if he wants a change in environment. There is, therefore, a prescribed alternative path to leaving the Order although if an individual selects this route, it is invariably interpreted as a sign of weakness and spiritual immaturity. The Order regards such a course as an escape rather than an act of transcendence. Sooner or later it is believed that the individual will have to return to face his problems. In the period of my study no-one took up this option.

THE NOVITIATE

The Belur monastery lies about five miles outside Calcutta on the Western bank of the Ganges, almost directly across the river from the Cossipore burning ghat where Ramakrishna was cremated. It is a powerful and evocative place for members of the Order. Extending more than 500 yards along the Ganges, the monastery compound contains the main monastery and several temples including ones dedicated to Ramakrishna, Vivekananda, and Sarada Devi (the wife of Ramakrishna). There is a guest house for visiting lay devotees and a novices' training area.

The average probationer group has about 35 members and

the intake is bi-annual. In the period between 1977 and 1979 there were 39 of whom only 30 completed their training. The probationers live apart from the main area of the monastery; the training centre has its own meditation room and is self-contained. The probationers only mix with other members of the Ramakrishna Order at mealtimes. Although they are under the formal control of the general secretary of the Mission, day-to-day supervision is undertaken by the staff of the training centre (the principal, vice-principal, and three assistants). These are not always senior monks but they are men selected for their piety and intellectual competence. Life at the training centre is intensive and probationers follow a set routine of meditation and study except on Sunday when they are expected to do their laundry and tidy their rooms.

When the assistant swami of the British centre visited the Belur monastery in 1969, he was given his own room overlooking the Ganges. It was even equipped with a fan to keep the room cool. But another probationer attending the training school in 1977 had to share a room with two others. Conditions can be difficult for non-Indians. The probationers sleep on a thin mattress on the floor and the diet is simple. Breakfast consists of two chapatis with some molasses. As a special concession Westerners are also given two boiled eggs and a banana. Lunch and the evening meal are composed of rice and/or chapatis, lentils, a vegetable curry, and some Indian sweets. Fish is served occasionally.

The probationer is expected to attend all the classes in the training centre, since it is the only time in a monk's career when a systematic study of the scripture is undertaken. The first year consists of a recapitulation and evaluation of the lives of Vivekananda and Ramakrishna and the other saints of the Mission. The probationer has to submit an extended essay on the life and work of Vivekananda and another essay on a theme of his choice. The second year is taken up with an examination of the principal doctrinal foundations of the Order. The key texts are the Vedantasara by Sadananda (a sort of Vedantic primer), the Samkhya Karika by Ishwara Krishna, the principal Upanishads with Shankara's commentary, the Bhagavad Gita, the Collected Works of Vivekananda, and Vedanta as expounded by Ramakrishna and the direct disciples.

Examinations are regularly held on these texts and the scripts are marked and returned to the probationers. The results are not made public since the system is not intended to be competitive. Unlike their Hindu counterparts, Western trainees are not expected to learn Sanskrit thoroughly, but most probationers return to Britain with the ability to read Sanskrit. They are the first to admit, however, that their knowledge of Sanskrit grammar is poor. Both my informants reported that they spent time pondering the relationship of Indian and Western thought, not simply out of an abstract intellectual interest, but also because they realized that sooner or later they would be expected to give talks and advice to Western householders.

The probationers' activities are tightly controlled and a careful watch is kept over their movements by the senior monks. But their time at the monastery is one of the few occasions when monastics are permitted to develop some form of friendly relationship with one another. This is designed to create a sense of identification with the Order and a similarity of orientation over and above national and regional differences and distinctions. For some, this is achieved, but others regard it as a claustrophobic intrusion upon their more individualistic dispositions.

The probationer's contact with the outside world is minimal; a trainee is only allowed outside the training centre with the permission of the principal. The probationer may make a pilgrimage to Dakshineswar, where Ramakrishna once lived toward the end of his life, but all secular visits are prohibited and an individual is only allowed to visit Calcutta if he is ill. Every so often a trainee is likely to be visited by a householder devotee from the British centre. These meetings are kept brief and take place outside the training centre in the monastery compound.

While at the Belur monastery it is impossible for a probationer not to realize the significance of the hierarchy within the Ramakrishna Order. Every four months there is a meeting of the Mission's Trustees at the monastery and these monks often give a guest lecture to the probationers in the training school. If they receive the permission of the principal, probationers are also allowed to sit with these monks after the evening meal when stories and recollections are told, sometimes into the early hours of the morning. In this way an oral tradition is maintained which supports mystical claims and sensibilities within the Order. But in some cases the entire process of talking becomes redundant when a trainee moves to a new dimension of experience. One monastic recalled his relationship with an elderly monk who lived in retirement in the monastery. It was a crucial aspect of my informant's training and convinced him of a deeper reality that transcended all cultural divisions. Perhaps for this reason he was a firm advocate of the necessity for probationers to go to the training school. He said:

'He was a man of few words but he loved us with a love I shall never be able to forget or do justice to. We used to serve him, either by gently massaging his head and legs, or by fanning him slowly, trying to fend off the numerous mosquitoes and at the same time attempting to bring a little breeze into that sultry room. We also had to lift him from his reclining deck-chair – on which he spent most of the day – and gently supported him as he shuffled two or three steps across the room to his bed. The swami would sit on the bed with his feet on the floor. We would then gently cross his legs and bring them up so that he would be sitting in a cross-legged position on the bed ready to take his meal. One or two novices would wait hours to perform this little task. Something happened when we were walking with the swami across his room and when we gently raised his legs into position on the bed. All I can say is that we felt, when we were touching him, that we were holding the universe, so elevating was the feeling that the swami transmitted to us. No words passed between us; we only felt his love and his power. There was nothing Eastern or Western about it, nothing Hindu or Christian. We only knew we were in the presence of a man of God.'

Even though the probationers have not reached that state, their contact with individuals who are believed to have done so gives forceful credibility to the system which has produced these saints who, finally, transcend it.

Initiation is a crucial aspect of the Mission's religious system. Indeed it is only through the controls imposed by initiation that an individual can become a novice and then a monk. These two stages do not by any means exhaust the overall concept of hierarchy within the Mission but they are necessary preconditions for entry into other areas of the Order.

Only candidate-monks and monks of the Order may attend the annual rites held on the celebration of Sri Ramakrishna's birthday. The following details are thus reconstructed from other accounts. The importance of secrecy in these rites is not only to keep esoteric knowledge from the layman, but also to give this type of knowledge a whole range of meanings beyond the ordinary and commonplace, so that the individual experiences a transformation in his position in the Order. He leaves behind his previous existence and takes his place in an ordered process that sharply differentiates him from the profane world of ordinary existence. In taking these steps his duties and relations to the organization are widened and stamped with a seal of a powerful authority. Indeed, it is only by virtue of that authority and its control over the initiatory complexes that the probationer's journey is assured and realized. It is, therefore, both the key and the passage to higher realities.

In India, the day goes from sunrise to sunrise and initiations of the candidate novice and monk take place at night at the end of the day. The initiation of the monk precedes that of the novice, but I will deal with the latter first.

Having completed the training programme and convinced the senior monks of his purity and motivation, the probationer meets the president of the Order who advises him on the nature and seriousness of the step he is about to take. The probationer is then released from classes one week before the initiation. The meaning of the various Sanskrit mantras to be used in the ritual are explained to the probationer. He is permitted to repeat them, but is not to write them down until after the initiation. A few days before the ritual the probationers have their heads shaved except for the small tuft of hair at the crown of the head (*sīkhā*) which symbolizes student status.

Three days before the initiation a ritual to Siva, called Siva

Ratri, is held at the Belur monastery. Siva is said to be the god of ascetics, and all the members of the monastic community attend, as well as lay devotees. One of the novices dresses up as Siva and dances around with a trident while the others sing and dance. At 10 pm most laymen leave the monastery and only the monks and a few privileged male householder devotees are permitted to stay. The singing and dancing continues until dawn, when the monastics eat the food which has been consecrated by the deity and then they catch some sleep.

The following day Sri Ramakrishna is worshipped. There is chanting and singing, and special lectures are delivered in the monastery compound. If the worship is on a weekday, it is repeated on a grander scale the following Sunday for the benefit of those laymen who missed it through work. The celebrations last until the evening service (*ārti*). This closes the public festivities. The probationers then prepare for their initiation. They bathe in the Ganges and try to get some sleep. Many will have fasted all day.

At approximately 3.30 in the morning, just before first light, the probationers assemble in the courtyard outside the temple of Sri Ramakrishna. As the newly ordained monks come out the probationers enter the temple. There is a sacrificial (*homa*) fire in the middle of the temple and the probationers sit around it in a semi-circle. Facing the candidates on the other side of the fire is a priest. On the candidates' right sits the Vice-President and a little further back is the President of the Order who presides over the entire proceedings.

The priest performs a small ritual offering in order to honour and placate the deities. The Vice-President rises and chants in Sanskrit. Below I give the translations given to me by a monk of the Order:

'The purpose of my life is to cultivate dispassion, to attain union with God, and to be immersed in the bliss of divine love. To attain these objectives I will do my utmost to live according to the ideals of celibate studentship.'

This is repeated by the initiates. Then a number of vows are undertaken. They are first spoken by the Vice-President and then repeated by the probationers. The initiates have some vilva leaves dipped in ghee and, as they make each vow, some of the leaves are offered to the fire. The vows include:

1 the resolve to meditate daily after having performed the necessary internal and external purifications;
2 the acceptance of the necessity to be pure in mind and to concentrate one's thoughts in meditation on the protection of Sri Ramakrishna;
3 the acceptance of the necessity to see work as devotional activity;
4 the control of the organs of perception and action while maintaining an attitude of cheerfulness;
5 moderation in eating;
6 the avoidance of bragging and conceit and the understanding that to examine one's own failings is more valuable than the criticism of others;
7 the adoption of the middle-way in every activity since over-exertion whether physical or mental is detrimental to one's spiritual development;
8 the recognition that the ultimate goal is God and that service to the highest takes precedence over the desire for 'women and gold', love of country, obligations to one's parents, and personal ambitions;
9 the recognition of the necessity to be continent in thought, word and deed and look upon all women as one's mother.

These vows are followed by the Ramakrishna Order's rendition of the Gayatri Mantra:

> 'Om. May the Paratman who is the Indweller of the three worlds – the earth, the heaven and the nether world – and the inspirer of the universe, inspire and guide me to spiritual unfoldment and protection. Om.'

After this each initiate goes to the President and receives his new robes. The outfit consists of a number of different pieces of white clothing. The colour symbolizes both purity and student status. The first is a *dhotī*, which is a light piece of cotton cloth nearly four feet wide and 15 feet in length. This has to be doubled and then beginning at the left hip it is taken once around the waist and then to the right hip where it is partially tucked in. The remaining material is brought back to the other side and it is pleated at the front. The second item is the shirt worn by the Order's monastics. This was introduced in the early days of the Mission in India. It does not have a collar and the sleeves are slightly open at the wrist. It also has a few pockets. The third item is the cotton blanket (*cādar*), which is roughly three feet wide and nine feet in length. It is placed around the shoulders like a shawl. The initiates are also given a loincloth (*kampina*) although most British monastics prefer to wear conventional briefs. Most of these garments are made from stitched cloth and the Order recognizes that this is a Western influence and a compromise with Hindu orthodoxy.

Those initiates who do not possess a sacred thread are then given one. This gives them a distinct cultural position, making the Westerner a member of the privileged twice-born castes. It is a significant status within Hinduism, opening the door to Vedic study bringing 'the unredeemed person into the company of the elect' (Kane 1953–73:2;193). The thread is a thin cord hung from the left shoulder to the right hip and it is always worn by novices of the Order. If it becomes frayed or tattered, a new one has to be put on before the old one is taken off. It is only removed before the ordination into monkhood and the novices are instructed to hold it in their right hand as they perform the Gayatri Mantra in their meditation.

By this time the newly ordained monks have returned to the temple and both the novices and monks ask for the blessings of Sri Ramakrishna that they may live up to their ideals. Both groups then go to the President's office where they are given consecrated food. They in turn give the President some fruit as an offering. After this they are given new names. Once a Westerner has gone through the pre-probationer stage, he is known as Brother David, Michael, or whatever his Christian name happens to be. Having taken his vows as a novice, he is given a new name – for example Veda or Bhakti – together with a second name shared by all fellow novices, Chaitanya. He is, however, rarely called that except on formal occasions. To his equals and superiors he will always be known by his Christian name, or, if he has been previously given an Indian name, by that instead.

For the next three days the novices are not allowed to eat in the monastery dining area. They have to beg for food from the dining hall and they must cook it themselves. Their diet consists of rice, lentils, and vegetables. This procedure harks back to the investiture with the sacred thread (*upanayana*) in which begging is an integral part of the ritual. This food is meant to be particularly pure and is part of the reciprocal obligations that exist between the student and householder (Kane 1953–73:2; 310–11). But although the concept of pure food is retained by the Mission, it is possible to detect an interesting transformation in meaning in that the exchange no longer symbolizes the mutual obligation of student and householder but of the novice and the Ramakrishna Order. The monastic community has become the paramount entity in this ritual complex.

After this period the novices return to their normal routine. There are some classes and a farewell celebration and meal. Most of the Indian novices immediately return to their respective centres but novices from the British centre go on pilgrimage for four or five weeks. They normally travel with a newly ordained Indian monk and stay at Ramakrishna Mission centres at night.

INITIATION INTO MONKHOOD

Having completed another four or five years in Britain the novice is eligible for ordination. The novice knows, however, that he should never enquire into his return to India for this purpose because such a question would indicate his inadequate ethical and spiritual direction. Indeed, he may well find that his initiation is postponed for three or four years if he does. Ordination takes place by the authority of the Order, not through the desire of the individual.

Those who are due to renounce arrive at the Belur monastery a few weeks before their initiation. It is a time to renew acquaintances and to pay respects to senior monks. A week before the ritual, the novices are moved into the library building in the monastic compound and some time in that week the novices have their head shaved except for a tuft of hair. Three days before the ritual, all the novices gather in a bamboo hut by the side of the Ganges. A Brahmin priest from Calcutta performs a funeral ritual and each novice conducts death rites for his father and mother and himself. The ritual lasts about three-and-a-half hours. In the days that follow the 'funeral' the novices must fast, sleep on the floor, and are forbidden to wear any stitched clothing or footwear. Instead they dress in loin-cloth, chadar, and dhoti made from rough material. Although this use of clothing is, as we have seen, only a temporary arrangement for the members of the Ramakrishna Order, it is a traditional practice incumbent upon ascetics and is similar to some of the taboos placed on mourners in Hinduism. Moreover according to Das (1977:126ff) the similarity is not accidental since both the renunciate and mourner are liminal entities outside the conventional classification system. But whereas the ascetic's liminality is permanent, the condition of the mourner is only temporary. Further, in Hindu religious thought death is a means by which the individual soul moves beyond the illusions of this world and realizes the eternal Brahman (Das 1977:121). This is accepted by the Mission and it reminded me that Vivekananda had told his followers that in the same way the worldly man loved life, so should the monk love death for only in this way could the latter sacrifice the ordinary self and achieve liberation.

After the death service the novices take part in Sivaratri and are expected to reflect on the meaning of the forthcoming initiation. My informants attested to heightening of emotion and strong sense of anticipation. About two in the morning the novices take a bath in the Ganges. They then enter the temple of Ramakrishna and the doors and windows are locked and sealed. The novices perform a full-length prostration to the life-size, stone image of Ramakrishna before taking their seats around the sacrificial fire. They then take their vows in Sanskrit. The English translation given to me is as follows:

'Om. Today with a view to embracing the Order of Renunciation for my own freedom from bondage and to work for the spiritual well-being of all beings, I am performing the Viraja Homa in the Fire named Sri Ramakrishna which is lighted before me. Om. May this resolve of my self-luminous mind, which wanders far and near during the waking state and withdraws into itself during the sleep, conduce to my spiritual progress. Om.'

The novices are given a plate of vilva leaves soaked in ghee to make their oblations to Ramakrishna. The deities are propitiated by the priest and then follows the process of purification. The novice offers himself to the fire and each oblation symbolizes the elements of the psycho-physical body which is believed to consist of the five senses (sight, hearing, smell, taste, and touch), the five organs of action (tongue, hands, feet, organs of excretion and generation), the five modifications of prana (the life-force which controls breathing, digestion, etc.) and finally the mind and intellect. Having totally renounced the body and the desire for family, the initiate identifies himself directly with Ramakrishna and then the Impersonal Brahman. He then returns from the formless and asks for the blessings of Ramakrishna.

In a drastic renunciation of worldly structures the initiates now take off all their clothes and perform a complete prostration to the president of the Order. My informants said that there was no sense of embarrassment at this point; they claimed that such an emotion would have been inappropriate since they had just renounced the body. The president then cuts the tuft of hair remaining on the head and places it on the sacrificial fire. He afterwards gives the initiates their new clothes. These are the same as those worn by novices but are ochre-coloured. The monks are then told the mantras known only to the monks originally initiated by Shankara in the ninth century AD.

The newly ordained monks then leave the temple and make their way down to the Ganges, singing and shouting as they proceed. They are provided with a wooden staff (*danda*) which they ritually break and, together with the sacred thread, throw these items into the Ganges. The casting off of the sacred thread by the initiates is easy to explain: it symbolizes a final rejection of their student status, but the breaking of the staff is a bit more puzzling. One monk explained to me that the staff is a symbol of the many ordinary Hindu ascetics and that because Ramakrishna had been initiated by the naked ascetic Tota Puri, Ramakrishna Order monks had transcended the need for external signs. As he put it, 'I have identified myself with the universe. Where is the form if the Universal Self (*ātman*) alone exists?' Obviously such a statement constitutes an ideal state of affairs rather than a literal description of their condition. Monks are well aware that they are not existentially united with the Universal Self.

After these events the monks return to the temple and join the newly initiated novices. They then receive their new monastic names. Although Ramakrishna's disciples chose their own names all monks nowadays are given them. They are composed by the senior monks and more or less randomly distributed except that, in the case of Westerners, simple and easily pronounceable names are bestowed. The names of monks always end in 'Ananda', meaning bliss. Thus a monk of the Ramakrishna Order is formally addressed as Swami Budhananda, Swami Ghanananda, etc. When this procedure has been completed, the monks go around and ask for the blessings of the senior monks of the Order.

Like the novices, the new monks are forbidden to eat in the Belur monastery dining room for three days. But unlike the novices who receive food from the Order, the monks must leave the monastery and beg in the streets of Calcutta. They are only permitted to eat vegetarian food and they are not allowed to accept money. This practice was recognized as conforming to the conventional role of the Hindu ascetic who having renounced ordinary society became a homeless wanderer wholly dependent on begging, unattached to pleasure and devoting his time to contemplation. This experience had a deep effect on my informants. One said:

'The begging experience was very interesting, because you could see how far your training had taken you. It's not that your training stops when somebody hands you these clothes. In fact it gets to a more difficult level – it reaches down to deeper parts of your being. You go out in your robe and stand outside a house while taking the name of the Lord. We went out in pairs. A tremendous reverence was shown. People would stop you. Little boys would grab you by the hand and ask you in. Then the grandmother would come out with a large stainless steel plate and fill up the piece of cloth that you held in your hands with dal, yogurt, and so forth. A lot of it would drop out. Then with great reverence she would hand the plate to someone else and in all the dust – and this applied to all grades of society rich and poor – they would touch your feet with their foreheads. There was no sense of pride. There was instead a tremendous sense of mutual reverence. They were paying respect to the cloth, to the ideal of the ascetic.'

After collecting the food, the monks walk back to the monastery where they give some of it to the President and other monks of the Order. They then proceed to the banks of the Ganges where they sit and consume their own portions. Overall these practices and exchanges reinforce the reciprocal link and meaningful position of a monk within the Order. But the begging transaction also demonstrates the significance of the hierarchical relationship between the monk and layman since it is only through the latter's charity that the monk is free to pursue a deeper truth.

After a period of three days, the newly initiated monks are permitted to put on stitched robes and footwear. Western monastics are generally allowed to make a pilgrimage. One informant, having already travelled around South India after his initiation into the novitiate, decided to go to North India. Accompanied by a monk from the Hollywood centre and staying at Mission centres at night, they visited Hardwar, Almora, Benares, Rishikesh, and Delhi. In the course of his travels he became intrigued by the romantic, if somewhat unlikely, idea that the mendicant tradition might take root in British society. On his return to Britain he talked of his trip to the Himalayas to some Western and Indian householders:

'There was a little temple and beyond that there was a cave made into the mountain by an ascetic. Over the other side of the crevasse was another monk. It was evening, about 7 o'clock. The atmosphere was incredibly peaceful so that one felt this was the spiritual life. Coming on top of the begging in the streets one really felt this was it. Returning to England I seriously wondered what would happen if with these clothes on, we took the name of the Lord and went begging in the countryside here. I think it could be done.'

But, of course, such visions do not last. But this general observation does not in any way diminish the significance of such experiences; rather it points to the necessity to contextualize them. Indeed my evidence suggests that these moments are crucial in that by liberating psychic energies credibility is given to the religious system which has, in a very real sense, informed and produced them. Although participants recognize that these occasions are only glimpses of the ultimate reality, it would seem that for them truth is powerfully revealed even when it is only partially perceived.

9
Hindu temple rituals in Britain: the reinterpretation of tradition

Kim Knott

The study of Hindu religious practice in Britain provides researchers with an opportunity to examine the question of religious change. What happens to a tradition when it moves to a new geographical and social location? How has Hinduism adapted in its meeting with the British way of life? Has it remained unchanged? Been engulfed by other ways of being? Developed new forms? In terms of the antiquity of its traditions the presence of Hinduism in Britain is a new phenomenon. Nevertheless in considering some aspects of its short history on these shores we are able to examine the process by which it determines its future in a new context.

> 'Since religion is subject to the passage of time religious leaders and believers are forced to respond to ever-lengthening perspectives. In particular the transmission of religion from one culture to another whether geographically or chronologically means that new cultural elements are introduced to the tradition and new demands are made upon it.' (Pye 1979:17)

In nineteenth-century India the interaction with British reformers, missionaries, and scholars led Hindus to consider the beliefs and practices of their religion from new perspectives. In the twentieth century, Hinduism has faced a challenge not from a powerful culture within its own midst but from its migration 'across the black waters' to countries in the first world. Unlike the travels of Vivekananda in the 1890s and the proselytizing of teachers and gurus, such as A.C. Bhaktivedanta Swami Prabhupada and Maharishi Mahesh Yogi in the 1960s, this migration has involved the transplantation to foreign shores not of intellectual Hinduism but of popular Hinduism.

The form this transplantation takes is not determined solely by the nature of the Hindu religious tradition. It is a process in which the complexities of religion and ethnicity become enmeshed. The relationship was noted by Abramson (1979:8): 'It is only in contact between cultures, as in the classic role of migration, that ethnicity and religion assume a dynamic and social reality of their own.' Religion is not necessarily a feature of the culture of all migrant groups. Some may well feel no need to develop their faith in their new location; others, like the South Asian religions recently established in Britain, feel a need to continue to practise and believe that which is familiar to them. For this to have any social meaning, that is for organizations to develop, traditions to be transmitted to new generations, and communal rituals to be continued, the migrants must have strong social ties. They must share a sense of distinctiveness recognized by themselves and by others. How groups of migrants then develop new ways of being depends on the nature of their social relationships, their response to the other groups with which they come into contact, their social, cultural, and religious traditions, and their commitment to a future in their new location.

It is the particular form or forms this process takes for Hindus in this country that is of interest here. Francis, discussing the relationship between religion and ethnicity in an American city, considered some of the ways in which transplanted religions might develop:

'It is the ethnic group which sanctions a particular church affiliation, and which supports a religious congregation and its institutions as an effective means for its own maintenance and the preservation of its cultural traditions. Thus, when religious affiliation and ethnicity are coextensive, both tend to support and sanction each other. In other cases, however, instead of increasing the unity and coherence of an existing group and of protecting it against the influences of the social environment so that assimilation is inhibited by religious taboos on intermarriage and apostasy, religious differences may weaken and divide ethnic groups, promote union with different ethnic groups, and facilitate transculturation, assimilation, and eventually absorption.'   (Francis 1976:157)

If we accept this analysis of the consequences of the relationship between ethnicity and religion we meet with particular problems when we turn to Hinduism. While it has been described as an 'ethnic religion' (Sopher 1967) as a result of its close and enduring relationship with its homeland, it is a religious system of enormous complexity which provides meaning and order for many quite different social and cultural groups from the Indian sub-continent. Therefore the migration of Hindus, and hence the transplantation of Hinduism to Britain, demands detailed examination. While the majority of the British Hindu population originates from two different geographical areas in India, Gujarat in the west of India and the northern state of the Punjab, the Sikhs are exclusively Punjabi. They comprise a group, by contrast to the Hindus, of whom it may be said 'religious affiliation and ethnicity are coextensive'. Like any group, the Sikhs in Britain suffer from internal differences but they are not divided by ethnic allegiances as the Hindus are, and have the advantage of adhering to a set of beliefs and practices of comparatively recent development, to a religious community described by Rose (1969:452) as 'a brotherhood which was forged in persecution'. As the selfconscious victims of a history of suffering and aggression, the Sikhs have sought to identify with the brotherhood (*khālsā*) and to maintain the traditions associated with it. This is no less true here than in the Punjab. The Hindus in Britain do not have the same natural advantages. Originating as they do from different geographical areas in the Indian sub-continent, they are divided by such things as language, culture, caste, and settlement history. In addition, unlike the Sikhs whose doctrinal position is to a large degree both unified and authoritative, their historical experience sanctions a diversity of differing cosmological and philosophical beliefs, ritual practices, cultural customs, and moral stances. How then have the Hindus in Britain coped with the situation in which they now find themselves? Have they become assimilated or absorbed, or have they succeeded in maintaining their social and religious distinctiveness?

The answers to these questions may vary for the different Hindu populations in Britain's cities. Leeds, where the field-work for this study was conducted, is perhaps an extreme case. In some areas where the population is exclusively Gujarati and belongs largely to one caste, the problems of religious and social diversity might not be so great. In Leeds, however, we find a small, mixed population of approximately 2,500, comprised of Gujaratis and Punjabis (with some Hindus from other Indian states) from a number of different castes (mainly Gujarati Mochi and Punjabi Khatri but also Suthar, Patidar, Lohana, and various Brahman castes). The proportion of Gujaratis to Punjabis is approximately 2:1, with the Gujaratis living in Burley and South Headingley, and the Punjabis in Chapeltown and Harehills with common language speakers, the Sikhs. What sense have these Hindus, with their different linguistic, cultural, and social backgrounds, made of their new situation?

As was suggested previously, the process of transplantation that is in operation here is one of popular Hinduism, not its intellectual counterpart. Two important issues arise from this. The first is that whether Hindus come to Britain from villages or cities in India their religious worldview tends to incorporate elements from what Redfield (1956) designated both 'great tradition' and 'little tradition'. Their beliefs and practices are a melange of pan-Indian and vernacular elements. The second issue concerns their degree of unselfconsciousness. Generally speaking religion was practised without question. It remained unarticulated. This was only natural when it was part of the fabric of everyday life. However, like the vernacular elements of a religion, this unselfconsciousness is under threat from the process of transplantation. When one religion comes into contact with another, and its beliefs, practices, and values become open to question in the new social context, the adherents of that religion become increasingly aware of its content. This is not without consequence for the persistence of a religion in an alien milieu.

In Leeds it is primarily through the temple that local Hindus have organized and maintained their religion. It is undeniably true that religious practice has persisted in the home, with women continuing to fast and to conduct regular pujas, and with families continuing to observe life-cycle rites. In addition, those with particular religious or cultural interests meet in small groups to worship, sing, and discuss their faith, and those with a common caste identity meet to organize functions, to raise funds, and so on. The small size of the Leeds population and its mixed linguistic and cultural background, however, makes it difficult for such groups to be socially and religiously effective. It is thus the temple and its chief functionaries which bring local Hindus together and serve their religious interests most successfully. Many of the particular requirements and needs of individuals relating to such matters as caste and sectarian allegiance are not met by the temple and its programme. It is the temple, however, which both presents the religion of the Hindu population to outsiders, and is recognized by Hindus as a focus for their religious identity. Many Hindus make infrequent use of the services of the temple, attending only for festivals and special occasions, and calling on the pandit only in times of need. In fulfilling these requirements alone the temple in Leeds provides an essential service, and a degree of continuity and support unobtainable elsewhere. Furthermore because of the complex role it plays as the symbol of official Hinduism – both to outsiders and to Hindus themselves – it has a social and religious significance which exceeds that of other local Hindu organizations. Thus it is in the temple that the creative process of transplantation can be seen most clearly.

In order to understand this it is necessary to know a little about the history of the temple and its identity as an institution representing the city's Hindu population. In 1968 a charitable trust was set up by the informal Hindu cultural society which had met in the city since the mid-sixties. The chief aim of the trust was the establishment of a temple and cultural centre for local Hindus, an aim the members achieved in 1970 when they obtained a small estate in Burley. The temple they opened, like the trust itself, had a strong Punjabi flavour. (Ten of the 16 original trustees were Punjabi.) A number of Gujarati men were involved in these early developments – one in particular was responsible for the temple's close links with the Indian Vishwa Hindu Parishad – but the Gujarati community at that time was relatively small. It was not until the mid-seventies, after the temple had suffered two very damaging fires, that the growing 'East African' Gujarati population began to take an interest. The Gujaratis, unlike the Punjabis who had to travel several miles to attend the temple, lived within easy reach. A number of them worked hard to renovate and redecorate a room for worship. It was this group which formed the core of temple management during this period, and which in 1975, in the absence of the Punjabis who had chosen to attend a temple in Bradford after the fires had destroyed their early efforts, invited a Gujarati pandit from Leicester to serve full-time in the temple and in the homes of local Hindus. This was not the last of the political swings and roundabouts in temple management, however. In 1979 a group of Punjabis took on responsibility for organizing a religious programme to correspond with the Divali festival. The success of this event stimulated Punjabi interest, and in 1981, six months after the second of these Divali celebrations, Punjabi candidates won a landslide victory in the temple management committee elections. Despite these radical changes both groups continue to use the temple and its facilities.

The arrangement in Leeds is thus very different from comparable arrangements in other British cities (e.g. Bradford and Coventry) where Punjabi and Gujarati communities are of sufficient size to fund separate places of worship. In Leeds, however, the total Hindu population is too small to warrant or finance more than one major temple and full-time specialist. Instead, both groups share the facilities, the financial burden, and the services of the temple and its priest for festivals and regular worship. Ethnic variations are not abandoned though.

Punjabis, for instance, rarely use the services of the pandit for rites of passage, and will pay a Punjabi Brahman to act for them instead, while the Gujaratis tend to use the pandit for all their religious requirements. Punjabis and Gujaratis also tend to support different rituals with Punjabis favouring the fire service (*havan*), and the festivals of Divali and Ramnavmi, and Gujaratis, the regular service of offering (*ārtī*), and the festivals of Navaratri and Holi. The two groups have also donated different religious objects, the Gujaratis, a picture of Shirdi Sai Baba, a popular saint from the west of India, and the Punjabis, an image of Hanuman, and a photograph of Satguru Jagjit Singh Ji, the saint of the North Indian Namdhari sect.

The religious culture of the two religio-ethnic groups is not only expressed overtly in these ways but has also been assimilated over the years into the basic fabric of temple religion. Since the early years both groups at some time have held control in temple management, and have been in charge of the provision of religious services. Both, therefore, have been in a position to introduce and effect changes in ritual practice. We will see how this has occurred a little later.

In the remainder of this paper two related questions will provide the focus for discusssion. What is the nature of 'temple religion' in Leeds, that is, what form has organized Hinduism taken as a result of its transplantation to a new location? And how have both the religious tradition and the various ethnic motives and interests of the Gujaratis and Punjabis been employed in the development of this new form? Religious practice in the temple, in particular the regular services of *ārtī* and *havan*, will provide us with an illustration of this process as it is in the fulfilment of this ritual role that the temple has its *raison d'être*. Although it functions as a social and cultural centre for Hindus, and plays a civic role in representing 'the faith' and 'the community' to outside bodies, it does so only because it operates first and foremost as a sacred space in which Hindu rituals can be performed. Ritual activity is a functional necessity which allows it to carry out these other roles. Without regular religious practices, festivals, life cycle rites, and irregular rituals for the making of vows (*vrat*) and the recounting of moral stories (*kathā*)

Hindus would feel no obligation to attend the temple, and its role in preserving and maintaining religious culture would be eroded.

Ārtī and *havan*, like other temple rituals, are performed in a context of 'Sanatana Dharma'. What local Hindus understand by this term is made clear in a handout produced by temple representatives several years ago:

> 'The Hindus call their religion Sanatana Dharma. Sanatana means Eternal. The word Dharma is difficult to interpret as it has no equivalent in English. Dharma means that which prevents one from going down, ruining oneself in any manner whatsoever and makes for one's welfare, progress and uplift all round. The word 'Religion' does not mean 'Dharma'. Dharma means the ethical and religious ideals, social and religious duties ... '   (Leeds Hindu Temple, n.d.)

The term is used to refer to 'that which remains of an ancient system of knowledge', to certain beliefs and practices of a traditional nature, such as transmigration and rebirth (*karma, saṁsāra*), liberation (*mokṣa*), divine incarnation (*avatāra*), duties according to one's caste and stage of life (*varṇāśramadharma*), and worship (*pūjā*) and service (*sevā*) to god. Local Hindus use the term with no apparent awareness of its nineteenth-century sectarian connotations. Even Punjabis whose sympathies lie with the Arya Samaj – a religious reform movement with nineteenth-century origins – remain silent on the subject. In the temple 'Sanatana Dharma' is held to be a system which incorporates all Hindus, irrespective of ethnic or sectarian divisions. It symbolizes temple religion: it is hailed in one of the final verses of the *ārtī* service with the phrase 'Sanatana Dharma *kī jay*'; it is the focus for dialogue with those of other faiths. Those temple representatives – the pandit, and the members of the Hindu Charitable Trust and Temple Management Committee – who have been responsible for articulating Hinduism to a non-Hindu audience and for compiling the temple's religious programme have 'standardized' this complex religion. They have developed the doctrinal and ethical components of Hinduism, those elements which can easily be recognized by non-Hindus.

They have stressed well-known deities such as Krishna and Rama, and have attempted to select key festivals and rituals which figure in the calendars of both Gujarati and Punjabi Hindus. As an inevitable consequence of this, particular ethnic and religious beliefs and practices have been subordinated in the interest of the general religious good. In becoming a self-conscious tradition in a new location the vernacular has given way to the pan-Indian, diversity has given way to a unified system of belief and practice, and ethnic identity has given way to 'community'. The content of those religious practices which take place in the temple – which form a part of 'Sanatana Dharma' – reveals the dynamics of this process, the development towards this new and standardized form of Hinduism.

Ārtī and *havan* are both performed regularly in the temple. *Ārtī* is undertaken twice a day at eight in the morning and eight in the evening, after and before the worship services in which the deities are cared for and worshipped. *Havan* is carried out each Sunday at 11.00 am before the communal meal (*samuha bhojana*). These two practices represent very different forms of worship, one devotional and the other ritualistic.

Havan, the older of the two rituals, has its roots in the fire service or Agnihotra of early Vedic ritual (*śrauta*), and like its ancestor is concerned with the power of sacrifice (*yagña*) to sustain order (*ṛta*) in the universe. The extensive history of Hindu fire rituals is a complex one, and contemporary *havan* seems to represent a fusion of several ceremonies related to fire with different functions and processes, and suited to different situations. While it is impossible to trace the history of fire practices in this account, a summary of certain developments is essential in order that we may understand the changes that have taken place in *havan*. The most important of these is the Agnihotra itself, a rite in which offerings were made at sunrise and sunset to Surya, Prajapati, and Agni. Srauta ritual demanded not one but three fires. The offerings were cooked in the household fire (*gārhapatya*) and offered in the celestial fire (*āhavanīya*). The third fire (*dakṣiṇā*) had a protective function, to ward off danger and preserve the celestial fire, the channel to the gods. The relationship between the fires and the rubric for their establishment, for the content of the offerings, and for the duties of the ritual specialists and householders were described in the *Samhitas* and *Brahmanas* of the *Yajur Veda*. Many of the verses which are recited weekly in Havan have their source in the *White Yajur Veda* or *Vajasaneyi Samhita*, and a number of the ritual actions which are performed are recorded in the companion text, the *Satapatha Brahmana*. Vedic ritual did not remain unchanged however, and the modern *havan* service reflects the course of its development.

> 'One may state that the Srauta Agnihotra, the most performed of the Vedic sacrifices, has left traces in several (daily) rituals. Its mantras, actions or implications play a role in sayampratr-homa (aupasana homa), the pranagnihotra (bhojanavidhi), the vaisvadeva (devayagna), the samdhya rites and (probably) in grhya libation sacrifices in general.'   (Bodewitz 1976:199)

Vedic domestic ritual (*grha*), however, expressed a move away from the practice of maintaining three fires (and their related specialists, utensils, and so on). Instead it was performed in the home with a single fire, by the householder for the family group. Of the five domestic sacrifices (*Pañcayagña*) it is the offering to the gods (*devayagña* or *vaiśvadeva*) which is the precursor of the modern *havan* service. In this ritual a portion of food was offered to the deities as an act of hospitality before the family ate their main meal. This domestic offering exhibits its influence on *havan* in three ways. First, the Leeds *havan* service is performed not at sunrise or sunset like the Agnihotra but at 11 o'clock, and is followed by a vegetarian meal prepared by the wife of the pandit, and eaten by the participants. Secondly, it is not only the deities who were paid homage in the earlier rituals (*śrauta*) but also those who became important at a later date who are invoked and praised. Not only are Agni, Surya, and Prajapati called upon, but also Chandramas, Brahma, Chitragupta, Ganapati, Buddha, and Durga. Thirdly, a number of mantras from the various *Grhya Sutras* have been incorporated in the modern fire service.

Although it is impossible to date the decline in the perfor-mance of the domestic fire rituals (*pañcayagña*) – it seems prob-

able that like some other Vedic rituals their practice was challenged by the rise of more devotional forms – their revival by
Dayananda Saraswati in the late nineteenth century suggests
that they were of minor importance by that time. The renewed
practice of domestic fire sacrifice became part of the Arya
Samaji commitment to the Vedic Age, its texts, rituals, and
philosophies. Dayananda Saraswati compiled a rubric for use in
the domestic fire offering (*devayagña*, also known in Arya Samaji
literature as *homa* or *havan-homa*) based on the *grha* rite but with
the addition of several introductory mantras locating the fire in
time and space, invoking the deities, and describing the primal
sacrifice. It is this form of service which constitutes the basic
Leeds *havan*, and it is as a result of the growth and migration of
the Arya Samaj movement in East Africa and Britain that *havan*
has been introduced into the temple programme. A number of
Punjabi settlers in the city had been influenced by the teachings
and practices of the movement, and as a result called for a
regular fire service to be carried out in the temple when it
opened in 1970.

Although the service has never attracted a large following,
as very few Hindus can understand the Sanskrit mantras and
most prefer a more devotional style of practice, temple representatives, both Punjabi and Gujarati, are proud of the temple's
weekly *havan*. According to some the Leeds temple is the only
one in the country to perform this ancient ritual on a weekly
basis. Its importance is on the one hand its antiquity, and on the
other its appeal to 'those who do not believe in idol worship'
(*Temple News*, Leeds Hindu Temple 1978).

Generally *havan* is attended by a small group of Punjabi males
and by a few Gujaratis with a particular commitment to temple
religion. Nevertheless, as we shall see later, this ethnic mix has
been influential in the development of the content of the *havan*
service. The majority of Hindus, however, prefer to attend the
temple in order to worship and serve Krishna and the other
deities manifested there. Annual festivals provide the most
popular opportunities for such activity but *ārtī*, a short service
conducted in Hindi, allows for regular worship of the same kind.
Little is known of the exact textual origins of *ārtī*, although

several verses can be traced to Upanishadic and Puranic sources. The style of practice falls firmly within the devotional tradition of serving and worshipping the deities with offerings (*tarpaṇa*).

Although *havan* has its roots in Vedic ritual while *ārtī* represents a later ritual development they are not entirely unrelated. Devotional features are not completely absent in the Leeds *havan*: some have been introduced in order to stimulate attendance; others have come about as a result of subsequent attendance patterns. For example, the verses now include several devotional songs to non-Vedic deities of which the *Mataji Puja* to Lakshmi is an illustration. In *ārtī* the opposite is true. Upanishadic mantras appear in between the songs (*bhajan*) and petitions (*prārthanā*) from later periods: *ārtī* draws to a close with a petitionary prayer from the *Brhadaranyaka Upanishad*. In both forms of practice attention to correct gesture and pronunciation is expected from the officiant, and participants are expected to conform to rules concerning purity and offering. This attention to duty and right conduct continues to provide a link between these two apparently dissimilar forms of worship.

We must now consider what takes place in the ritual processes of *havan* and *ārtī*. *Havan* is the longer of the two practices. It generally lasts for approximately an hour and a half, the last 15 minutes of which are set aside for an *ārtī* service which terminates the ritual procedure. Although only a dozen or so people attend *havan* itself, others may join them for *ārtī* and the communal meal which follows it. The fire service itself is conducted by the pandit, assisted by two participants. Together they sit on the floor around a fire grate (*kuṇḍ*). The remaining participants sit behind them reading from copies (photocopies, in Gujarati or Hindi script) of the *Sanatana Agnihotra* text. Before the fire is lit the pandit and his assistants perform a series of purification rituals: red powder (*kaṅkuṅ*) is placed inside the grate and on the foreheads of those present, and purified water is sipped (*jalācman*). Various mantras are recited. These include a non-Vedic mantra locating the *havan* in time and space, a mantra calling for the success of the *havan*, and a mantra from the *Yajur Veda* in which participants ask for help and protection in their performance of the sacrifice. After these initial actions and verses have been performed and recited the fire is ignited. Clarified butter (*ghī*) is poured into the grate and lit with a stick of incense (*dhūpa*):

'In this yajna-grate which is in contact with the earth and which represents the centre of the universe, we light the holy fire of sacrifice with the hope of success.' (*Agnisthapan Mantra, Vajasaneyi Samhita 3,5* in Knott 1982:216)

The deities are then invoked and invited to be seated before the fuel is placed in the fire. This consists of small pieces of bel wood (*śamīdh*). As each stick is ignited Agni is invoked and petitioned. After each of the verses the participants repeat a phrase (*tyāga*) in which they shun the fruits of their actions ('This is for Agni, not for me'). After a further act of purification the participants take it in turn to offer clarified butter or grain in the fire whilst first Vedic and then non-Vedic deities are hailed. Lakshmi and Shiva are then praised, and petitioned for good fortune and mercy, and Agni is asked to forgive any errors made in the sacrifice. The participants bow their heads, the *Shanti Mantra* is recited, and *havan* is concluded.

Havan is followed by an *ārtī* similar to that performed in the temple each morning and evening and during festivals. In Leeds the short service consists generally of about a dozen different prayers, songs, and verses. The participants, the numbers of which vary, stand facing the central image upon which worship is focused (*mūrti*). Before the singing begins the pandit prepares a tray with purified water (*arghya*), lights the incense, and places small candles of cotton wool and clarified butter (*dīvī*) in the branches of a small candelabrum, which is then placed on the tray. His wife or another woman brings a covered bowl of food in from the kitchen, and this is placed near the central image. The first song is then sung to an accompaniment of bells, tambourines, and clapping, while the pandit rotates the lamp in front of the image as an offering to the deity. The prayer ends with the phrase 'Homage to Krishna' ('Jay Srī Kṛṣṇa'), and the participants bow their heads. The pandit then performs a gesture in which by pouring water around the tray he symbolically effects the circumambulation of the image for those present. As he does this he recites the *Pradaksina Mantra*: 'With each step of this circumambulation may the sins of this and the previous life be eliminated' (Knott 1982:195). This is followed by the communal recitation and singing of a series of petitionary prayers and songs to Narayana, Shiva, and Gauri, and an impersonal prayer for peace. The pandit turns slowly to each of the pictures and images in turn, passing his right hand across the flames from the lamp in the direction of each of the representations. Everyone then chants a short Upanishadic mantra calling for guidance before hailing the deities in turn. They finally pay homage to their tradition with the phrase 'Sanatana Dharma ki jay'. The lamp is then passed amongst the participants on a tray. In turn they offer money, purify themselves with the light of the flame, and bow to the lamp. The singing begins anew – either a Gujarati prayer or a Hindi song – while sacred food (*prasāda*) is given to those present. The meeting may continue with further devotional songs but *ārtī* itself comes to a close after the sacred food has been distributed.

The main tone of *ārtī*, unlike *havan*, is clearly devotional. The participants petition and praise the deities. They make offerings to them, and pay them homage. They focus their attention on Lord Krishna but call on a variety of other popular deities. In addition, they recite a number of older impersonal petitions such as the circumambulation mantra, the peace prayer, and the verse from the *Brhadaranyaka Upanishad*. Unlike the *ārtī* prayer and the songs to Vishnu and Shiva, these are not directed to specific deities. Thus, although *ārtī* provides a marked contrast to *havan* in stressing devotional attitudes rather than ritual actions, it still includes older forms of petition more akin to some of the requests for success and guidance in the fire sacrifice than the later songs of praise and homage to Vishnu and Shiva. This is all the more striking if we compare the Leeds *ārtī* to the service described by a Coventry Hindu (Jackson 1981: 72–3). The *ārtī* also takes place in a Krishna temple but here the emphasis seems to be placed more squarely on Krishna than it is in the Leeds service. The 'Prayer of the Holy River Jamuna' is sung at the beginning of the service, and the phrase 'Hare Krishna, Hare Rama' is frequently repeated at the end of the *ārtī* songs. Although the commentator mentions the Upanishadic mantra his account does not refer to the other impersonal prayers that appear in the Leeds service. This seems to suggest that at the Hindu temple in Coventry greater emphasis is placed on later devotional verses (particularly to Lord Krishna) whereas in Leeds these are combined with short requests for universal well-being rather than personal benefit. We could speculate on the reasons for these variations – the mixed ethnicity of the Leeds population, the social and religious unity of the Coventry Suthar caste, the religious background and knowledge of the cities' ritual specialists and so on – but we need to know far more about the nature of these and other Hindu communities before we can confidently compare their interpretations of tradition.

We can be aided in this process, however, by adopting a strategy for understanding temple practices irrespective of where they are performed. In Hindu religious practice, as in the practices related to other world faiths, there is a prescribed form and structure to which practitioners aspire. Moreover, Hindus – be they religious specialists or lay participants – have a duty to fulfil the ritual demands made of them. The majority of these demands pertain to practices that can be carried out in the home although some, particularly festivals, are better suited to the provisions offered by a temple (*mandir*). In theory, at least the shape and layout of the temple would be prescribed according to tradition; rites would be performed in a correct manner with attention to right pronunciation and gesture; they would take place at the right time of day, month, and year, and in consideration of auspicious and inauspicious periods; and the practitioner, according to family tradition, would be brought up and educated to perform temple rites to a particular deity in the highest possible state of purity. Few temples in India fulfil all these requirements, and in Britain such prescriptions are still harder to meet. In Leeds, for example, where the temple is situated in a Victorian stable building, where the ritual specialist only recently assumed the role of pandit, and where the Hindu calendar is set in the context of Christmas and the cold British winter rather than the Indian monsoon, traditional rules are hard to obey. Nevertheless, as we have seen, temple practices are of immense communal importance in this new geographical and social location, and serious attempts are made to observe traditions. Installation ceremonies (*pratiṣṭhā*) are viewed as essential, inauspicious days are avoided as far as possible, and more confidence is inspired by Brahman specialists than those from other castes who have taken on ritual responsibilities.

Religious practice in the temple thus continues to involve attention to certain basic features, to ritual space, to time, and to the role of the practitioner or specialist. In addition, although the temple exists primarily to serve God, it also functions to allow Hindus to act dutifully in accordance with their family customs and social position. Religious practice in the temple therefore would seem to be the performance of a ritual process, with its associated meanings, by a religious specialist and a gathering of participants in a prescribed space and time.

It is possible for us to see more clearly the way in which Leeds Hindus have interpreted their traditions if we apply this defin-ition of religious practice to the two regular rituals described earlier. Both *havan* and *ārtī*, as we saw, are traditional Hindu practices despite their different origins and historical develop-ments, and their distinctive religious styles. What seems a little surprising, if we consider these differences, is that both of them should be performed by the same people in the same sacred space. *Havan*, despite its elaborate ritual specifications and re-quirements, is directed to deities through the medium of the fire rather than through figurative images. However, although the sacrifice is not directed to the temple image a number of partici-pants pay homage to Krishna by bowing to the image before the start of the service. In addition, in the *ārtī* which follows *havan* attention is turned from the fire to the images and the pictures of deities around the walls. In a sense, the practitioners of *havan* have flaunted the Arya Samaji principles of formless or 'non-idolatrous' worship in adapting the service to suit the style of its surroundings and the needs of its participants. *Ārtī*, however, is well-suited to the temple's style and layout. Worship is directed to the deity manifested in the image. Homage is paid, offerings are made, and love and praise are lavished. The temple might be said to fall short of expectations in one respect, however: it inhibits the participants from circumambulating the focus of worship. They must content themselves with the pandit's symbolic enactment of this ritual duty.

Similar modifications have been made in regard to the times at which these rituals are performed. As we saw *havan* descends in this respect from *grha*- and Arya Samaji-fire ritual (*devayagña*) undertaken before the family meal rather than at sunrise and sun set. It is not performed daily, however, as past fire sacrifices were, but just once a week on a Sunday morning in order to suit British working conditions and Christian congregational traditions. The same process of adaptation has occurred in relation to *ārtī*: sunrise and sunset have been standardized to 8.00am and 8.00pm to encourage attendance.

The roles of the religious specialist and the participants can be observed to follow the same trend. Both rituals have been led on occasions by non-Brahmans, generally from artisan castes. While this is unwelcome to most Hindus they have no choice but to accept such a situation, which is itself a natural corollary of their migration to Britain. Brahman families are in a minority in the community, and like other families have to consider their incomes and standard of living: religious duties are poorly rewarded. The Gujarati pandit in Leeds, though previously a railway employee in Baroda, was from a Srigaud Brahman family which, by tradition, provided guardians of the *Yajur Veda*. Therefore, the establishment of the sacrificial fire was a part of his traditional religious duty, just as it was for the ritual specialists (*adhvaryu*) of early Vedic ritual (*śrauta*). In this respect the *havan* is carried out according to prescription. In the past, however, a single fire does not appear to have been used for communal purposes. In both *śrauta* and *grha* rituals individual households, with or without the help of a priest, established and maintained fires.

As we saw earlier other features are worthy of note in the composition of the participant group. Gujaratis and Punjabis attend both *ārtī* and *havan*. This is not surprising in relation to *ārtī*, as devotional worship is popular with the majority of

Hindus from both states. The practice of *havan*, however, is not customary in Gujarati temples, as a consequence of which few Gujaratis understand the language of the service or its formal ritualistic and non-devotional orientation. The same is true for many Punjabis, particularly women. A number of Punjabi men, however, through their past relationship with the Arya Samaj in India or East Africa, have become accustomed to *havan*. However, although these Hindus were responsible for introducing the fire service into the temple programme at an early date it is not they but the Gujaratis who have effected most change in its performance. It was to encourage their attendance that selected devotional verses were included, and that xeroxed texts of the service were made available in Gujarati script. In addition, regular Gujarati attenders, who are generally those with most commitment to religion, have contextualized *havan* within their own devotional styles of worship. Before and after the service they perform an act of homage or obeisance (*praṇāma*) to Krishna and offer him money and food. As the petitionary verses of *havan* are recited they put their hands together, bow their heads, and close their eyes. When the post-*havan* *ārtī* begins they are joined by other devout Gujaratis from the kitchen, reception area, and living quarters.

A number of fundamental changes can clearly be seen to have occurred when we consider *havan*. The performance of a regular *havan* had no place in traditional Gujarati religious culture (although Gujaratis had experienced similar fire services in marriage rites and special ceremonies). *Havan* certainly meant more to the Punjabi Arya Samajis who were responsible for its introduction. However, to these men both the addition of songs to non-Vedic deities and the devotional attitudes adopted by some of those who take part must represent new and perhaps unwelcome developments. *Ārtī* is less dramatic in this respect. Far from being new or controversial in its essentials it can be said to form a blueprint for an understanding of the content of the majority of popular temple rituals.

On the question of ritual content in Chhattisgarh, Babb observed:

'The four ritual performances I have described display wide variations in ostensible purpose and content ... Nevertheless,

the striking fact is that despite this obvious diversity the four
rituals described share certain features with each other and
with most Chhattisgarhi ceremonial.' (Babb 1975:47)

The three common features to which he alludes are 'purity',
'pranam', and 'prasad'. While these represent a substantial
part of the content of Hindu rituals they are inadequate for a
thorough analysis. First, the absence of 'offering' as a separate
analytical category suggests that Babb has united offering with
'*prasad*' under a single heading. If this is the case it would ignore
the important question of food status: food offered to the gods
(*naivedya*) has no special status, food that is shared at the end of
a ritual has been made sacred by the gods (*prasāda*) during the
ritual process and is thus of superior status. Second, the features
Babb describes take no account of the verbal element of ritual.
The content of *ārtī* and of other rituals seems to suggest therefore not three, but six common features which together constitute
the ritual process: obeisance or homage (*praṇāma*), purification
(*śuddhī*), petition (*prārthana*), praise (*bhajana*), offering (*upacāra*),
and sharing sacred food (*prasāda*). They do not necessarily
occur in this order, although some form of obeisance and purification generally precedes the offerings, and the sharing of
sacred food often concludes the process. As a general rule the
word '*upacāra*' can be used to describe all acts of service and
offering including obeisance and praise. In this context, however, it is used specifically to refer to offerings of food, light,
incense, water, and so on. In addition, although petition and
praise generally refer to the spoken part of the process there is
no rigid division between the verbal and practical elements. The
purification of objects, for example, is often accompanied by
appropriate verses which describe the action of purification
rather than petition or praise the deity.

From the description of *ārtī* given earlier it is easy to see how
these elements combine to form the ritual process. When participants enter the temple they remove their shoes (*śuddhī*), and
they greet and pay homage to Krishna (*praṇāma*). The pandit,
having bathed and dressed in clean clothes, prepares the utensils and objects for use in the service (*śuddhī*). Food is brought
into the room in a covered bowl, and placed near the central

image (*upacāra*). Prayers and songs are sung in which the deities are petitioned (*prārthana*) and their qualities described and praised (*bhajana*). While these are sung the pandit rotates the *ārtī* lamp, directing its light to the various deities portrayed in the pictures and representations (*upacāra*). The participants hail the deities and the eternal tradition or 'Sanatana Dharma' to which they belong (an action known as '*vandana*', in which the two offerings of *praṇāma* and *bhajana* are combined). Money is offered (*upacāra*), and those present purify their eyes with the light from the flame (*śuddhī*). Food made sacred by the deities during *ārtī* is then shared among the participants (*prasāda*).

In this short service the six elements can be clearly observed. They occur also in festivals and other rituals which developed in the tradition of worshipping the deity with offerings (*tarpaṇa*). *Havan*, the origins of which predate this development, is more complex. In the core of *havan* ritual, when the fire is established and the grain and butter offered, the main elements are purification, offering, and petition. Obeisance and praise are of less importance. As the deities are not invoked (*āvāhana*) until the fire is lit no initial obeisance takes place unless the participants choose to pay homage to Krishna before *havan* begins. It is not until the end of the service that those present bow their heads in homage. In addition, it is clear that the majority of the *havan* mantras either describe the actions or petition Agni, Surya, and Prajapati. It is only really the additional verses introduced by local Hindus, particularly the one directed to Lakshmi, in which praise is offered. Finally, although the deities are offered grain and clarified butter, they are not asked to consecrate food for consumption by those present. The communal meal which follows *havan* has an important social function but does not represent the sharing of sacred food (*prasāda*). All the elements but this final one can be observed in the ritual process of *havan*. Those with a more devotional orientation (*praṇāma* and *bhajana*), however, seem to be contemporary developments rather than original constituents.

Although participants perform ritual practice in part for its own sake, because it is their duty to do so, they generally have other objectives as well. In addition, the content of a ritual generally gives some indication of its purpose or function. It is these underlying reasons and purposes that constitute the meaning or meanings of a ritual. It could of course, be said, that each ritual has a unique content and meaning. Nevertheless, just as it was possible to draw out certain common elements pertaining to the ritual process, we can perceive different types of shared meaning. Three of these seem to bear a specific relation to the Hindu tradition ('pleasing the gods', 'personal karmic benefit', and 'sustaining and regulating the cosmos') while the others may have wider application to rituals in general (religious intensification, social rebellion, status elevation, and conferment). The aims most closely related to Hinduism are commonly expressed in prayers and songs, and frequently articulated by participants to explain their attendance. The more general purpose of religious intensification, however, whether it be doctrinal, social, moral, or experiential, tends to remain implicit. Therefore, though we can see from the content of the *ārtī* ritual process that its major purpose lies in 'serving and pleasing the gods', while in *havan* the objective is 'to sustain and regulate the cosmos', we might also find that the regularity of the two services serves to intensify and reinforce social bonds or matters of doctrine. This is certainly true for the major festivals which are often high in mythological or moral content, and which encourage large attendances and that which Victor Turner has called 'communitas' (1974).

This last point brings us back to the main issues of this paper: the perpetuation of a tradition in a new social location, the problems this generates, and the forms it takes. Religious practice in the temple, whether it be a regular ritual like *havan* or *ārtī* or an annual festival, provides an opportunity for the intensification of social relationships and the reinforcement of religious traditions. This is the *raison d'être* of the temple, without which it would cease to control the destiny of Hinduism in the city. If this function were not fulfilled the maintenance of the tradition would depend upon the efforts of individuals to consolidate and transmit the important features of Hindu religion and culture. While this might result in the private retention of valuable vernacular traditions ignored in the temple's current religious provision, it is difficult to see how Hinduism as a religious and social system could be perpetuated in an alien environment without undergoing some kind of institutionalization.

This is a difficult process for Hindus to undertake in the name of their religion: leaders struggle to find unity in its diversity; ethnic and caste divisions invite political and religious instability; the awakening of religious consciousness creates new interpretations. In Leeds, as we have seen, the solution has been 'standardization'. The temple's representatives and leaders, by developing a particular kind of religious provision and by presenting the religion to Hindus and non-Hindus alike in a particular way, have stressed certain beliefs and practices and neglected others. 'Sanatana Dharma', as it is perceived and presented in Leeds, represents on the surface something akin to 'text-book Hinduism': the fundamental beliefs of karma, re-birth, liberation, duties according to one's social position, etc., and the pan-Indian but nonetheless popular practices of *puja*, *ārtī*, life-cycle rites and festivals, with the addition of a Vedic *havan*.

The examination of *ārtī* and *havan* enabled us to see the complex processes at work behind this awe-inspiring symbol of unity and community. While both had firm roots in Hindu tradition a number of adaptations had taken place: times of performance had been modified, the surroundings were un-orthodox, the roles of the specialist and the participants had changed, and the rituals had new meaning in their new location. Therefore, despite the avowed conservatism of Hindu ritual, changes took place. Verses or practices popular with either the Gujaratis or the Punjabis were incorporated in rites like *ārtī* and *havan*, just as their favourite festivals were included in the Leeds Hindu calendar. (Navarātri continues to attract a Gujarati attendance while Divali is dominated by Punjabis.) Thus, though standardized, the religious programme is able to find room for some degree of ethnic expression, although the major outlets for the affirmation of specific, regionally related cultural, religious, and social interests continue to be the home and the various societies and groups that coexist with the temple.

The process of adaptation that has taken place with regard to

Hindu rituals is itself a process of reinterpretation. *Ārtī* and *havan* are undoubtedly similar in many ways to their Indian counterparts. Nevertheless, in adapting to suit their new location – the host society, the climatic and geographical conditions, their minority status, and the social and religious complexity of their own community – Leeds Hindus have selected, modified, and developed their traditions. They have been guided not only by established Hindu obligations and prescriptions, but also by the interpretations of modern reformers like Dayananda Saraswati and Mahatma Gandhi, in their preservation of this 'ancient system of knowledge'. This process of retraditionalization, of rejuvenating and giving new meaning to traditional beliefs and practices, characterizes the transplantation of Hinduism to Leeds. This process, commensurate as it is with the gradual erosion of ethnically related religious and cultural interests, is the price of its survival as a socially meaningful tradition in a new location.

10

Legal pluralism in the Hindu marriage

Werner Menski

While the topic of arranged marriages among South Asians has generated some interest among researchers (Ballard 1977–78; Brah 1977–78), is often taken up by the media, and remains of tremendous importance to the South Asian communities in Britain themselves, nothing has, to my knowledge, so far been written about the effects of the British legal system and its requirements on South Asian customs and practices with particular reference to the solemnization of Hindu marriages.

The presence of large communities of South Asian Hindus in British cities has imported into this country interesting elements of legal pluralism (Hooker 1975); indeed, the perceptive observer can detect numerous instances of competition between conflicting obligation systems. We are not concerned here with the implications of this situation for the English legal system (the prevailing view seems to be, at any rate, that little if anything has changed as a result of the presence of Hindus, Muslims, and Sikhs in the UK; see Bromley 1981); we are concerned with the effects of legal pluralism in a British context on the institution of Hindu marriage and on the Hindu spouses themselves, who as parents of the next generation of South Asians in this country will have a decisive role to play in the maintenance or abandonment of Hindu culture in Britain. So our considerations of past and present patterns of marriage solemnization among Hindus naturally have implications for the question whether and how Hindus in Britain can maintain their culture in an alien socio-legal context.

This essay, then, describes elements of legal pluralism, with particular reference to marriage solemnization, within Hindu culture in South Asia. It discusses the effects of the transfer of this plurality to the British social context, and it tries to analyze the present rather confused situation with regard to marriage solemnization among Hindus in the UK.

While we find an abundance of material on Hindu marriage in India, written both in India and abroad (see Kapadia 1966; Mayer 1960), we have very little published information about Hindu marriage in Britain. Kanitkar and Jackson (1982:17–19) give a general description of a Hindu marriage ritual in Britain, but do not make it clear enough that there are tremendous variations between different regional and social groups in the UK; Khera (1981:105–07) puts forward some comments on Hindu marriage, but is exclusively concerned with the topic of arranged marriage. Our lack of information is, of course, partly due to the fact that the phenomenon of Hindu residence in the UK is a fairly recent one. Hindu marriage does not appear to be a topic that interests the English lawyer. The assumption is that immigrants and their descendants are governed by English law, which is clear and familiar. That there may be problems of adjustment for Hindus, Muslims, and other immigrants is conveniently overlooked; the prerogative of the rule of English law is assumed without a clear understanding of the legal background of immigrant cultures. More dangerously, there is a general assumption that South Asian laws themselves are largely, if not exclusively, the same as English law, so that there is no need to teach, study, or research into such laws with special reference to Hindus, Muslims and other communities. Such attitudes are utterly wrong: India's Hindu law, though much reformed on Western lines, is alive and constantly developing, also on traditional lines.[1] Much better known is the fact that the

Muslim laws of South Asia form vigorous legal systems with much control over the Islamic population.

The fact that modern legislation dominates Indian family law does not mean that traditional Hindu law is dead (but see Derrett 1978). True, much of it is abrogated or reformed beyond recognition, but the majority of Hindus do not appear to be aware of modern laws issued from Delhi or some state capital, and the further one goes away from the capital, the less people appear to know that there exists something like the Hindu Code, a conglomerate of four Acts of Hindu law.[2] Many aspects of traditional Hindu law have been codified in those Acts, which are not just a wholesale import from the West, as is often believed. The Hindu Marriage Act (HMA) has left absolute scope for custom in the field of marriage solemnization and has not even tried to reform this area of the law on Western lines. Registration of marriages, the crucial legal component in the West, is not a requirement under Hindu law, so a uniform demand of the state's law at the point of solemnization of a marriage does not exist and the customary plurality of solemnization patterns is maintained in full strength. We shall see below how the demands of a Western legal system, with its emphasis on certainty and written, documentary evidence designed to facilitate administrative processes, not only change patterns of behaviour relating to the solemnization of marriage itself, but may have wider repercussions on culture and its maintenance in a fast-changing environment.

LEGAL PLURALISM IN HINDU MARRIAGE IN INDIA

The aim of this section is to describe the relationship between the different sources of legal authority in Hindu India, i.e. customary, Brahmanical, and state law, and to show how they tolerate and legitimate different forms of marriage. We shall then examine how relevant these sources of authority have remained in contemporary Britain.

We have to emphasize the importance of the well known concept of Hindu 'unity in diversity' (see Derrett 1979). Hindus in Tamil Nadu, Gujarat, the Punjab, or Kashmir may be governed by totally different customary rules, but we would refer to them as 'Hindu law'. Regional and local diversity has always been of enormous importance in the subcontinent as a parameter in defining rules of law. Apart from that, social class, whether measured in terms of ritual purity and caste membership, or less traditionally, in terms of socio-economic status, adds to the plurality of customary legal rules and concepts.

The crucial and central notion of Hindu *dharma*, be it as a set of duties and rights pertaining to a particular individual (*svadharma*), as the global notion of *dharma* affecting the whole universe, or at any of the intermediary stages (the *dharma* of the family, the clan, a particular profession, a whole state, or human society) leads by definition to a system of law not characterized by uniformity. What is 'right' and 'wrong', in a Western sense, appropriate behaviour in different life situations, is determined from case to case and varies according to circumstances. Traditional Hindu law, therefore, being largely customary, is not a legal system that can prescribe identical behaviour in many different situations and for many people. It is highly localized and particularized. Facts and circumstances of a particular case weigh more heavily than any abstract rule, so that in theory no two situations are completely alike. On the other hand, identical life situations, like marriage, constantly arise, and certain repeated patterns of behaviour evolve, acquiring a superior status when it comes to laying down rules of appropriate conduct.

At such a crucial point as the rite of passage of marriage, then, quite apart from Sanskritic rules of a ritual nature, the position of the individual Hindu as a member of a certain family, clan, caste, or any other social group will largely determine how a particular marriage is solemnized. It also matters, for example, whether the bride is presumed to be a virgin or not, and whether a spouse is widowed or not. So the basic pattern that we find in Hindu India is an immense variety of customary forms of marriage solemnization, locally and socially determined and observed.

In a complicated relationship of mutual dependence with the customary Hindu law we find what may be called the Sanskritic Hindu law. This adds to the customary 'unity in diversity' rather than acting as a unifying force, at least in the realm of marriage solemnization. In the literature, the impression has been created that Sanskritic models of marriage solemnization among Hindus have provided an element of unity and of cultural continuity. While this is no doubt true to a certain extent (see also Kanitkar and Jackson 1982:18), statements of social scientists to the effect that contemporary Hindu marriage rituals are nothing but true copies of their ancient Vedic models have not proved right (for details, see Menski 1984). In reality, Sanskritic Hindu law is based on an enormous variety of written sources, some of them unknown to the present day, others like the famous *Manusmṛti* (also referred to as the *dharmaśāstra* or handbook of *dharma* by Manu) overvalued and overinterpreted as a 'Code of Hindu law', implying uniformity where even the text itself does not warrant that kind of interpretation. Thus the *Manusmṛti*, for example, says almost nothing at all about ritual details of marriage solemnization. It merely lays down (8.227) that a particular ritual, the *saptapadī*, when completed with the seventh step, signifies legal validity of the marriage. This means, in particular, that from that point onwards the bride/wife would be classified as a widow should her husband die.

The rite of *saptapadī* appears to have a special position even in present-day India (Mayer 1966:229) and also in British Hindu marriages (Kanitkar and Jackson 1982:18), but the Sanskrit texts that deal with marriage solemnization in great detail are by no means uniform. There is an abundance of such texts, and they tend to differ in points of detail when it comes to the various rites that make up a complete marriage ritual. Some of the texts expressly state that the local variations in marriage solemnization should be given preference, while others merely state what appears to be common to all.[3]

The evolving pattern seems to have been that of an age-old continuous competition between local customary traditions developed and controlled by the family and clan elders and more-or-less localized Sanskritic traditions propagated and interpreted by the Hindu priests. This seems to have led to two developments: the professional priests with an interest in the performance of elaborate marriage rituals designed to give maximum profit to all participants supported a trend to perform long and complicated rituals lasting for days rather than hours (see also Mayer 1966: 228). This practice was justified and legitimized by the Hindu theory of marriage as a sacrament (*saṃskāra*), which means that the performance of elaborate rituals is deemed to have a beneficial effect on the spouses and their environment and creates, in fact, some awareness in the minds of the spouses that they are getting married. This theory was apparently readily accepted by the higher sections of the highly stratified Hindu society. On the other hand, many communities that were not so highly placed in the ritual hierarchy of Hindu society and the caste system (and they seem to have maintained that lowly position) appear to have abandoned Sanskritic rituals of marriage altogether and have developed customary forms of marriage which may stress the acceptance of the bride and the union of the couple, adding at times some rudimentary forms of dramatization of crucial marital expectations, such as progeny, which would be expressed through fertility symbols. It is thus not correct to assume that all Hindus marry in elaborate Sanskritic fashion, but we appear to know very little about the simpler forms of marriage.

For the average Hindu, however, solemnization of marriage as a crucial step in an individual's life is an occasion on which to call a priest and to celebrate with elaborate rituals. While the ritual aspects of marriage are largely delegated to the priest, the social functions of the event seem of crucial importance to the families and individuals involved. Considerations of whom to invite, what presents to give, and what to expect from others seem prominent rather than concern over the ritual aspects of the marriage, though the latter are by no means unimportant (see Mayer 1966:227ff).

In conclusion, we see a largely harmonious coexistence between the customary and the Sanskritic laws of marriage solemnization in traditional India, both supporting and supplementing each other, thus creating the confusing plurality with which we are concerned here.

As far as the state law is concerned, one must note that there was no legislative interference with the Hindu patterns of marriage solemnization until the HMA of 1955. Legal validity of a particular Hindu marriage was determined socially on the basis of community recognition (hence the importance of the publicity of rituals) and depended, if at all framed in ritual terms, on the performance of the rituals customary to particular communities. This position was not disturbed by the HMA of 1955. Section 7 of that Act reads:

'S.7 Ceremonies for a Hindu marriage:
(1) A Hindu marriage may be solemnized in accordance with the customary rites and ceremonies of either party thereto.
(2) Where such rites and ceremonies include the *saptapadī* (that is, the taking of seven steps by the bridegroom and the bride jointly before the sacred fire), the marriage becomes complete and binding when the seventh step is taken.'

Thus, also under contemporary Indian law, any customary form of Hindu marriage solemnization leads to a lawful union. The definition of 'customary' is found in Section 3 of the HMA of 1955:

'(a) The expressions 'custom' and 'usage' signify any rule which, having been continuously and uniformly observed for a long time, has obtained the force of law among Hindus in any local area, tribe, community, group or family: Provided that the rule is certain and not unreasonable or opposed to public policy; and Provided further that in the case of a rule applicable only to a family it has not been discontinued by the family.'

So we see that even a family custom, under the conditions described, may be employed to solemnize a valid Hindu marriage. This rule gives tremendous discretion to Hindu spouses and their parents, but has created many problems for courts, since it has proved to be a most difficult task to decide what, in a particular case, is a valid custom. Under the influence of English concepts of law, the rule that valid customs must have been observed 'for a long time' (see S.3 of the HMA quoted above) was interpreted very strictly, and new customs were denied judicial recognition. This led to many unjust and socially unacceptable decisions and prompted special legislation in Tamil Nadu.[4] A recent case involving neo-Buddhists in Maharashtra has, however, given judicial recognition to newly developed customary forms of marriage solemnization (see note 1 above).

The confusion in this area of the law has been increased due to a one-sided interpretation of Section 7(2) of the HMA (quoted above). That section has picked out one particular rite as more important than others and is thus in line with the rule found at *Manusmṛti* 8.227. Even though the wording of the section implies, clearly enough, that a *saptapadī* need not be performed in all Hindu marriage rituals, many Hindu law cases have ruled otherwise (Gupte 1976:153) and have created problems for spouses who, after many years of marriage, found themselves deprived of status and, often, property rights (see, for example, *Bibbe* v. *Ram Kali – All India Reporter* 1982 Allahabad 248).

Now, what actually is a *saptapadī*, that crucial rite of seven steps? Our efforts to find an answer may serve to illustrate the gradual process of development and change in a fluid ritual field characterized by a plurality of rules and models. The most ancient forms of the *saptapadī* point to a dramatization of friendship, not exclusively in the context of marriage rituals (for details see Menski 1984:580ff.), but particularly between husband and wife (see the translation provided by Kanitkar and Jackson 1982:18). Yet originally the seven steps of the ritual were not taken *around* the sacred fire; significantly the HMA stipulates 'before the sacred fire', i.e., perhaps, in the presence of the holy fire. It is obvious that if one circumambulates a fire, more than seven steps may be needed, and seven circumambulations are not the same as seven steps! In some Hindu communities, the fire is circumambulated four times only, in others five times, but still one speaks of *saptapadī*. Most Hindus are unable to give us a clear answer, and the Hindu law books are confused too. Some knowledge of Hindu ritual patterns helps to disentangle this confusion. The so-called *saptapadī* of our days is in reality the ancient Hindu ritual of circumambulation of the fire, called *agnipariṇayana* (leading around the fire), which, in Vedic times, was performed four times. This ritual appears now merged with the real ancient *saptapadī*, in which the bride (or both spouses) would take seven steps in one direction, either east or north (Menski 1984:581–82). The latter ritual seems to have lost popularity and from my observations appears to be performed only in marriages involving very traditional and learned families in India. Such ritual niceties are, however, not widely known, and the general public is more concerned with the social and culinary aspects of marriage than with the ritual.

To summarize this section: by the time large numbers of Punjabis and Gujaratis left India for East Africa and .Britain, redefined ancient customary traditions of Hindu marriage solemnization with all their local and social variations were being observed. Hindu marriage had the definite aura of sacrament, at any rate for the higher castes, and the Hindu priests were in more or less full control of the ritual sequences to be followed.

LEGAL PLURALISM IN HINDU MARRIAGE IN THE UK

It has already been indicated that, from a certain viewpoint, it may be disputed that one can talk of 'legal pluralism' with regard to Hindu marriages in the UK. Hindus domiciled in Britain are, like everybody else, subject to the *lex loci*, and English law as a uniform legal system with no special marriage rules for members of different religions (apart, however, from some special rules for Jews and Quakers) does not take notice of the fact that certain spouses may be Hindu, but requires them to solemnize their marriages in a form that has legal validity in the eyes of, and according to, English law. Whilst we cannot dispute that Hindus in Britain are subject to English law, there is evidence that the individuals concerned also continue to be guided by Hindu law and have been put under pressure to work out compromises between conflicting legal demands. How this works in detail we shall see below. It is apparent that elements of Hindu law have almost imperceptibly been added into the fabric of English law, which is subtly changing under the influence of the multi-cultural population it is supposed to govern, because the alternative would be to allow a system of coexisting personal laws, as in modern Indian law. England does not seem ready for that, even though Muslims in particular would welcome such an arrangement.

On the other hand, the strong compulsive force of the uniform legal system makes itself felt in that it demands compliance with its rules or threatens with sanctions. This also means that the traditional sources of Hindu law, as outlined above, have no standing *vis-à-vis* English law: no form of Hindu marriage solemnized in the UK has legal validity under the *lex loci per se*.

Now, it may be argued, and seems indeed the case, that the vast adaptive potential of Hindus, a consequence of the customary plurality of legal authorities outlined above, has made it comparatively easy for Hindus in Britain to follow the rules of English marriage law. For an English lawyer the matter may end here, and on a satisfactory note. But while we may now assume almost total compliance with the English law of marriage solemnization among Hindus (there is much evidence that the picture was quite different 10 years ago), it is certain that Hindus in Britain are also maintaining their customary forms of marriage solemnization. I know of very few Hindu couples who simply had a registered wedding and no more. In those cases, the reason given for not celebrating a Hindu wedding as well was a financial one, the aim being apparently to avoid double expenses and extra costs related to the Hindu wedding. Public opinion among Hindus, however, is not in favour of such arrangements.

How, then, have the majority of British Hindus adapted to the new socio-legal environment? It is clear that a Hindu couple in Britain, whose marriage was solemnized in an elaborate ritual by a Hindu priest, in a hall hired for the purpose, or in a temple, and in the presence of many invited guests, is not valid under English law unless it was, or is subsequently, registered. Thus, if the couple enjoyed the 'first night' and consummated their marriage as Hindu husband and wife, and the next day the husband decided to abandon his spouse, the woman and her relatives would have little remedy under English law. They could, at best, try to bring back the defaulting husband through community pressure. It must have been a tremendous shock for some Hindu parents and their daughters to discover that a

purported husband could get out of marriage without any difficulties and without further liabilities under English law.[5] I have
tried to trace court records of such instances, but have not been
successful. It appears that Hindus, and Gujaratis in particular,
have been very reluctant to go to court over such matters. The
information I have is from individual cases that came to my
notice, and in all those cases the girl's family has taken steps to
look after her. The considerable element of shame involved
seems to have contributed significantly to the rather rapid learning process among 'Asians' in this area of the law, because it was
immediately and forcefully brought home to them that adjustment to, and compliance with, the new legal framework was
necessary for one's own protection. As a result, 'Asians' have
become even more careful when it comes to arranging marriages,
preoccupied as they are with female chastity and the reputation
of their female family members.

What does a Hindu couple have to do in order to avoid pitfalls
and to get validly married? Like everybody else they would have
to apply for a certificate or licence from a Registrar. There are
a number of different procedures with which we are not concerned here (for details see Bromley 1981:45ff), but the choice
of procedures is limited if either spouse has come from abroad,
as is often the case.

But the solemnization of marriage in an English registrar's
office does not make the marriage legally valid in the eyes of the
Hindu spouses and their families. They will, therefore, make
arrangements for a Hindu wedding, which could be held at any
time up to several months later. Meanwhile the couple would
continue to live in their respective homes, and the bride/wife
would not consummate the marriage (see also Pearl 1972–73:
71,73).

In the early stages of 'Asian' residence in the UK this was the
only satisfactory and safe procedure, since celebrating the
Hindu wedding first and subsequently registering the marriage
could create considerable problems, as outlined above.

As the immigrant communities in Britain grew in size and
began to establish themselves more firmly in certain areas during the 1970s, an option offered by the Marriage Acts 1949–70

became available to more and more Hindu couples, and is now exercised in many cases – though obviously there are tremendous local variations within Britain. Some sections of the Marriage Act 1949 provide the machinery for registering certain buildings for the solemnization of marriages (see Bromley 1981: 48). A 'registered building', however, must fulfil certain criteria in order to qualify for this special status: it must be certified as a 'place of religious worship'; it must be a separate building; and at least twenty householders must support the application and certify that the building is used by them as their usual place of public religious worship.

David Pearl (1972–73: 67) has complained that the above conditions 'are so restrictive that few immigrant communities would be able to obtain benefit from the provision'. He has outlined three difficulties facing applicants attempting to secure registration:

'(a) the building in question must first have been certified under the Places of Religious Worship Registration Act 1855.'

This appears as a mere administrative formality, but certification (which carries with it certain benefits) could be refused to buildings other than Hindu temples, e.g. Hindu community centres, on the ground that they are not places of worship.

'(b) It is necessary to prove that the building is a "separate building" and that the whole building is used as a place of worship.'

According to Pearl (1972–73:68) this has created 'a difficult stumbling-block to the immigrant communities seeking to register their religious buildings for the solemnization of marriages'. In the early stages of 'Asian' immigration to Britain, these conditions must indeed have been difficult to fulfil; with regard to the situation before 1972 Pearl is certainly right. But matters have changed considerably since then. Hindu communities all over Britain have gained enough strength and financial support to establish their own, communal places of worship in the form of Hindu *mandirs* (temples). This process still continues, as smaller groups and sects beginning to assert their separate identity follow the older, established temples on this way. While a preference for the use of redundant church buildings may be noticeable, this need not be a general trend.

In some cases, it may still be difficult to satisfy the condition of 'separate building'. Moreover, most Hindu temples in the UK seem to comprise a large hall or some other form of accommodation which can be used for lectures and other public functions, and for marriages. The whole building may, therefore, not be used as a place of religious worship, and for that reason some Hindu temples appear to have met with difficulties in registering their building. What the picture is throughout the country would be very interesting to know.

'(c) The worship in the building must be public worship.'

Pearl (1972–73:68) wrote that this rule posed no problems, and I have not heard of any. It should hardly be difficult for a temple committee to get 20 signatures of householders. But it must be noted that the above rules of law lead to, and presuppose, a somewhat distorted picture of the role of Hindu temples. The fact that Hindus traditionally worship in the home rather than at temples (most Hindu families in Britain have a *pūjā* corner in their home) is overlooked or ignored.

Here, then, are significant changes of Hindu socio-religious practice in this country: the temple in Britain has become more than a place of worship (on this see Jackson 1981:65). It should also be noted that traditionally solemnization of marriages did not take place in Hindu temples. Still, not all Hindu temples in Britain have the necessary accommodation to cater for weddings and the pattern common in India, i.e. that one hires a suitable hall for the solemnization of the marriage and subsequent celebrations, recurs in Britain. Hindu marriages in Britain are, then, often solemnized 'in the temple' because it is such a large, convenient hall. Otherwise there is little connection with the temple itself, though I have observed that some Hindu couples, *before* the solemnization of their marriage, enter the *mandir* to pray for blessings and good luck, and in one case a priest even performed some small ritual with the couple to the same effect.

What percentage of Hindu couples is actually using the facilities offered by 'registered buildings' would be interesting to know, but we appear to have no figures. It seems very common for Hindu couples to marry in a registrar's office and then to have a Hindu wedding plus celebration in a hall, independent of any temple, but with the help of a Hindu priest. Here again, local circumstances will determine the range of options.

If a Hindu temple has been given the status of 'registered building', this means that Hindu couples can register their marriage there and undergo the Hindu rituals on the same day, a matter of some convenience, especially in view of the liminal state that follows a registered wedding. In the temple, there will be a registrar present, or an 'authorized person' to ensure proper registration of the marriage. Apparently the English Law Commission in its Working Paper on Solemnization of Marriages presumed that the registrar and 'authorized person' would also be able to keep an eye on the Hindu marriage solemnization. I find this somewhat pretentious, and indeed a common practice seems to be that a marriage between two Hindus in a 'registered building' is first solemnized by the registrar, who then retires and leaves the couple to undergo whatever Hindu form of marriage they want. Thus, the picture that emerges is that the state's agents are concerned to ensure the proper registration of marriages (see in general terms for English law Bromley 1981:39) and are not interested in 'ethnic' forms of marriage. We also have evidence that the formal requirements of the short secular ritual of registration (see Bromley 1981: 47–8) have not been observed to the letter, since many Hindu spouses have not been able to make the stipulated declaration in English, but have still had their marriages registered.

While it could thus be said that the English law and its machinery are only interested in proper registration of the marriage, for the sake of evidence of the legal status of the parties, more recently some government departments like the DHSS have begun to ask for proof of Hindu marriage solemnization in addition to the document of registration. This amounts to a silent recognition of the legal importance of the Hindu rituals of marriage in the UK. The communities themselves have maintained throughout that, for them, the Hindu form of marriage solemnization is more crucial than the English one.

A series of informal interviews and discussions with Hindu individuals and youth groups in 1982–83 yielded some interesting insights into how Hindus in Britain have adjusted to the new socio-legal environment and how they have reconciled the two forms of marriage solemnization expected of them.[6] To begin with, very few people we spoke to did not agree that both forms of marriage solemnization were important. Overwhelmingly the Hindu marriage was thought to be of greater importance, but then many respondents had second thoughts and added that the registration of the marriage was just as important. Older people especially were aware of the crucial role of the latter: for tax purposes, all kinds of benefit, immigration, and travel abroad, and official paperwork. The most important aspect of the Hindu wedding, for the older generation, appeared to be that it helped to maintain Hindu culture in an alien environment. Young people, while readily agreeing that Hindu marriage solemnization was necessary, were much less specific as to why this should be so and seemed to think that the social function connected with it was an important element. From this viewpoint seems to derive criticism of the Hindu marriage as too lengthy and too costly, as reported by Jackson (1981:65).

We also found that the registration of marriages preceded the Hindu form of solemnization in almost all cases, that there was no consummation of the marriage until after the Hindu wedding, and that the registration was in effect looked upon as a form of engagement. The lesser importance attributed to the registered wedding is also shown by the fact that fewer people are commonly invited to celebrate this form of marriage, indeed there may be no celebration at all: we have come across cases where a spouse went straight off to work after the ceremony in the registrar's office. And lastly, it is significant that wedding anniversaries are counted from the day of the Hindu wedding, if indeed one celebrates such dates, as it is not a Hindu tradition.

The Hindu wedding of a couple, however, is most regularly accompanied by a big social function and it is then that public acknowledgement that the spouses have become husband and wife is shown.

These findings left us somewhat unsatisfied. Even if the registration of the marriage preceded the Hindu solemnization of marriage by only a few hours there were indications that the latter was considered crucial and was given more importance. Even then, not many guests would attend the short ceremony in the registrar's chambers (numbers have often been restricted, anyway), while the Hindu ceremony was part of a big function. Was the Hindu marriage more important?

It took some time to realize that to discuss the matter in terms of relative importance was inappropriate. There are clearly two distinct forms of marriage solemnization, supplementing each other and leading to a marital union that is fully legitimized from every viewpoint. Clearly, the two components of this complex process of solemnization are not identical, neither in form nor in substance. A brief look at both of them should show what is meant here.

The ritual drama of a registered marriage comprises essentially of an interaction between the registrar as a representative of the state and the couple. This, at least, is how Hindus seem to view it. Even though at some point in the ritual the spouses have to make a declaration which refers to the other spouse, the registrar's ceremony does not appear to establish a relationship of intimacy between the two spouses. The conclusion is inevitable that the couple here make a contract with the state, more or less reluctantly, because required to do so by law, and that the burden is now on the state to give the spouses a number of rights.

The ritual drama of the Hindu marriage, however, emphasizes the polarity of the wife-giving and the wife-taking family, of husband and wife, male and female, and dramatizes expectations in that framework. The major level of interaction is found between the two spouses who, step by step, approach the position of husband and wife through the performance of the marriage rituals which consist essentially of rites of separation and rites of incorporation. The end of the marriage rituals appears, in view of lack of public knowledge about the precise meaning of individual rites, to signify that groom and bride have become husband and wife. In this sequence of rituals the modern state is conspicuously absent, but the crucial element of community participation in the marriage is provided for by the more or less attentive crowd that attends the wedding.

For Hindus in Britain, then, the registered marriage has indeed largely remained a 'legal formality' (see Ballard 1978: 189 with similar evidence for Sikhs), while only the Hindu wedding is taken to establish conjugal links between the spouses.

We do not have to look far to find out why this should be: Hindus are not content to consider the narrow, secular approach to marriage solemnization, as taken by English law, as appropriate for themselves. Getting married, for them, is more than a matter of a contract between two individuals; it has, in the context of the Hindu notion of *dharma*, implications for the world at large. The requirements of the English law of marriage have thus been built into the British version of the Hindu world view without much friction: the added ritual of solemnization in the registrar's office has simply become a further element of the traditional, but constantly evolving and redeveloping legal pluralism. British Hindus, outwardly westernized, seem to continue to act in terms of *dharma*, even though much of what is done happens at the subconscious level.

It is quite a different matter to look at the Hindu marriage rituals themselves and to ask what changes may have occurred on the way from India to Britain, or via the East African sojourn. Some observations on this as yet largely uncultivated field of study may be added here.

It is quite well-known, I think, that Hindu marriage rituals in this country, compared to India, are shorter and less complicated in ritual terms. In particular, many preliminary rituals contained in the traditional handbooks of marriage solemnization are no longer performed. Still Hindu priests find themselves constantly under pressure to shorten rituals or to abandon some peripheral ones, so that we can already observe marriage rituals which consist of little more than the crucial *mangalpherā*s or circumambulations of the holy fire. Generally, however, Hindu priests will insist that a more or less complete marriage ritual be performed. I have seen an old priest waiting patiently till everyone had had their meal and the spouses were ready for their departure to the new home, so that he could perform the send-off ritual without which, in his own opinion, his function was not satisfactorily completed. He was perfectly aware that, had he gone home, nobody would have cared to perform this little ritual, but he considered it his duty to ensure its performance.

Considerable pressure is exercised on the priests to perform marriage rituals, even on inauspicious days. In Britain, the weekends are the most convenient time for marriage functions, so clients may insist that their priest perform the marriage rituals on a convenient day and in disregard of astrological factors. Priests who refuse to do this may suffer loss of remuneration, so many seem to adjust to the new situation by making it clear that their performance of auspicious rituals may well be fruitless on such a day and that they would not give any guarantee about the success of a marriage thus solemnized.

As far as the ritual substance is concerned, Hindu priests seem to exercise almost total control and face little supervision from participants in the marriage. Only once have I observed a priest interrupted in the middle of a ritual; this was so that he could repeat it in a form known to, and preferred by, some old ladies, the guardians of a particular local or caste tradition. In this case the priest was a Gujarati and the spouses were immigrants from Fiji originating from Uttar Pradesh, evidently subject to different customary traditions.

Priests have shown me how they select and compose their own variants of marriage rituals from a number of ritual handbooks, and how they vary the rituals depending on the caste status of the spouses and particular circumstances. Rarely would a family specify what rituals they wanted performed: the priest as ritual specialist is trusted; he has, after all, a certain reputation due to the fact that he acts for a number of local groups (rather than one particular caste only) which makes him experienced in the customary traditions of many people. In fact a versatile priest can considerably shape the customary forms of marriage solemnization for different castes by introducing and maintaining ritual variants (see also Menski 1984:875). I doubt whether this is even noticed by the lay Hindu who seems remarkably uninterested in the performance of marriage rituals.

Recently, however, as a reaction to frequent complaints by Hindu youngsters that the Hindu marriage rituals are cumbersome and 'meaningless', many Hindu priests have started to give a running commentary in English or one of the Indian languages of what they are doing and why certain rituals are performed. This often takes the form of sermon-like little speeches. Here is not the place to elaborate in detail on new interpretations introduced by contemporary priests. The trend seems to be to overlook the finer points of the Sanskritic ritual and to give a popularized version of what the rites are thought to express or to achieve. The phrase that a particular rite is performed for good luck appears, of course, rather often in this context.

I see two main problems for the future of Hindu marriage solemnization in Britain. The first is that in the foreseeable future there will be a lack of committed and experienced Hindu priests, who alone could uphold the ancient traditions or their more recent variants in a socio-cultural environment that seems unconducive to the perpetuation of notions of *dharma*. The presently active older generation of Hindu priests is going to die out over the next two decades. Few Hindu youngsters in Britain seem to envisage a career as *paṇḍit*. The recent recruitment of a number of young priests from India has not been altogether successful, as some of those attracted did not possess the desired expertise and seem to have been more interested in the 'green pasture' overseas. Priestly activities are, after all, financially lucrative, but if, as I have heard in London, certain priests exploit their ritual monopoly by demanding excessive payment (a pound for every *om svāhā*, of which plenty could be added at will in the course of a marriage ritual), it is understandable that there is a counter-reaction among those Hindus who are concerned to cut down the expenses connected with a wedding and as a result may decide not to have any Hindu marriage rituals at all.

The second risk for the future of Hindu marriage solemnization in Britain appears to be a growing ignorance of Hindu youngsters about their cultural traditions and the value of those traditions. While it would, perhaps, go too far to argue that it is crucial for Hindu spouses to know exactly what the ritual elements making up a Hindu marriage mean, some basic knowledge about the function of these rituals would, I think, be very beneficial. After all the Hindu marriage rituals place the two individuals in a cosmic context as well as in a very real social context (the publicity of rituals) and dramatize the change of role experienced by the male and female spouse. The major concern is therefore not with the expectations of the individual *per se*, nor with those of a partially abstract legal entity like the modern state, but with the spouses as part of micro- and macro-cosmic constellations that force the individual to consider the needs and demands of others just as much as his or her own. In some forms of Hindu marriage rituals, the spouses' responsibility for each other, in particular, is beautifully expressed and dramatized in solemn vows. If spouses remain unaware of such basic Hindu notions, there may indeed be little need for elaborate Hindu marriage rituals. The price Hindus might have to pay could be the same degree of marital instability as currently experienced by those legal cultures that emphasize the needs of the individual above everything else, and they might have to go as far as to accept the bitter pill of irretrievable breakdown of marital unions on the ground that one partner, for his or her own selfish reasons, has lost interest in the relationship.

Since Hindus in Britain are ideally placed to study the pros and cons of modern marriage laws at first hand, there is every likelihood that a trend not to abandon Hindu notions altogether will prevail. In view of this prognosis English lawyers might do well to reconsider their silent assumption that Hindus in Britain will, in the not too distant future, behave 'as the Romans do'. Hindu elements within modern English law deserve serious consideration and detailed study. Perhaps the fact that more 'Asians' are entering the legal profession will provide greater incentives for as yet largely unsuccessful efforts to increase official awareness of the workings of elements of Hindu culture in the British context.

NOTES

1 In the area of marriage solemnization, customary law has recently won a major victory. In *Baby* v. *Jayant Mahadeo Jagtap* (*All India Reporter* 1981 Bombay 283) the High Court of Bombay accepted that new customs can indeed develop and that the modern law will eventually have to recognize them if many people are involved.

2 They are the *Hindu Marriage Act* of 1955 (HMA), the *Hindu Succession Act* of 1956, the *Hindu Adoptions and Maintenance Act* of 1956, and the *Hindu Minority and Guardianship Act* of 1956.

3 See, for example, *Āśvalāyana-Gṛhyasūtra* 1.7.1–2 as translated by Oldenberg, Hermann. 1973. *The Gṛihya-Sūtras*. Part I. Delhi reprint: Motilal.

4 The *Hindu Marriages (Madras Amendment) Act*, 1967, inserts a section 7A behind S.7 of the HMA to the effect that Hindu marriages in Tamil Nadu may be solemnized in less elaborate forms than seem stipulated by S.7 HMA; this was done in reaction to early cases that denied legal recognition to the so-called self-respect marriages. For details I refer to Derrett (1970: 299).

5 Hindu law in India would put him under an obligation to maintain this wife, because she is a 'Hindu wife' under S. 18 of the *Hindu Adoptions and Maintenance Act* of 1956.

6 I am grateful to my student Ismail Mehta, now a barrister, who conducted most of this research for an undergraduate project.

11
Changing conceptions of Hinduism in 'timetabled religion'

Robert Jackson

'Timetabled religion' refers to the subject which has compulsorily appeared under various names (such as Divinity, Religious Instruction, Religious Education, or Religious Studies) as part of the curricula of county schools in England and Wales since 1944. The subject is, in theory at least, taught in accordance with agreed syllabuses produced under the terms of the 1944 Act by conferences set up within each local education authority. The conferences are comprised of committees representing the Church of England, other denominations, the local authority, and representatives of the teachers, each committee having a single vote. Differing ideas on the nature and aims of 'timetabled religion' influence the content of syllabuses, the attitudes of teachers and pupils towards their objects of study, and the approaches and methods adopted by teachers of the subject. This chapter addresses two questions on Hinduism and education in Britain. First, how have broad societal changes in post-war Britain influenced and sustained a philosophical debate among educators concerning the nature and aims of 'timetabled religion'? Second, in the context of this debate, what changing images of Hinduism have been presented to the school population of this country since the implementation of the 1944 Education Act's clauses on religion in schools?

THE SHIFT FROM RELIGIOUS NURTURE TO RELIGIOUS EDUCATION

One of the most important developments in 'timetabled religion' derives from a changing view of its aims. Many local authorities now see their responsibility to be in developing children's understanding of religions, rather than nurturing them in a specific religion. By religious nurture I mean the range of processes through which children are reared as members of a faith-community. Some of these might be described as informal – various aspects of socialization within the family which may not be consciously identified by parents as the transmission of religion. Others could be described as semi-formal – the regular participation in family prayers or visits to a place of worship, for example. Formal religious nurture, however, might involve such activities as the instruction of children by a religious specialist or attendance at a religious school.

Until the mid 1970s most local education authority syllabuses identified the content of 'timetabled religion' as a species of this formal religious nurture. It was generally assumed that pupils shared a common Christian background. Any denominational rivalries, it was hoped, could be avoided by having a largely biblical syllabus, while a 'conscience clause' enabled dissenting parents (more likely to be Roman Catholic, Jehovah's Witness, or Jewish than atheist) to withdraw their children from religious classes. Though new syllabuses in the 1960s tended to reduce the amount of biblical study and to involve older pupils in discussion and debate about religious and moral issues, the assumption prevailed of a common Christian commitment among both teachers and pupils.

It was not until the emergence of new syllabuses in the mid- and late-1970s that some local authorities began to heed the advice of religious education professionals that 'timetabled religion' should be concerned not with religious nurture but with religious education. Recent agreed syllabuses have tended to characterize religious education as having two interrelated concerns: one is to develop children's understanding of religion or religions through an impartial study of material drawn from several religions (usually with particular reference to Christianity); the other is to encourage pupils to grasp the significance of their studies for the development of their own personal views. Thus, while religious education sets out neither to establish nor to weaken the personal commitments of pupils, many educators would affirm its concern to encourage a reasonable accommodation of newly encountered material to the range of views the pupils already hold (e.g. *Agreed Syllabus of Religious Instruction*, Birmingham 1975; Hampshire 1978; Berkshire 1982; Warwickshire 1985).

The shift from formal religious nurture to religious education was influenced by several factors. At the level of educational theory, developments in the study of religion in universities, new writing in the philosophy of education, and research into religious education were all influential, while at the most practical level, the increasing professionalization of general education was accompanied by corresponding developments in religious education. Bodies such as the Christian Education Movement, the Association of Religious Education, the Shap Working Party on World Religions in Education, and latterly the Professional Council for Religious Education have encouraged 'professional' values and standards in teachers rather than relying on piety or 'character' as marks of teaching quality, and have supported the work of religious educators through conferences and the publication of journals.

Both theoretical and practical developments reflect a changing socio-political context exhibiting features such as a decrease among the general population in formal Christian allegiance; a 'world-shrinking' effect resulting from dramatic improvements in travel and communications; the shift from the old imperial order to the formation of a Commonwealth of Nations which is egalitarian in conception; and the increasing religious pluralism of Britain, consequent on the arrival and settlement of immigrants from the New Commonwealth and Pakistan. This context provides the setting not just for changing aims in religious education, but also for a shift in subject matter from biblical studies and Christian morality to 'world religions' (including Christianity as a world phenomenon and as the historic faith of Britain) and moral issues seen from secular and humanistic as well as religious perspectives. It is within this context that changing conceptions of Hinduism in 'timetabled religion' need to be understood.

THE COMPARATIVE RELIGIONIST APPROACH

Prior to the 1970s many agreed syllabuses, which assumed that religious education was identical with formal religious nurture, suggested a limited amount of work on religions other than Christianity. With the exception of the occasional representation of such material in fifth form (15–16 yrs) work (e.g. *Syllabus of Religious Instruction*, Sunderland 1944), the majority of syllabuses suggested courses in comparative religion as options to be studied in the sixth form.[1] The truth of Christian revelation was regarded as axiomatic, and Christianity provided the 'standard' by which other religions should be judged. Thus the West Riding of Yorkshire syllabus of 1947 asserts:

'The teacher should not only aim at describing the outstanding features of the great religions of the world but should also bear in mind that the study is to be a comparative one, i.e. resemblances and contrasts and the relations between the different religious systems should be emphasised. The pupil should be led to appreciate that while each great religion has made its contribution at some period of the world's history, either to man's knowledge of God, or to man's relations with God or to his fellow men, all these contributions are unified and on a higher plane in the Christian religion.' (1947:73)

The representation of Christianity as combining the 'best' features of other faiths is also illustrated by another early syllabus:

'This review of the great religions of the world should lead us to see that whatever is good in these religions in the conception of the character of God and of man's moral duties is found unified and elevated in the Christian Religion. Thus the practical goodness of Confucius, the valiant courage of Islam, and the contemplative patience of Hinduism or Buddhism all have their place in the revelation of God's character and man's duties in the life which was lived among men in Palestine 1900 years ago. Christianity, moreover, provides something which no other religion affords – a Saviour from sin and a present Source of power and strength.'

(Sunderland 1944:88–9)

Turning specifically to the treatment of Hinduism, it is possible to find passages which could have come from the pen of mid-nineteenth century missionaries, writing for their fellow Victorian, white Anglo-Saxon Protestant readers. Take this passage, for example, from a syllabus published in 1944:

'Hinduism, with its roots in the pre-historic past, was, and is, a gross polytheism with crude conceptions of its gods and a rigid caste system. The ill-treatment of widows and the recently suppressed practice of "suttee" were the direct outcome of a cruel and immoral polytheism. Its solution to the problem of evil was sought in the doctrine of Karma which asserted that a soul passed from one body to another by successive transmigration until it was purified of all desire and was thus fit to enter Nirvana [sic], Heaven of Hinduism, which might be likened to the ocean of infinity which absorbed the individual soul thus purified of all desire – and, we might add, of all individuality.' (Sunderland 1944:87)

The section of the Sunderland syllabus entitled 'A Comparative Study of the Great Religions of the World', from which this quotation comes, was adopted by other local authorities such as Durham (1946), Derbyshire (1948), and Cheshire (1949), thus establishing the comparative religionist approach in a wider geographical area and for a longer period of time than its authors may have anticipated. A more dramatic example of educational time warp is derived from the West Riding of Yorkshire syllabus of 1947 from which a few extracts will suffice for the purposes of illustration.

'Hinduism: earliest form is Brahmanism ... In its purest aspect it was monotheistic ... Later Hinduism polytheistic. Crude

conceptions of the gods ... the practice of "suttee" now forbidden by the Government ... Doctrines of transmigration
(Khama) [sic] and of emancipation from re-birth (Nirvana)
[sic] ...

This material is reprinted unrevised in the Coventry 1962
Agreed Syllabus of Religious Instruction, a document that is still the
official syllabus of an education authority that includes about
6,000 Hindus. In the comparative religionist approach the conception of Hinduism is largely governed by the presuppositions
of Christian theology and Western civilization, the superiority of
which remains unquestioned. Hinduism, like Christianity, is
seen as a unified religion, rather than a loosely knit, complex,
and pluralistic tradition. Hindu categories are not examined in
their own terms but are judged rather from a stance rooted in a
Hebrew understanding of the unity and personality of God and
of morality. There is little attempt to grasp key concepts from
the Hindu tradition and it is notable that factual errors and
category mistakes are made when such concepts are mentioned
directly – e.g. 'Nirvana, Heaven of Hinduism' (Sunderland,
1944), 'transmigration (Khama)' (Coventry, 1962). Neither syllabus refers to the important concept of *dharma*, yet without
explanation both draw attention to the practice of *sati*, described
by the 1944 Sunderland syllabus as 'recently suppressed' just
115 years after Bentinck's regulation was passed to abolish it,
and as 'now forbidden by the Government' in the 1962 Coventry
document – reprinted, of course, from a syllabus published
before Indian independence. In brief, in the focus on polytheism,
sati, the rigid caste system, and the absence of individuality one
is presented not so much with an understanding of Hinduism on
its own terms as an assertion of the superiority of Christianity in
the light of which Hinduism appears as the inversion, if not
perversion, of the values of Western Christian civilization (see
also Turnbull 1985).

FROM RELIGIOUS ASSERTION TO HUMAN UNDERSTANDING

The comparative religionist approach has been considerably
reduced in influence over the last ten to fifteen years; in its place

have come a number of approaches to the teaching of 'time-tabled religion'. Although these approaches have important internal points of difference (elaborated below), they all emphasize the importance of human understanding in coming to know another religion and they all emerged in reaction to the comparative religionist approach.

One of the first voices in this shift was that of Professor F.H. Hilliard, a religious education specialist whose booklet *Teaching Children About World Religions* was published in 1961. Prior to the 1960s there were no textbooks on Hinduism written specifically for pupils.[2] Agreed syllabuses recommended, for teachers and sixth formers, popular works on comparative religion by such writers as A.C. Bouquet, W. Paton, F.H. Smith, and T.H. Robinson. In contrast to the agreed syllabuses of the period, Hilliard offered non-comparative religionist reasons for the study of world religions in schools. The first is a kind of 'world studies' argument, based on the 'world shrinking' effect of modern communications and the media. The second is that 'many older children in the Secondary School themselves ask for some teaching about other religions'. The third is a Christian theological argument – one which sets out to converse with other faiths, not to judge them. Hilliard showed himself familar with what has now become known as the literature on 'interfaith dialogue' and he referred to the work of such Western scholars as Hocking, Toynbee, Cragg, and Warren in addition to Asian writers such as K.M. Panikkar. He also claimed – and he cites an example of a particular sixth form's course – that a study of world religions is likely to help students to understand their own religion better. It is worth recording that his bibliography on Hinduism includes works by Indian as well as European authors, and books on popular Hinduism supplement general introductions and anthologies of texts.

Hilliard's publication had, however, little influence on the new syllabuses produced in the 1960s. The pressing issues for most religious education teachers at that time were not the scope or even the aims of their subject but the question of how far younger children could understand religious ideas, and the issue of providing subject matter for older students which was relevant to their concerns. Thus, many of the 1960s local authority syllabuses, while retaining a Christian theological base, were reacting against the 'content' dominated syllabuses of earlier years. The publication of Ronald Goldman's research[3] on children's religious thinking influenced syllabus-makers and producers of teaching materials to excise much explicitly religious material from primary school RE and to substitute an exploration of some Christian ideas and values in contemporary life-theme material; 'Caring' and 'Courage' tended to replace the Good Samaritan and David and Goliath. At the secondary level – partly under the influence of the writings of Harold Loukes[4] – syllabuses also made an effort to make religious education relevant to the experience of young people, and the 'discussion' method was widely advocated. From the third or fourth year of schooling onwards, syllabuses tended to emphasize the exploration of moral and social issues from a Christian point of view.

At the sixth form level the treatment of 'comparative religion' was on the pattern of earlier syllabuses, with some local authorities simply reproducing all or part of their material from earlier syllabuses. At least one new syllabus, however, suggested 'world religions' as its topic for 13–16-year-olds. That this part of the syllabus comes in a subsection called 'Facing World Problems' in the section on 'Christianity in the Modern World' illustrates the West Riding syllabus makers' difficulty in accommodating the study of world religions to an experiential approach to religious education. Paragraphs on 'world religions' follow entries on 'mass media', 'world hunger', 'work and leisure', 'politics', 'gambling', 'alcohol and drugs', 'the colour problem', 'war', 'refugees', and 'illiteracy'.

A notable absence from Professor Hilliard's list of reasons for teaching children about world religions was an argument based on the fact that there were adherents of religions other than Christianity residing in the United Kingdom. Although teachers in many inner-city areas were gradually becoming aware of religious pluralism, it took the publication of books such as Desai's *Indian Immigrants in Britain* (1963) to make information about Asian religious minorities more widely available. What could not fail to make an impact, however, was the wave of migrations of South Asians from East Africa which began in the late 1960s resulting from Africanization policies in such states as Kenya and Tanzania. The syllabuses of the late 1960s do at least reflect this changing pattern and they contain short articles such as 'Immigrant Children and Their Religion' (West Riding 1966) and 'Religious Education in a Multi-racial Community' (ILEA 1968). The 1968 Lancashire syllabus states: 'In view of the families arriving from the Commonwealth and the need for a more sympathetic understanding of their problems, there is a need to introduce pupils to the main faiths held by many Afro-Asian peoples' (p. 163). In spite of this concern, the approach taken by such syllabuses to religions other than Christianity remained essentially 'comparative religionist'.

Not surprisingly, many religious education professionals were becoming increasingly dissatisfied with the dogmatic approaches to their subject still being advocated by new agreed syllabuses. In response to such factors as the obvious decline in religious practice in British society at large, the effect of television and other media on people's awareness of the world scene, and – as has been noted – the evident religious pluralism of many urban areas, many teachers were seeking a new rationale for the treatment of religion in schools. Much original work was done at the grass roots, some in multi-cultural schools, resulting in the kind of material published by the Yorkshire Committee for Community Relations under the title *Religion in the Multi-faith School* (Cole 1972). A theoretical underpinning for such experiments appeared partly in recent work in the philosophy of education (e.g. Hirst 1965) and more significantly in developments in the academic study of religion. From a study of recent literature three different approaches to religious education – the 'phenomenological', the 'experiential', and the 'dialogical' – can be discerned. The aims of these approaches and their respective portrayals of Hinduism are presented below.

PHENOMENOLOGICAL APPROACHES

The main impetus for the phenomenological approach in religious education dates from the setting up of the Department of

Religious Studies at the University of Lancaster in 1966. This Department, under Professor Ninian Smart, was particularly influential in changing the pattern of teacher education in religion, through its influence on the curricula of Colleges of Education in the 1970s and through the Schools Council Secondary Project on Religious Education (established in 1969) and the second Schools Council Primary RE project. Smart was concerned to broaden the scope of courses, partly through the introduction of studies in a range of world religions. This was seen to be appropriate in a secular university. He was also concerned to introduce what he called descriptive studies of religion (especially using phenomenology as a method) alongside theological, philosophical, and textual studies, both to give students a better grasp of the nature of religion than might have been obtained on earlier courses, and to begin the development in this country of studies already well established in Europe and North America (Smart 1967).

Smart's writings (e.g. Smart 1964, 1968, 1969) and views profoundly influenced the working paper of the Lancaster based Schools Council Secondary Religious Education Project. This document – called *Religious Education in Secondary Schools* (Schools Council 1971) – advocated what it called the 'phenomenological' or undogmatic approach to religion in schools. In the working paper's words:

'This sees the aim of religious education as the promotion of understanding. It uses the tools of scholarship in order to enter into an empathic experience of the faith of individuals and groups. It does not seek to promote any one religious viewpoint but it recognises that the study of religion must transcend the merely informative.' (p. 21)

For many teachers the working paper was their first encounter with the phenomenology of religion. Although the discipline has been represented in different ways (Waardenburg 1978), the principal writers have endeavoured to 'bracket out' their own pre-suppositions when attempting to understand another's faith and to study parallel phenomena in different religions in order to elicit basic structures and forms which give insight into the essence of religious reality. The first of these aspects of phenomenology has had much more influence on religious educators than the second. The notion of an impartial study of religion, as it is or has been lived by people, with teacher and pupil alike attempting to suspend their own presuppositions in empathizing with religious believers, was appealing to the many teachers who found theologically loaded approaches to 'timetabled religion' distasteful. As we shall see, this characteristic of phenomenology has influenced significantly the way in which Hinduism has been presented in textbook and resource materials. With few exceptions (one is Marvell 1976) religious educators have been less influenced by the phenomenologist's concern to grasp the essence of religion, preferring instead to leave such issues to the scrutiny of their classes. Nevertheless the practical activity (if not the phenomenological method) of studying common features of different religions thematically – rites of passage and sacred writings, for example – has become widely practised in religious education (e.g. Butler 1975; Davies 1981; Cole 1981). One might conclude that while the phenomenology of religion, in its scholarly form, is itself a rare phenomenon in schools, its influence upon writers and teachers desiring an impartial approach to religious education has been considerable.

The concerns of academic religious studies and the insights of teachers from multi-cultural schools were brought together in 1969 by the formation of the Shap Working Party on World Religions in Education whose first publication (Hinnells 1970) includes an essay by Ninian Smart on 'The Structure of Comparative Religion' and a chapter by Professor Geoffrey Parrinder on 'The Ethics and Customs of the Main Immigrant Peoples'. The Shap Working Party has continued to make an important contribution to the study of world religions in schools through the regular provision of short courses, through its annual *Shap Mailing* (retitled *World Religions in Education* in 1986), and through its books. The first full-length book on Hinduism specifically for teachers was produced by the Shap Working Party (Hinnells and Sharpe 1972). It is important to note that all the contributors on the teaching of Hinduism in schools make a point of drawing attention to Hindus in Britain. In this context mention should also be made of Peter Bridger's text *A Hindu Family in Britain* (1969) which predates Hinnells and Sharpe by three years. In spite of its oversimplified discussion of caste and deities, this little book introduced a wide audience to the fact of a Hindu presence in the United Kingdom; it traces the migration of the Shah family to England from Gujarat and includes such topics as a Hindu festival (*Divali*), death, caste, a wedding, and Indian stories. Indeed a keynote of the better-quality phenomenological materials that have appeared since the mid 1970s is their awareness of and sometimes direct involvement of Hindus in Britain.

The City of Birmingham *Agreed Syllabus for Religious Instruction*, published in 1975, was the first in this country to reject unequivocally the view that religious education should nurture pupils in the Christian faith. (It is perhaps no coincidence that the Birmingham Conference was also the first to include in its membership representatives of religions other than Christianity.) It prepared the ground for later syllabuses which adopt this view (e.g. Avon 1976, Hampshire 1978, Humberside 1981, Berkshire 1982) and its publication encouraged publishers to commission more material on world religions. The Birmingham syllabus asserts that religious education should be directed towards 'developing a critical understanding of the religious and moral dimensions of human experience and away from attempting to foster the claims of particular religious standpoints'. Hinduism is specifically mentioned as offering appropriate material for the religious education of children at all school ages, including the 3–8 age-range. Teaching material designed to resource the ideas suggested in the syllabus is to be found in *Living Together, A Handbook of Suggestions for Religious Education* (Birmingham 1975). This handbook includes a basic course in Hinduism drawn up by Eric Rolls with a panel of practising Hindus and Birmingham teachers. In a more developed form this material later appeared as *The Hindu Way* (Schools Council 1978), one of the most successful course units in the 'Journeys into Religion' series, associated with the Schools Council Religious Education in Secondary Schools Project. Rolls aimed not to offer an encyclopaedic treatment of Hinduism but 'to so present that faith that the pupils will gain some authentic flavour of what the Hindu way of life means in practice' (Rolls 1977). The resultant course emphasizes religious practice rather than belief, encourages pupils to enter imaginatively into the Hindu way of life, and sets before the students a series of opportunities to investigate and discover for themselves, rather than simply to be the recipients of information directed by teachers.[5]

Under the heading of phenomenology, attention should also be drawn to books and other resources produced locally by groups of teachers and published by teachers' centres or local education authorities. Such materials are generally cheaply produced and are written to meet the immediate needs of teachers in multi-cultural schools. Coventry's Minority Group Support Service has published various materials on Hinduism, including the illustrated booklet *How a Hindu Prays* (MGSS n.d.), while resource centres in such places as Peterborough (1981) and Bedfordshire (n.d.) have produced material on the festival of *Divali*. These examples are all about Hindus in Britain, and all have involved members of Hindu communities in their compilation. The most thorough and detailed of the locally produced resources is *A Handbook of Hinduism* published by Newcastle upon Tyne Education Committee (Killingley 1980). This excellent piece of work, which in an expanded form has now been published commercially (Killingley 1984), results from the collaboration of a scholar, a practising Hindu, and a group of teachers. One should also mention here the many visual and audio-visual resources on Hinduism, most of which adopt a phenomenological methodology and many of which feature Hindu communities in Britain (see Kanitkar and Jackson 1982; a wide listing is appearing in 1987 in the Shap Working Party's *Handbook on World Religions*, published by the Commission for Racial Equality).

EXPERIENTIAL APPROACHES

We turn now to religious education which either emphasizes the emotional, religious, and moral experience of pupils (rather than simply introducing data from the world's religions), or claims that alternative approaches have taken insufficient account of the experience or 'life-world' of children and young people.

One experiential approach associated with the 1960s was grounded in a Christian natural theology of human experience, influenced by such Protestant theologians as Paul Tillich and advocated by a number of influential religious educators, including M.V.C. Jeffreys and Ronald Goldman.[6] Jeffreys's assertion that religious truth is 'ordinary experience understood at full depth' (1950) serves well as a summary of the stance. Agreed syllabuses of the late 1960s (e.g. West Riding 1966, ILEA 1968), particularly in sections dealing with younger children, were strongly influenced by this approach (though, as has been stated above, no impact was made on the parts of syllabuses dealing with comparative religion). Guided by new agreed syllabuses and by teaching materials associated with the work of Ronald Goldman, many primary school teachers taught a brand of religious education which ruled out much overtly religious material, replacing it with an exploration of emotions such as 'wonder' and 'love'. This approach may be seen to have influenced the work of Elizabeth Wilson on the teaching of Hinduism in primary schools (Hinnells and Sharpe 1972). This writer, however, does retain explicitly Hindu material which she seeks to relate to various emotions and values that are within the experience of young children. These are:

1 A cosmic sense of awe and wonder at the mystery of life and the universe.
2 Joy in movement and rhythm, creation and beauty.
3 A sense of unity with all creation and reverence for life.
4 Recognition of suffering, loss, death, and change.
5 Compassion and caring for people, animals, plants, water, and the air we breathe.
6 The satisfaction of doing what is right for its own sake, and courage to bear witness to the truth as we see it.
7 A sense of gratitude, loving tolerance, and humility.

In addition to relating overtly Hindu material to such experiences the writer also recommends various Indian children's books which explore such themes as joy, compassion, and friendship, all of which she regards as inherently religious.

Another approach which is also rooted in existentialist theology, and which gained currency in the late 1960s and early 1970s, concentrates on certain 'ultimate' questions about human destiny and the purpose of life which are of universal human concern and with which the various religions of the world have grappled. According to this position, an exploration of such questions in the context of a study of religions helps pupils to clarify and form their own beliefs and values (see, for example, *The Fourth R – The Durham Report on Religious Education*, Durham 1970). Although this approach can be seen to have influenced some of those writers on Hinduism already discussed – notably Eric Rolls – its most detailed application is in a chapter written by Simon Weightman. Weightman argues that since the application of *any* scholarly systematics to Hinduism inevitably results in a distorted picture, teachers of religious education should not hesitate to select from the tradition those aspects which meet their needs.

> 'For children in schools ... we can take material – why not at random and out of historical sequence – that is the answer to real religious questions. By the answer I mean an answer, as clearly to every religious question different faiths have provided different answers. What matters for children is that through this material we can implant in them the questions.'
> (Weightman 1978)

The basic problem with the first experiential approach is that a particular Christian view of religious experience not only influenced what was selected from a religion for presentation to children, but also *determined* what was regarded as religion. The danger with the second approach is that teachers with little knowledge or experience of Hinduism might introduce the religion through an idiosyncratic range of topics. It is notable that Weightman's own selection of examples – they include key concepts, ideas of deity, the *margas* (paths to salvation), and personal mystical experience – reveal an extensive knowledge of the Hindu tradition and an ability to identify its distinctive features.

One of the biases of the experiential approach is that it assumes the superiority of natural to revealed theology. A recent version of the experiential approach, originated by Michael Grimmitt, sidesteps this and other theological difficulties by concentrating, not on the ways religions have dealt with fundamental questions, but on exploring with children the various 'models of the human' provided by different religions and philosophies (Grimmitt 1982). Such an exploration involves pupils in both evaluating their understanding of religion in personal terms and in evaluating their own understanding of self in terms of the religions being studied. The kind of material from religions that Grimmitt would hope teachers might use with children would include themes of particular significance for personal growth and what he calls 'human shaping'. The skilful teacher could marry such themes with the pupils' own concern with self-understanding. In this way they might both increase their comprehension of the nature and purpose of the spiritual or religious quest within different religions, and be encouraged to reflect on the implications that the adoption of a religious view of life would have for their own understanding of self and their consequent development as people. Such an approach assumes, of course, that all school children are willing or ready to be challenged personally in this way.

An important feature of recent experiential approaches is their attention to the life-world of children and young people. It is recognized, for example, that some children have direct experience of religious practice and that young children may have complex sets of religious or secular beliefs, even though they might find difficulty in expressing them in adult language (Gates 1975, 1976, 1977, 1980, 1982). Advocates of experiential approaches wish to encourage children to express and share their beliefs and judgements. The implications of this view are significant both for the contribution that Hindu children might make to 'timetabled religion' and for the reciprocal benefits they might gain from religious education. Hindu children might, for example, contribute personal experience of festivals and weddings or of prayer and worship. They may also share their beliefs and doubts with classmates. Their contributions would be of particular value, for they represent a unique and rapidly evolving part of the Hindu tradition. At the same time, Hindu children may learn from teachers, textbooks, and other resources new material about Hinduism which increases their own regard for their inherited tradition.

Finally it should be mentioned that certain recent agreed syllabuses (e.g. Birmingham 1975, Hampshire 1978, Berkshire 1981) have attempted to preserve balanced accounts of religions and at the same time to engage pupils and to allow an evaluative element in religious education by combining phenomenological and experiential approaches (for further comment on this see Jackson 1984).

THE DIALOGICAL APPROACH

Reference has already been made to F.H. Hilliard's suggestion that religious education should involve some study of the relationship of religions to one another. The presence in Britain of substantial numbers of adherents to faiths other than Christianity has highlighted the urgency for such studies and has influenced their direction. John Hick, for example, states that his professional involvement in inter-faith dialogue as a theologian and philosopher was stimulated by living in a religiously plural city, namely Birmingham (Hick 1973). The main academic source of writing in this field is Christian theology and several important works have appeared on the relationship between Christianity and Hinduism. Some of this literature is studied as part of the Associated Examining Board's Advanced Level syllabus in Religious Studies. Further, some of the major issues about the relationship between religions are also simply and sensitively introduced in a widely used O level and GCSE textbook (Cole 1981, 1985).

Other important initiatives in this area were the formation in 1973 of the Standing Conference on Inter-Faith Dialogue in Education (SCIFDE) and of the Religious Education Council of England and Wales. SCIFDE was set up 'to convene, or encourage the convening of, national and regional inter-faith conferences concerned with education in school and community, including religious education, and to circulate or publish reports of the proceedings or findings of those conferences.' Several national conferences have been held, which have included Hindu speakers and delegates, and books have been published on initiation rites (Prickett 1978), on beliefs and rituals about death (Prickett 1980), and on marriage and the family (Prickett 1985), all of which contain contributions by Hindu writers. The Religious Education Council provides a forum for over forty national organizations concerned to promote religious education in schools and colleges. Its membership includes bodies wholly or substantially concerned with religious education in county schools or higher education, as well as groups whose main concern is the educational work of their own organizations. Currently this latter category includes one Hindu member, the Ramakrishna Vedanta Centre.

The aptness of the dialogical approach, if not as an approach on its own then as a supplement to other approaches, is underscored by one researcher's study of multi-racial schools which showed that the school is where pupils meet the plural society for the first time in personal terms (Marvell 1973, 1975). The most obvious context for dialogical teaching is the interaction between pupils of different religious and secular backgrounds in religious education classes.

HINDUS IN BRITAIN

This discussion of Hinduism in the syllabuses and books used in 'timetabled religion' has tried to make two points. First, the ways in which Hinduism is presented have been strongly influenced by the theological and philosophical presuppositions which underpin various approaches to the study of religion. Secondly, these changing theological and philosophical presuppositions cannot be viewed in isolation from the broad socio-political changes which have taken place in post-war Britain. At the ideological level, at least, the old imperial order has given way to a commonwealth of nations in the world and a plural society at home. For some English and Welsh school children a Hindu is as likely to be one's neighbour as a person of a different faith living in a distant land. The shift from religious nurture to religious education and the change of focus from Biblical Christianity to world religions have gained, if not in force at least in sense, in the context of these social changes.

However, to what extent have Hindus in Britain themselves participated in the negotiations which determine the curriculum and approach to the teaching of Hinduism in the educational system?

For the present it would seem that most Hindus are interested in working within the 'county' school system rather than establishing Hindu 'voluntary' schools within the state system. Many Anglican and all Catholic schools have 'aided' status; and the fact that there are a few Jewish voluntary aided schools has lent support to the lobby from various Muslim organizations to establish Muslim voluntary aided schools in such cities as Bradford and London. As far as Hindu communities in Britain are concerned there has been little pressure to establish Hindu nurture within the state educational system. To date, only one serious attempt has been made to establish a Hindu voluntary aided school (V.P. Kanitkar 1979). The proposed co-educational comprehensive school was to be situated in North or West London, catering for around a thousand children from Hindu families. The steering committee failed to get the full support of Hindu communities and local education authorities in London, and the project was abandoned in 1981. Reasons for the failure of the venture are various, but they included fears of racial divisiveness and a desire on the part of some Hindu communities to place formal religious nurture in locally run supplementary schools and classes (Jackson 1985).

There is a striking diversity among such supplementary schools; their style and content reflecting the organizers' Indian regional origin, educational level, and sectarian allegiance. In some instances religious instruction is inseparable from the teacher's principal aim of teaching mother tongue or Hindi. The following examples illustrate the diversity. Children at a Swaminarayan temple may be listening to an exposition in

Gujarati of Swaminarayan's *Shikshapatri*, a compilation of rules of conduct; while the children of Sathya Sai Baba devotees answer multiple choice questions in English on human values, sing Sai *bhajans*, or practise elementary meditation. Arya Samajis participate in the recitation of Vedic Sanskrit mantras around a ceremonial fire or prepare speeches against the caste system and meat eating. The younger children of ISKCON (Krishna Consciousness) devotees colour in duplicated outlines of Lord Krishna and enjoy stories from the Bala books, published by ISKCON (Jackson and Nesbitt 1986).

As for the teaching of Hinduism within the 'county' school system, there is no question that the presence of Hindu communities in Britain has made an impact on the coverage of Hinduism in 'timetabled religion'. Many recent books and resources take account of Hinduism in Britain and members of Hindu communities have acted in an advisory capacity to authors and publishers (in addition to Yogeshananda 1973 (see n.5, p. 222), see also Ramachandran 1979; Pancholi 1982; Aggarwal 1984; V.P. Kanitkar 1984, 1985; Sharma 1984; Mitter 1985; Ray 1985). In at least three cases (Birmingham 1975; Dudley 1979; ILEA 1984) Hindus have served as members of agreed syllabus conferences. That Hindu members have had to sit on committees representing 'religious denominations other than the Church of England', however, shows that the 1944 Education Act's agreed syllabus conference arrangements are in need of urgent reform. (Authorities such as Berkshire and Warwickshire, who were genuinely keen to involve non-Christian religious groups in the production of their recent syllabuses, chose to consult Hindu organizations rather than to bend the law and include them on the 'other denominations' committee.) The presence of a Hindu organization on the Religious Education Council of England and Wales is significant, though a wider representation is desirable. One should add that Hindu temple committees have welcomed visits from school parties and representatives from Hindu committees have visited schools as guest speakers. Further, there is a small number of Hindu teachers of religious education, who, in addition to being trained to teach several world religions, are able to draw material and insights from their own experience and knowledge.

In case this summary sounds over-optimistic, several notes of caution should be sounded. First, decisions about curriculum philosophy and content in Britain are highly devolved, which means that there are British schools in which Hinduism is either never mentioned or in which it receives an over-simplified treatment. Second, agreed syllabuses and teaching materials are not the sole factors determining the quality and effectiveness of religious education. Local education authorities, school heads, and boards of governors may not necessarily place value on religious education. Moreover, about half the teachers of religious education in secondary schools have no formal qualifications in the subject.[7] And in infant and junior schools the religious education teacher is usually just the class teacher. Finally no detailed studies have yet been carried out which satisfactorily examine the way in which the material on religious education is received and refracted by pupils in the light of their own experience. This is clearly an important problem, now that students are less likely to be nurtured at school in the faith to which they have been socialized at home. But despite these problems in the implementation and effectiveness of curricula, it can be said that the liberalism of official policies expressed through recent agreed syllabuses and the quality of some currently available materials on Hinduism point to a situation which is very different from that which existed a decade ago.

NOTES

1 In using the expression 'comparative religion' I am referring to the 'old style' of comparative religion which compared religious systems rather than particular features of religions and which set other religions against the yardstick of Christianity. Many contemporary scholars use the term 'comparative religion' to refer to various combinations of the history and phenomenology of religion (Sharpe 1975).

2 The 'Christian Approach' series (Edinburgh House Publications) was not written specifically for teachers, though volumes (including Winslow 1958) are recommended by some agreed syllabuses.

3 Goldman, R. (1964) *Religious Thinking from Childhood to Adolescence.* London: Routledge & Kegan Paul.

4 Loukes, H. (1961) *Teenage Religion.* London: SCM.

5 Other recent examples of the phenomenological method should also be mentioned. In *Many Lights*, subtitled *World Religions: an Anthology for Young People*, Butler (1975) presents religions and ideologies through extracts from textual materials of various types. Each translation, or 'version' as the author prefers to call it, was evolved after consultation with scholars of the source languages, members of the faith or culture represented, teachers, and pupils aged eleven to fifteen. There are 24 pages of Hindu material from a variety of sources, including the *Rig Veda, Brahmanas, Upanishads, Bhagavad Gita*, and *Laws of Manu*, as well as a selection of Ramakrishna's sayings. An early textbook written by a Hindu author and marketed by a commercial educational publisher is *The Way of the Hindu* by Swami Yogeshananda (1973). This volume (aimed at lower secondary school children) introduces a range of topics integrated within the central theme of pilgrimage and combines an insider's insights with a commendable sense of balance and detachment. A quite different approach is offered in John Ewan's (1977) *Understanding Your Hindu Neighbour* which echoes *A Hindu Family in Britain* in telling the story of a Hindu family (this time the Patels) who have migrated from Gujarat to England. The two children, Sumitra and Krishna, make friends with Susan and her brother Peter, and the English children learn a great deal about Hindu faith and culture from the Patel family. By focusing on Hinduism in the life of a family, the book includes much information (e.g. birth ceremonies, the first haircut, and domestic worship) that would have been unlikely to figure in a more general treatment. Finally there is Patricia Bahree's *The Hindu World* (1982), a beautifully illustrated children's book which brings to life Hindu concepts and institutions. The quoted views of some Indian teenagers on their beliefs and on caste, for example, make concrete some usually rather abstract notions, and are the kind of personal statement to which pupils will relate.

6 Jeffreys, M.V.C. (1950) *Glaucon.* London: Pitman. Goldman, R. see note 3 above.

7 Department of Education and Science surveys of staffing of Religious Education in secondary schools in 1977 show that 59 per cent of all RE teachers had no qualifications in religious education

and that only 23 per cent had studied religious education as their main subject or had religious education as their highest qualification. See *Religious Education Provision 1984*, published by the Religious Education Council, 1984.

Conclusion: The perpetuation of Hinduism in an alien cultural milieu

Richard Burghart

The search for an understanding of essential characteristics of Hinduism is likely to begin with key religious doctrines and practices and the social institutions in which they are embedded. The historical antecedents of these characteristics testify to the antiquity of Hinduism; its perpetuation becomes the story of the adherence of a people to their doctrines and practices.

Greater familiarity with Hinduism leads one to realize that it is not only the outside observer who seeks to reveal its essential characteristics. Other observers, including Hindus themselves, have done so over several millennia. The perpetuation of Hinduism appears bound up with the way in which various individuals have changed Hinduism while making claims about its changeless essential nature. That the historical continuity of Hinduism, as the 'world's oldest religion', cannot be understood solely in terms of the adherence to certain practices is evident in the fact that many institutions of contemporary and historical Hinduism are non-Hindu, or at least pre-Hindu, in origin. For example, the vegetarianism of Brahmans, the quasi-historical mode by which Vaishnavite pilgrimage places are consecrated, and the formation of militant Saivite orders have antecedents in

Jainism, Buddhism, and Islam. Such examples are unremarkable in that social phenomena are not formed *ex nihilo*. Of interest, though, is the way in which the perpetuation of Hinduism is bound up with its native spokesmen who reinterpret their beliefs and practices in the light of other native and alien traditions and then authenticate their reinterpretations with reference to the timeless Brahma from whose invisible essence the entire universe derives its existence.

I would suggest, then, that Hinduism be considered as something more than a *given* body of doctrine and practice to be explained solely with reference to itself, for it is also a product of its spokesmen, both Hindu and non-Hindu. The transplantation of Hinduism to Great Britain provides us with a different context in which to understand the perpetuation of this religion, but the fact that Hindu spokesmen in Britain are changing Hinduism by redefining it in relation to other beliefs is as old as Hinduism itself.

WHAT IS HINDUISM?

Most Hindus practice their religion without ever asking themselves what Hinduism is. If questions are asked they concern such topics as the procedures of worship and the benefits to be gained from it. Questions about the nature and extent of one's religious life arise only in the context of something not being religious, or not being one's own religion: the answer is in terms of boundaries of belief. Similarly most people in Britain do not question the nature of Hinduism, although they might note that Hindus have different religious beliefs and practices, and might also ask what these observances mean in order to understand why Hindus perform them.

Yet for some people – both Hindu and non-Hindu – the question does arise in some form; and in answering it, they become spokesmen to a certain audience about Hinduism. Traditionally the privileged spokesmen of Hinduism have been Brahmans and ascetics; more recently indologists and social scientists have described the nature of this religion. In the context of that questioning, religious life is structured and delimited and becomes something which is officially claimed to be 'Hinduism'. Understanding the logic of question and answer is essential in analyzing Hinduism in Britain, for 'British Hinduism' is being shaped by the kinds of questions which non-Hindus, as much as Hindus, ask of it.

Questioning by non-Hindus is intrinsic to the formation of Hinduism: this becomes evident when we consider the historical context in which the term 'Hinduism' emerged. The term 'Hindu' was originally applied to the people of the Indian sub-continent by Muslim raiders in the early second millennium AD. The term applied to Buddhists and Jains as much as to 'Hindus', for the Muslims considered these religious differences to be insignificant variations in the idolatry of a country (Smith 1964:62). The institutional eclipse of Buddhism and Jainism from much of the subcontinent meant that the term came to denote those people who accepted the everpresent Brahma as the source of the universe and who respected the ritual status of Brahmans as the human embodiment of that everpresent Brahma. After some time these so-called Hindus began to refer to themselves as Hindus and to their religion as Hindu dharma; but not in relation to one another (in which context terms such as Saivite and Vaishnavite were more apt), only in relation to outsiders, namely the Muslim 'Turks' from Central Asia and the Christian 'Firangi' from Europe (see O'Connell 1973).

Similarly, the concept of Hinduism was established by outsiders. The earliest instance of its use as a term that I have found is in a paper published in 1808 by Colonel 'Hindoo' Stewart (cited in Kopf 1969: 140). Yet the sense of the term had been prevalent for nearly half a century before. East India Company officials referred to the religious life countenanced by Brahmans as Hindoo religion, Hindoo faith, the doctrine and law of the Gentoos (a term which, like caste, the British took from Portuguese usage), or Brahman religion (a review of this literature may be found in Marshall 1970). Implicit in these designations was the assumption that there was a religion on the South Asian subcontinent which formed (or which at one time formed) a coherent system of beliefs and practices: Western scholars provided an intellectual space for a systematic description of Hindu religious beliefs and practices.

In a very loose sense this enterprise was anything but new, for Hindus systematically described their religion in terms of the concept of dharma. There are numerous senses of this term, ranging from order to religion, duty, and consciousness, but one widespread meaning is the everpresent moral order of the universe (*sanātan dharma*). In this sense, dharma is an absolute term. It would be inaccurate to state that the *sanātan* dharma is the 'Hindu way of life'; rather, from the Hindu point of view it is *the* way of life. All beings throughout the universe – men, animals, and even gods – are subject to dharma. The term also specifies and legitimates the relative duties of each person according to his caste (e.g. the dharma of Brahmans is to know the Vedas) or his vocation (e.g. the dharma of thieves is to steal) in the perpetuation of this great cosmic order. This dharmic order is valid for the entire universe in that it is given in the everpresent Brahma, of whom the universe is a materialization in time and space and for whom the members of the Brahman caste are the terrestrial spokesmen.

Another widespread meaning of the term dharma is that of a universal order, constituted and transcended by a particular deity, which may also be transcended by devotees in reunion with their deity. This other sense of dharma is roughly equivalent to the Western understanding of religion; indeed, it is the term which Hindus use in translating religion – Christianity and Islam being rendered as 'Christian dharma' and 'Muslim dharma'. This second sense of dharma, therefore, can be used in the plural. Hinduism includes various dharmas, such as Siva dharma and Krishna dharma. Each of these dharmas, or paths of salvation, has been formulated by ascetics into a system of religious knowledge and authenticated by their realization of the transcendent deity (Siva, Krishna, etc.) as a form of the everpresent Brahma. These formulations were universal descriptions by virtue of the claim that they were derived from knowledge of the god who constituted and transcended the universe.

The intellectual space conceived by Europeans for the description of 'Hinduism' was rather different, however, from the systematics of Brahmanical spokesmen about *the* dharma or ascetic spokesmen about *a* dharma. This space was based on human understanding, not on divine apprehension or realization; and the reality to be understood was of the diverse Hindu beliefs and practices that existed on the subcontinent, not of the changeless reality of Brahma. For Europeans the Hindu universe was enclosed by the distribution of Hindu beliefs and practices; for the Hindu the universe was enclosed by Brahma, not by Brahma's many forms – or what Europeans would call beliefs and practices. From the very start, attempts to make *a* system in human understanding of this universal moral order and the myriad methods of personal salvation have dogged the Western understanding of Hinduism, creating artificial unity (e.g. that there is *a* religious system called 'Hinduism') where there is actual diversity, artificial diversity (e.g. great and little traditions), where there is unity (e.g. the dharma).

Moreover, the methods for knowing Hinduism are different. Brahmans take themselves to be icons of Brahma and ascetics see themselves as 'moving temples'. It is by virtue of their divine nature that these persons can apprehend the divine Reality. The methods by which Brahmans and ascetics become fit to know god entail the enactment of rituals of purification and concentration. One comes to know the divine by realizing the divine in oneself; it is only by virtue of being god that one can find union with god. The Western understanding more or less accurately rewords the metaphysics of Hinduism, but in gaining access through texts to divine knowledge, Western scholars perforce disregard the metaphysical basis of Hindu religious methodology. Scholars are not terrestrial gods; and they gain their knowledge by being objective, not by becoming divine. Their objectivity is based upon the awareness of the meta-terms of their investigation and an ethic of personal detachment. The difference in approach comes out clearly in comparing Jackson's material on religious education with that of Carey on religious initiation in the Ramakrishna Mission. In spite of the European influence on the Ramakrishna Mission in respect of their pedagogical methods, the kind of knowledge transmitted and its mode of acquisition are quite different. In the case of the Ramakrishna Mission (and for the Hare Krishnas as well) the probationer purifies himself, undertakes certain vows, and is then invested with a sacred thread. He becomes a Brahman so that he might be a fit receptacle for the religious knowledge he later receives at initiation. The aim of initiation is to render the novice fit for the universal experience of union with god. In religious education one comes to understand the method and purpose of religious knowledge in Hinduism; but in achieving that understanding, one disregards both the method and purpose of religious knowledge in Hinduism.

Without wishing to labour the rather obvious difference between religious knowledge and human understanding, it is nevertheless important to stress that in Western civilization one lives in a world of understandings. When a scholar makes understanding his method of investigating some object of study, his method of inquiry and description feels so 'natural' that it becomes transparent. By virtue of this transparency, the description of the object of understanding appears authentic. Understanding, however, only makes one aware of Hinduism; it does not enable one to represent it authentically. Far from being a transparent medium, it colours the object of study. This may be illustrated with reference to Taylor's contribution on the Community of the Many Names of God. From the point of view of Western scholarship one might understand there to be an equivalence between Lord Krishna and Jesus by virtue of their similar meanings in Hindu and European civilization. In so far as the comprehension of this equivalence is a lingual problem, the equivalence is achieved by an act of translation whereby Krishna and Jesus are roughly identical instances of a third term, a meta-term, be it god or whatever. At the Community of the Many Names of God it would probably also be agreed that Jesus and Krishna are equivalent names of god. That the members of the Community see the matter this way is from the Western scholar's point of view a successful case of inter-cultural understanding. Yet from Guru Subramanium's point of view the equivalence of Krishna and Jesus has nothing to do with human understanding, much less a meta-theory of meaning in the relations within and between cultures. Rather the universe is a materialization in time and space of Lord Subramanium. Krishna, Jesus, and the many other names of god are but divine forms of Subramanium's omnipresent formlessness. The meta-level which makes Jesus and Krishna equivalent is ontic. It lies beyond time and space. It does not see itself as having anything to do with human understanding. Indeed, from Guru Subramanium's point of view it would exist regardless of whether human beings understood it. The equivalence of Jesus and Krishna in Western scholarship, however, is totally dependent on human understanding. If it does not exist in understanding, it simply does not exist.

The difference between these two ways of describing Hinduism systematically is not solely an academic question; for these different spokesmen authenticate in their own way the reality which the one calls dharma and the other, Hinduism. The fact that the Community of the Many Names of God near Llanpumsaint, Wales, is an abode of the transcendant deity Subramanium has been authenticated by the fact that the god Subramanium answered the request of his devotee Guru Subramanium to establish a temple in the West. For the devotees of Lord Subramanium everything in connection with the found-ing of the Community, including the 'miraculous' way in which the Guru was able to obtain a mortgage on the temple property while lacking both funds and a bank account, is authentic testi-mony that the god Subramanium is, indeed, lord of the universe. Similarly, Western scholars authenticate Hinduism in giving expert testimony based upon their understanding of this world religion. Several contributors to this volume have given evidence in both civil and criminal proceedings about Hindu religious practices and the customary law of castes; and their testimony has influenced the outcome of the trial. Indeed, even swearing on oath in courts of law has presented problems for Hindus in Britain, since there is no Hindu text (except possibly the putative source of Hinduism in the Vedas) which is equivalent to the Bible for all Christians and the Koran for all Muslims. The recommendation by scholars, therefore, that the *Bhagavad-gita* be used or not be used for the swearing-in ceremony authenticates the Gita as being, or not being, the essence of Hinduism for all Hindus (see on this Schofield and Channan 1974). Finally one might mention the debate, summarized by Jackson in this volume, about the best approach to understanding Hinduism in which scholars have negotiated the curriculum used in the teaching of Hinduism in British schools.

So far only two different spokesmen for Hinduism have been presented. Some of the contributors to this volume imply that there is a third, namely the Hindu laity. Knott observes that at the Leeds temple both Gujaratis and Punjabis participate in the worship and in the management of the temple. The two regional groups, however, prefer different forms of worship: the Gujaratis customarily worship god in the offering of light (*ārtī*) and the Punjabis with the fire offering (*havan*). The outcome of their different preferences has been the incorporation of features of the one into those of the other. Temple services have become standardized, in part with a view to attracting the attendance of both Gujaratis and Punjabis. In a sense their procedures for revising the worship service are like that of a scholar in that they focus on the distribution of elements in the service rather than make claims concerning the ontic basis of the procedures. This might be expected, of course, in that none of the laymen on the temple committee claim to speak on behalf of the everpresent Brahma, as would be the case of an ascetic who has realized Brahma or a Brahman who can refer to his divine texts. It is significant, though, that the Hindu laity of Leeds, instead of calling upon ascetics or Brahmans, negotiated the form of the service themselves.

Could this mean that the laymen have taken on a privileged role and now authenticate their own religious observances? This cannot be said on the basis of the information from Leeds, but it would seem to be the case with the National Council of Hindu Temples (UK). In their information pamphlet, entitled 'An Introduction to the World's Oldest Religion', they state:

'India's timeless spiritual culture is a mystery for many. The rituals, the customs and the 'many gods' seem inexplicable to the observer and often standard reference works on Hinduism do little to clear the confusion.

> Here for the first time is a concise yet comprehensive intro-
> duction to Indian culture presented by those who know it best
> – not the scholars nor the mystics, but the people who prac-
> tise it as a daily way of life.
>
> The National Council of Hindu Temples (UK) offers you
> this booklet as the authoritative statement on the tenets of the
> Hindu religion, confident that you will gain from it a true and
> clear understanding of the oldest religious tradition in the
> world.'

The text goes on to present a comprehensive view of Hinduism
which, in fact, is rather partial to Vaishnavism. Saivite gods are
mentioned in passing, but the emphasis is on the *Bhagavad-gita*,
the message of Krishna, non-violence, and vegetarianism; in
brief, the hallmarks of urban, middle-class Hinduism. But what
is of interest is that the statement claims to be authoritative yet
rejects the two modes of knowing Hinduism, that of the mystic
and that of the scholar. Instead, authenticity lies with the people.
It is ordinary people, as bearers of their culture, who reliably
know the beliefs and practices of Hinduism. They are the
privileged spokesmen. It is the practice of Hinduism that gives
knowledge of Hinduism, not the understanding of scholars or
the divine realization of mystics.

The idea that Hinduism is an ethnic religion, so rigorously
affirmed by the National Council of Hindu Temples (UK), is
further supported by Bowen's material on Bradford. He notes
that in establishing their caste temple, the Shree Prajapati
Association decided to eschew all caste and sectarian divisions.
They settled for a central image of the deity Ram, but installed
images of other Vaishnavite and Saivite gods as well; and called
their temple the Shree Hindu Temple. The name is highly
unusual, for temples are personal abodes of a deity. Hence they
are invariably known by the name of the deity in the central
shrine. By calling their temple the Shree Hindu Temple rather
than the Shree Ram Temple, the Prajapatis were calling attention not to the deity in the temple but to the community that
worships the deity.

The conception of Hinduism as an ethnic religion and the

role of lay practitioners in its authentication is not, strictly speaking, a 'social change', for these notions have been prevalent for some time. Ever since the Muslim conquest of the Indian subcontinent, the concept of Hindu dharma has been taken to mean not only the moral order of all men and gods in the universe but also the moral order of a people who believe such things to be true. Thus the awareness of an ethnic constituency, if not basis, of Hinduism is anything but new to the late twentieth century. Nor is it new that lay practitioners are entitled to authenticate their religious observances. Indeed, the traditional basis for establishing the customary law of castes has been to call upon the testimony of 'men of good character' and to ask them what they remember the behaviour of the reputable men of their caste to have been in the past. The spokesmen sought to establish the behaviour of the caste from time immemorial, and their testimony carried the authority of the ancestors of their particular regional caste. Such procedures – entailing the memory of practices – were not used, however, to authenticate the everpresent dharma of the entire universe. Only Brahmans or ascetics who apprehended or realized Brahma could speak about the universal dharma. It would seem, therefore, that authoritative statements from respectable Hindu laymen about the universal dharma is a new departure for Hinduism.

In considering the circumstances surrounding the emergence of lay spokesmen, the presence of non-Hindus in Britain has been influential in two respects. First, many non-Hindus in Britain see Hinduism as the religion of an ethnic group. From the point of view of Hinduism's Brahman and ascetic spokesmen this is in certain respects inaccurate. The Hindu civilization (*saṁskṛti*) perpetuated by Brahmans is thought to transcend the regional cultures of Hindu South Asia. Furthermore the religious traditions of ascetics, such as the Ramakrishna Mission and the Sathya Sai Babas, recruit members from all peoples of the world. But the cultural awareness of Hindus has been sharpened in an alien cultural milieu, and they are ready to believe – as many non-Hindus do – that Hinduism is an ethnic religion. Second, there is a Western folk model that culture is a system of meaning such that a person can understand accurately only his own cultural experience. Hence the citizens of a democratic and plural society are ready to acknowledge ordinary Hindu citizens – that is to say, laymen – as authentic spokesmen of their religion. Other facts do not completely support this belief. Carey, for example, reports that the Gujarati devotees of Krishna at the Hare Krishna temple at Watford found the presence of an American guru to be unusual, but they did not think him inauthentic. Indeed, they even sought initiation from him. Nonetheless the fact that in British society the members of each ethnic group are thought to be the ones entitled to speak on behalf of their community serves to legitimate authoritative statements made by Hindu laity about their religion. Thus the redemptive Hinduism of Hindu religious traditions, with its ascetic spokesmen, sees itself as being neither ethnically Hindu nor British; and paradoxically it is a very British form of Hinduism, with its Hindu lay spokesmen, which claims with force to be ethnically Hindu.

THE RITUAL BASIS OF COLLECTIVE IDENTITY

In Hindu society any group that constitutes itself as an autonomous social body will usually worship as a collectivity at the shrine of a deity. By worship I refer to an asymmetrical relation in which a devotee makes an offering to a god and the god bestows his grace upon the devotee. To this relation the devotee brings acts of veneration, service, remembrance, and faith and the deity replies with liberality, mercy, potency, and fortune. This relation is an interpersonal one, but social groups may also place themselves under the protection of a deity. Such is the case with the family that collectively worships its household deity, the lineage that worships its lineage or ancestral deity and the regional caste assembly that worships either a universal deity or a deity specific to their caste. Even the notorious 'criminal castes' of thugs, who robbed and plundered the merchants and landlords of central and upper India in the nineteenth century, constituted themselves as auspicious ritual groups in the service of some deity, for example, Kali. In brief, rituals of worship may serve to organize social relations among diverse groups of people.

Both Menski and Michaelson have dwelt on the implication of this ritual relationship. From the point of view of British law a temple, like a church, is a social institution separate from the household; from the Hindu point of view worship is an aspect of each and every auspicious social institution. Hence temples may be found not only in 'temples', but also in the household, community centres, factories, and schools. Further, according to the Western secular categories which inform sociology Hinduism is a particular field of study within the sociology of religion, separate from other equivalent sub-disciplines such as the sociology of crime or the sociology of the family. From a Hindu point of view, however, all aspects of social life may be structured ritually in a relation of worshipper and worshipped. Thus if such a discipline as 'Hindu sociology' could exist, then crime, the family, etc. could all be investigated under the rubric of the sociology of religion.

The significance of worship in establishing group identity may be highlighted by contrasting it with the significance of belief in Christianity, where the group establishes its identity by affirming its belief in a common creed. The question of belief may be paramount in monotheism where the presence of one true god discounts the possible existence of all other gods, but nothing could be further from the spirit of Hinduism. An illustration may clarify this point. Certain castes of untouchables from Maharashtra have in recent years sought to escape from the stigma of their untouchability by converting to Buddhism, a religion in which caste status receives no canonical recognition. Such conversions have taken place in the Indian state of Maharashtra as well as among Marathi-speaking untouchables living in Birmingham. It has been reported from India that upon their conversion the Marathi Buddhists did not destroy their village temples; rather they adopted the customary Hindu procedure for dispatching a god. They took the images from the temples and consigned them to a nearby river. Upon relinquishing the images to the water, the newly converted Buddhists did not say: 'We no longer believe in you'; nor did they say: 'You no longer exist', or 'You have never really existed'. Rather they said: 'Please forgive us, please forget us'. That the gods exist, therefore, is not a matter of belief; they simply exist. The problem for the group is not to affirm their collective belief in the sole invisible god but to establish, by means of service and devotion, personal relations with a beneficient god.

Such relations have a dual aspect: there is the relation between a god and a devotee and there is the relation between devotees which stems from their co-relations with the same god. Has the formation of British Hinduism brought about any changes in the summary of co-relations which link Hindus as a collectivity of worshippers? In comparing the material of Michaelson, Taylor, and Knott, one difference emerges in the procedures of worship used by different types of social groups. For the members of a family, lineage, or caste group worship is seen as a means of constituting the group as a social body which is autonomous of all other equivalent social bodies and dependent only upon the god whom they worship. The physical basis of family, lineage, and caste solidarity is signified by the fact that worshippers partake of the consecrated food leavings and the water with which the feet of the god have been washed. The reasoning which underlies this is pervasive among Hindus. Water as well as certain kinds of processed foods are thought to take on the moral qualities of the food handlers. Members of the same social body accept water and cooked food from one another because they consider themselves to possess identical qualities. Hindus also accept food and water from persons of higher status who possess superior moral qualities, but they will not do the same for persons of lower status because the absorption of the inferior qualities of the lower caste will pollute their own mind and body. In the case of worship it matters not that food and water have been consecrated by god; if the priest who handles the consecrated food is of low or undetermined caste status, higher caste worshippers will not accept the food or water. Alternatively if the priest or worshippers are of high status, they may not let persons of low or undetermined status pollute their temple.

It is interesting to note, however, that in temples and devotional congregations that recruit 'ethnic' Hindus of diverse families, lineages, and castes a reduced form of worship is present. Two popular modes of worship include devotional hymns (*bhajan*), described by Taylor, and the offering of light (*ārtī*), described by Knott. In the latter case the endeavour by Gujarati and Punjabi Hindus to establish standard procedures of worship at the Leeds temple implies that they are beginning to see themselves as an auspicious collectivity; otherwise there would be no reason to standardize the procedures. It is significant, however, that the prevalent forms of worship in temples with an ethnic constituency are the offering of light and the singing of devotional hymns. Participants in *ārtī* do not run the risk of becoming contaminated by other worshippers or by the priest, should these other persons have ritually inferior bodies. Nor do singers of *bhajans* court such a risk. In sum, the formation of temples with a self-styled ethnic Hindu constituency using standardized procedures of worship suggests that ethnic groups may be beginning to see themselves as social bodies. The absence, however, of a substantively strong commensual relation between worshipper and worshipped in the ritual service at these temples indicates that the internal, physically conceived, boundaries of family, lineage, and caste are still of considerable importance among Hindus in Britain. A 'Hindu' identifies with an ethnic constituency, but a 'British Hindu' does not see himself as being member of a corporate group.

THE PERSONAL MEANING OF RELIGIOUS EXPERIENCE

There is no doubt that Hinduism means something to its individual practitioners and that meaning is intrinsic to human experience: yet the categories of religious meaning and human experience are not in themselves invested with religious value in transcendental Hinduism. These categories do, however, have value in European civilization. More particularly they have value for Europeans attracted to Hinduism and, it would seem, for some Indians in Britain as well. The indications from several contributors are that this is one of the changes which is taking place in the transcendental aspects of Hinduism in Britain.

That religious meaning and human experience were not, and are still not, significant in many Hindu religious contexts can be readily demonstrated. Hindu rituals are usually thought to be effective regardless of whether or not the actor actually understands the ritual; all that is important is the correct enactment of the procedures. It is true that Brahmanical schools formulated commentaries on divine texts in which the spoken word of god became the object of some interpretation, but still the ritual actor himself did not feel obliged to explain his actions either to himself or to others. Moreover, even for Brahman interpreters their exegeses were secondary to the word of god which was intrinsically significant regardless of how, or even how well, it was understood. Action, not meaning, received the stress; and when divine words were uttered, it was their sound, not their meaning, which was critical.

Like the category of religious meaning, so also human experience does not figure prominently in Hinduism. That is to say, Hindus may have a personal experience of their religion and they can speak of both experience (e.g. *anubhava*) and mankind (e.g. *nar* and *manuṣa*), but in religious contexts human experience does not have a specifically religious value. For example, one of the well known notions of Hinduism is the transmigration of souls whereby each soul in the universe wanders over time, suffering rebirth in various bodies until it obtains release from conditioned existence. Liberation from this cycle entails the realization that the soul is the divine element in man (and in animals as well). The union of worshipper and worshipped or individual soul and Supreme Soul is possible because of man's divinity, not his humanity. In such transcendental contexts human experience has no significance. The experience (*anubhava*) of the devotee refers to the inkling of his divine proto-consciousness awakened by spiritual discipline, not to the construction of his personal history.

Meaning, however, is fundamental to the experience which modern man imputes to his humanity. Life is expected to hold some meaning; and more often than not that meaning is seen to lie in the extension or development of one's self as remembered or anticipated in one's personal history. The difference between

Western secularism and Hinduism with regard to the value of human experience is evident in the fact that biographies and autobiographies are Western literary genres which, for the most part, were absent from Hindu South Asia until the period of British rule. Instead of biographies, in which an author recounts the development of a person's individual character as it was forged in the course of life experiences, one had hagiographies in which an author recounts either the signs that a person was already a great man from birth or the signs that his greatness would eventually become manifest. Some modern Hindu ascetics (e.g. Mahatma Gandhi and Swami Yoganand) did write autobiographies, but the fact that they either wrote in English or had their work translated into English indicates the cultural presuppositions of their readership.

Further evidence of the difference in the value of human experience may be found in the contributions to this volume. In Guru Subramanium's personal account, recorded by Taylor, of the founding of a religious community in Wales there is no information about the founder's search for the meaning of existence nor about the formation of his character or 'the lessons he learned' in the mobilization of people and resources. Instead the narrative theme is that of Lord Subramanium manifesting his purpose through the life of his devotee Guru Subramanium. The emphasis is not on the history of the guru's considerable effort to establish the ashram but on his request that the ashram be established and the signs by which Lord Subramanium indicated his accession to that request. The human effort was not to gain an uncertain future; nor did this effort have any religious meaning, for both god and his devotee shared the foreknowledge of the events to come. This may be compared with the conversion stories of Europeans at the Ramakrishna Mission where the theme was the meaning of human existence. When the probationers avowed that life had no meaning until they had found the message of Ramakrishna, they were implying that they were guided by the conviction that life should have some meaning. The problem was that it did not for them, but in actively searching for it, contentment eventually came. Of course, Indian Hindus may similarly undergo conversions, before which they may wander in a state of doubt and confusion, searching for the right spiritual path. The difference is that the European is looking for fulfilment in his life; the Indian is acknowledging that his life is incapable of fulfilment.

The material presented by several contributors to this volume suggests that Hindus in Britain are increasingly concerned about the meaning of their religious beliefs. Menski notes that Gujarati youth in Leicester find the Brahmanical marriage ritual, spoken in Sanskrit, to be virtually 'meaningless'. Some caution is necessary in accepting this remark, for it may not be the sense of the ceremony that gives purpose to the participants. Rites of passage are often more meaningful for the audience than the participants. One can hear British youth saying that they are getting married for the sake of their parents or their prospective children but not for their own sake. In other words, one can content oneself with the knowledge that the ritual will have a purpose for someone. What seems to be different for Hindu youth is not that the ritual has no purpose, but the expectation that the sense of the ceremony ought to give purpose to the marriage. Michaelson similarly reports that Lohanas are occasionally pressed by their English neighbours, colleagues, and friends to explain their Hindu religious practices. The explanation is solicited in Western terms; that is to say, Westerners will try to understand why Hindus observe such practices by learning what the rituals mean. When the Lohanas are unable to explain the meaning, they put this down to their being in Britain. In India, they reason, people are aware of the meaning of these beliefs and practices. Fieldwork in India, however, does not confirm the existence of a greater awareness of religious meaning than in Britain. Rather, it would seem that Lohanas have come to think about the meaning of their way of life in the alien cultural context of Britain.

This evidence points only to the expectation that rituals have a meaning, that it is central to the ritual enactment and should be understood by the actors. Evidence that meaningful experience and personal identity have a religious value comes from the initiation procedures of the Ramakrishna Mission. Carey reports that prior to undergoing initiation, the guru explains to the probationer the meaning of the various Sanskrit formulae, or mantras, used in the ceremony. The probationer is allowed to repeat the mantras, as a way of practising them, but not to write them down until after the initiation. This procedure is of interest when compared with my field material on the Ramanandis, a Vaishnavite sect of India and Nepal which was formed several centuries before the arrival of the British on the subcontinent. I never sought to become the disciple of a Ramanandi guru and hence I was not entitled to receive their initiatory mantra. After more than a year in the field, however, I did persuade a Ramanandi to let me know the mantra. My request to obtain the mantra without having been rendered ritually fit was highly irregular, as was the ascetic's accession to the request. He asked for a pencil and wrote the mantra on a sheet of paper; and then with the tip of the pencil pointed to the different letters, explaining the meaning of each. The one thing he did not do was to pronounce the mantra, either in its entirety or syllable by syllable. For the Ramanandi sound, not meaning, was at the centre of the mantra. That was the one thing he refused to divulge in my ritually unfit state. Explaining the meaning, however, was not central; nor was committing the mantra to paper a means of personally appropriating it. Exegesis helps the disciple integrate the mantra in his personal consciousness, but that aspect of the mantra which can be personally appropriated in consciousness – namely its meaning (sense) – has no meaning (purpose) for the Ramanandi. All that has purpose is the meaningless sound of mantra, which is also the sound of one's divine proto-consciousness. Initiation awakens the disciple to the fact that one is, and always has been, the personal vehicle of the mantra. Thus one does not by means of meaning, make the mantra part of oneself; rather by means of sound one realizes that one is part of the mantra.

INTRACULTURAL AND INTERCULTURAL CONTEXTS OF HINDUISM

These changes in the value of religious meaning and human experience among British Hindus are of interest, for they give some indication of the way in which Hinduism is transformed in the context of culture. In social anthropology culture is still a poorly understood, or at any rate greatly contested, concept. It is often thought to be a system of meaning or of communication in which internal relations are logically or coherently ordered and in which external relations are discretely bounded with other cultures. This at least is the implication when anthropologists claim that 'Hindus think this' or 'Hindus do not do that'. It is also the implication in the notion that Indian immigrants in Britain, or their offspring, are 'between two cultures'. One almost has here the image of culture as a nation state, complete with immigration offices and a no-man's land between frontiers in which people do not know how to think or act. But such notions of systematic, autonomous cultures are an ideological distortion of culture. This, at least, is what the material suggests with regard to the changing significance of religious meaning and human experience for Hindus in Britain.

If one were to cast intercultural relations in the idiom of translation theory then one might say that in an alien cultural milieu a people may see themselves through foreign eyes, and find meanings in their own culture which are roughly equivalent to those of the other culture. Such meanings as not 'exchanged' between cultures, but functionally equivalent meanings are established; and some potential for meaning is actualized within a culture. A case in point was mentioned in the Introduction. Bengali reformers of the early nineteenth century, such as the founders of the Brahmo Samaj, conceived of Hinduism, or at least its Vedic origins, as being based on rational principles. The Western idea of science provided the Bengali intelligentsia with a concept through which to see and legitimate their own religious heritage. In other words, science figured as a meta-term in an imperial discourse which enabled subject Hindus to identify in their own culture something which was equivalent to the idea of science in Western civilization. Thus the boundary between English and Bengali culture was not so absolute that the Bengali elite could not objectify their culture through foreign eyes and then find in their own society some experience which could be described with reference to a foreign concept.

These remarks suggest only that intercultural boundaries are not absolute. The same example also indicates that such boundaries are not discrete. The focus on intercultural relations in situations of 'cultural contact' accentuates the differences between cultures and blurs the differences within a culture. Yet these intracultural differences are also critical. In the nineteenth century science served as a meta-term not only in the relations between European and Hindu society but also within European society. Throughout this period diverse groups of intellectuals in Europe began to see their knowledge as a species of science; as in 'political science', 'social science', and 'scientific socialism'. In the same way that Hinduism's spokesmen in an intercultural context began to see themselves in the light of science so too did Christianity's spokesmen in an intracultural context. The formation of Christian Science and the Unitarian Church are cases in point. Thus as a meta-term in a discourse on knowledge, science figured in both intracultural and intercultural contexts. To revert to the idiom of translation theory, translation is an activity of consciousness which occurs in various cultural contexts – within specific cultures, between them and between much broader cultural areas.

The field material on the value of religious meaning and human experience is too fragmentary to draw as complete a picture as can be done for that of science in the nineteenth century. There is sufficient evidence, however, from Menski's and Michaelson's material to indicate that meaningful experience and personal identity are becoming important values for some Hindus in Britain. Moreover, in coming to see their religion in this light, they have begun to see Hinduism through foreign eyes. One should add, though, that the designation of this value as a Western value is not specific enough, for it operates within an intracultural context rather like that of science in the nineteenth century. One might mention here the work of such mid-twentieth century theologians as Tillich and Robinson who have interpreted their faith in the light of the secular values of meaningful experience and personal identity. In sum, the changing expectations of some Hindus in Britain are occurring in the context of culture, but that context is as much an intracultural as an intercultural one.

Lest this attempt to de-essentialize culture be thought con-
voluted, several comments in clarification should be made.
Anthropologists have defined culture with reference to its structure and to its content. In the former case culture appears as the
formal or modal procedures of consciousness by which cultural
content is combined; in the latter case culture appears as the
content itself – that is, the beliefs and practices of a specific
people. In neither case does the structure or content of culture
constitute a discrete world of difference. If the structure of
culture formed a world of difference then the communication
between anthropologist and informant would be so deficient that
points of cultural difference could only be located, but not
understood. Nor is the content of culture uniformly distributed
among a people. McDonald notes the variety of family traditions
among Gujaratis. Moreover, within Hindu society there are a
variety of regional traditions. Certain Gujarati rituals, such as
sīmanta celebrated in the seventh month of a woman's first
pregnancy, are not found among Tamil Hindus. Tamil parents
do, however, celebrate the first menstruation of their daughter.
But when a Gujarati Hindu woman in east London received an
invitation to such a ceremony from a Tamil friend, she was
shocked to discover that Tamil Hindus celebrate publicly what
for her had been such a shameful experience. In the event she
was too embarrassed to attend (McDonald, personal communication). Not only may cultural content be *unevenly* distributed
within a 'culture'; it may also be *evenly* distributed across 'cultures'. For example, the wet/dry and hot/cold classification
of foods by which Gujarati women manage the health of the
parturient mother can be found throughout much of the Asian
continent from the Middle East to Indonesia. The picture that
emerges, therefore, is a pepper and salt pattern of cultural
content. It is impossible to specify where one culture begins and
the other ends. Without specifying the context, it makes no
sense to speak of cultural differences. This does not deny the
possibility that the content of culture in some context is alien to
another context, but even here functionally equivalent notions
may be found to link contexts. Without such linkages it is

impossible to explain how alien concepts are taken up and understood by a people.

Such an analysis does not, however, explain why a participant in social interaction should want to take up an alien concept. The reason for this seems to lie outside the communication act itself. In a humanist age understanding or 'dialogue' may be an end in itself, but such purposeful understandings do not necessarily have value outside the bounds of humanist intentions. Indeed, not all cultures or religions – and especially those with divine spokesmen – would wish to be so 'humanized'. Many nineteenth century encounters between Hinduism and Christianity were not so much 'inter-faith dialogues' as mutually unreciprocated monologues. And those Brahmans (*qua* Brahman), who did familiarize themselves with Christian doctrine, did not want dialogue but debate in which there was a clear sense of winner and loser (see Young 1981 for examples). But who set the terms of the debate? Certainly each side tried to do so; and in so doing found the other side morally deficient. From the Brahmanical point of view Englishmen were uncivilized and untouchable. From the English Christian point of view, as noted by Jackson in his description of the comparative religion approach, Hinduism appeared as a religion devoid of individuality in which human freedom was constrained by the 'rigid caste system'. The Englishman valued his freedom; the Brahman called it licentiousness. Occasionally something approaching a dialogue did occur, yet self and other were not equally engaged in the task. Very few Englishmen, but some Hindus – whether modernist, humanist or scientific Hindus – sought to address the other using the other's terms. In so doing, they took up alien concepts and evaluated themselves in their light, either finding themselves deficient on foreign terms (e.g. the Indian babus), equal on foreign terms (e.g. Ayurveda as the Hindu equivalent of Western medicine), or superior on foreign terms (e.g. the claim that nuclear weapons, lasers, and spaceships, recently discovered in the West, were known to ancient Indians). For the British the imperial mission might, in some contexts, have provoked a debate, but the terms were of the dominant, not the dominated.

RELATIONS BETWEEN RELIGION AND CULTURE IN
HINDUISM

In resorting to translation theory to de-essentialize anthropological notions of culture, one also comes to recognize the
ideological value of essentialist notions. That is to say, such
accentuated intercultural differences as the type 'Hindus think
this' and the 'English do that' are not observable from a neutral
position between 'cultures'; rather they achieve their ideological
focus from relations within a culture. Given the complexity of
intracultural relations, one might expect the boundaries between
cultures to be constituted differently from different intracultural
points of view. Or, indeed, an intracultural point of view may not
recognize boundaries at all between cultures. To return to the
theme with which this Conclusion began, there are different
spokesmen for Hinduism and each spokesman may see the
culture differently from his religious point of view. Not all
Hinduism's spokesmen necessarily see Hinduism as having anything to do with 'culture'; or indeed *a* culture. Lacking a cultural
basis, it may also lack a cultural constituency. Other spokesmen,
however, firmly identify Hinduism with the cultural life of a
people. If one is to consider the way in which Hindus conceive
the perpetuation of their religion to be a cultural problem then it
is necessary to discern how the relation between religion and
culture is constituted by Hinduism's different spokesmen.

One might begin by identifying in Hindu society the concepts
which are functionally equivalent to the Western understanding
of religion and culture. It has already been mentioned that the
term dharma comes closest to the notion of religion and that this
term has two relevant meanings: the everpresent order of the
universe to which all beings – gods, men, and animals – are
subject; and a universal religion which is constituted and transcended by a deity who releases his devotees from their endless
cycle of rebirths. As for the concept of culture there are also two
native terms which are roughly equivalent to the English understanding. The first term is *deśa*, which describes the people of
a particular region with their own language, customs, and environment (as in Bangladesh, or the country of the Bengali

people). The second term is *saṁskṛti*, that is to say, Hindu civilization with its arts and sciences.

These four concepts of everpresent order, religion, ethnic group, and civilization are brought into relation differently from different intracultural points of view. From a classic Brahmanical point of view civilization figures as a unitary concept. There are diverse ethnic groups throughout the Indian subcontinent (and indeed throughout the world), each with its own customary way of life, but there is only one civilization. The way of life of each particular ethnic group is legitimated with reference to ancestral authority and ascertained by the memories which reputable men of that group have of their forbears' behaviour. Civilization, however, is authenticated by divine authority. Artistic and scientific knowledge, in so far as it is recorded in texts, was divulged by celestial deities. The carriers of this civilization are Brahmans whose function in the everpresent order is to know the Vedas and whose ritual status is that of a human god. The distinction between ethnic group and civilization had its lingual counterpart in the distinction between Prakrit and Sanskrit languages. Prakrit languages comprise the vernacular speech of different peoples of the Indian subcontinent, e.g. Gujarati, Bengali, and Tamil. By contrast, Sanskrit is the language of the gods. It was in that divine and perfect language that the texts of civilization were compiled. There was horizontal translation between vernacular languages and vertical translation between Sanskrit and vernacular languages. Ideologically speaking, civilization was neither opposed to ethnos, nor was it seen to entail inter-ethnic relations with other civilizations. Instead, civilization was, by virtue of its divine basis, an ethnically neutral phenomenon.

This classic Brahmanical point of view is not asserted by Hindu laity in Britain. Rather the laity have modified Brahmanical civilization in their cultural awareness that they themselves as Hindus – rather than, say, Gujaratis, Bengalis, or Punjabis – constitute an ethnic group. For such Hindus civilization is seen to have an ethnic rather than divine basis. Thus *saṁskṛti*, instead of referring to universal civilization, has come to mean more specifically Indian civilization. In spite of this shift from a divine to an ethnic interpretation of civilization, the concept of *saṁskṛti* still appeals to Hindus as a basis of trans-ethnic unity. This comes out clearly in Bowen's paper in which the initial Gujarati organization in Bradford was an ethnic organization (for it included even Gujarati Muslims but not Punjabi Hindus), yet the official basis of the organization and the programme of activities was concerned largely with matters of civilization; that is to say, the staging of dance programmes and music recitals and the celebration of festivals. Similarly the Hindu Cultural Society, run mostly by the Punjabis of Bradford, was dedicated to the promotion of Indian civilization. Ostensibly membership in these societies was open to all Hindus yet recruitment was largely along regional ethnic lines. On the one hand, one might read into this the significance of Indian civilization in the integration of the Hindu peoples of Britain; on the other hand, one might read into it the attempt by a regional ethnic group to speak in the name of all Hindus by promoting Indian civilization. Regardless, however, of these integrative and divisive uses of an ideology of unity, the implication is the same. Civilization has come to have an ethnic, rather than divine, basis for the Hindu laity of Britain.

The relation between culture, civilization, order, and religion is different from an ascetic point of view. Here the entire universe is seen to be a manifestation of the everpresent Brahma or of some universal deity – such as Siva for the Sathya Sai Babas or Krishna for the Hare Krishnas. Reality is not of this transient world but of the formless unconditioned state which transcends the universe and yet is immanent in it. Both civilization and ethnic group are of this universe and thus they are transcended by the redeeming deity. This fact comes out clearly in Taylor's remarks about the way in which the Sathya Sai Babas construe their transcultural recruitment of devotees in terms of the universality of their spiritual tradition. One should add that other religions are also of this universe; thus they are also transcended by the true universal deity. A remark by Carey may illustrate this point. The Ramakrishna Mission claims that its message is not a Hindu one; rather it helps to make a Hindu into a better Hindu, a Christian into a better Christian, and a

Muslim a better Muslim. Such a message implies that the path established in the name of Ramakrishna transcends, and hence is superior to, these other religions. This is also the implication in the life of Ramakrishna who is said to have 'tried' Islam and 'tried' Christianity and after having experienced everything which these religions had to offer – it took him only a few days – he carried on in his meditation to higher states of consciousness. The notion that there is *a* religious reality which transcends other religions also figures in the ambiguous situation at the Community of the Many Names of God. As Taylor notes, Lord Subramanium is a god who transcends not only the religions of other gods, such as Christianity, Judaism, Sikhism and Hinduism, but who also transcends the form of Subramanium himself.

If one takes culture to refer to the way of life of a people, one may note that there are intercultural relations among Hindus, as in, say, the relations between Gujarati and Tamil Hindus. From the point of view of Hinduism's spokesmen, however, these intercultural relations do not necessarily entail any specifically cultural problems in the perpetuation of Hinduism. If the spokesman takes himself to be a god or the vehicle of a divine agent then the perpetuation of Hinduism becomes a religious phenomenon, not a cultural one. From the perspective of divine Sanskritic civilization as well as that of the everpresent Brahma (or of Siva-Sakti for the Sathya Sai Babas, Lord Subramanium for the Community of the Many Names of God, or Lord Krishna for the Hare Krishnas) cultural differences are seen to have no bearing on consciousness. The 'problem' of the perpetuation of Hinduism is solely the religious one of realizing divinity or preserving religious knowledge. Similarly the boundaries of social interaction are hierarchical and ritual (e.g. touchability and initiation) rather than egalitarian and cultural (e.g. exclusive ethnic membership). If, on the other hand, a spokesman for Hinduism takes himself to be a human being then Hinduism is rewritten as the spiritual culture of a people. Intercultural re-lations among Hindus, such as Tamils, Bengalis, and Gujaratis, are considered to be intracultural ones and the boundary be-tween Hindus and non-Hindus becomes the one that ideologically marks a world of cultural difference. Whereas a divine spokesman for Hinduism might exclude a foreigner from a Hindu organization because of his untouchable or uninitiated condition (or include him following his initiation as in the case of the Ramakrishna Mission and ISKCON), a human spokesman might exclude a foreigner because of his alien cultural origin. Similarly human spokesmen for Hinduism would think that Hindus might preserve their religion in Britain by preserving their culture and their vernacular language (see on this problem, Pocock 1976).

These perspectives on the relation between religion and culture accord with different views from within Hindu society about the values of hierarchy and equality. For divine spokesmen society is structured in a hierarchical manner. Ascetics and Brahmans cast themselves as human gods and they take lay persons and men of lesser castes to be their subordinates. In the ritual integration of ethnically diverse regions of South Asia ethnicity was not ideologically salient. Brahmans and ascetics were recruited from all the major regional cultures of the South Asian subcontinent. Innate mental and physical virtues, ritual initiation and spiritual discipline, not cultural consciousness, determined one's access to different levels of religious consciousness, and hence of ritual status. People of low ritual status, such as untouchables, were unable to attain higher status not because of the ethnicity of their caste or tribe but because of the supposed physical and mental deficiencies of their group. For human spokesmen of Hinduism, however, their religious awareness stems from their ethnic consciousness which is distributed equally among all Hindus, for it is derived of their common birth and upbringing in an ethnic group. In asserting that Hinduism is the 'timeless spiritual culture' of an ethnic group, the National Council of Hindu Temples implies that Hinduism has always been an 'ethnic religion', although from an anthropological point of view it is only in an alien cultural context that it has become so.

In sum, Hinduism takes its form from those who shape it; and ethnic Hinduism, with its human interpreters, has become a Hinduism for Britain. From an anthropological perspective a different sort of Hinduism has emerged, but ideologically speaking this is not so. What – to the outside observer – appears to be a change, is said not to be a change and the absence of any such change is now legitimated not with reference to the timeless Brahma, but to 'timeless culture'.

Bibliography: Hindus and Hinduism in Great Britain

Helen Kanitkar

The bibliography includes references from papers appearing in this volume, supplemented by a listing of published works dealing with Hindus and Hinduism in Britain, and sources of background information on Hindu religion and culture. Articles and books dealing with the treatment of Hinduism in multiethnic education syllabuses in Britain's schools are also listed. Unpublished material, except for theses, is not included.

The bibliography is arranged alphabetically by author, and entries are numbered consecutively. These numbers provide a location coding for use with the classification by subject which follows the bibliography, and which, it is hoped, will help readers interested in tracing material on a particular sect or community to locate additional entries quickly.

Some authors have multiple entries, and these are listed chronologically under author's name. Two or more items by the same author published in the same year appear alphabetically by title under that year within the author's total listing.

1 Abhedananda, Swami (1950) *Swami Vivekananda and his Work.* 3rd ed. Calcutta: Ramakrishna–Vedanta Math.

2 Abramson, H.J. (1979) Migrants and Cultural Diversity: on Ethnicity and Religion. *Social Compass* **26**(1):5–29.

3 Adriel, J. (1947) *Avatar: The Life Story of the Perfect Master Meher Baba.* Santa Barbara, Calif: J.F. Rowny Press.

4 Aggarwal, M. (1984) *I am a Hindu.* London: Franklin Watts.

5 Allison, J. (1970) Respiratory Changes during Transcendental Meditation. *Lancet* **7651**(18 April):833–34.

6 Ambroise, Y. (1982) Hindu Religious Movements: a Sociological Perspective. *The Journal of Dharma* **7**(4).

7 Amitabh, Swami Prem (1982) Shree Rajneesh Ashram: a Provocative Community. *Journal of Humanistic Psychology* **22** (1):19–42.

8 Ananthanarayanan, N. (1970) *From Man to God-Man: The Inspiring Life Story of Swami Sivananda.* New Delhi: Indian Publications Trading Corporation.

9 Ananyananda, Swami (1970) *Essentials of Hinduism.* Bourne End: Ramakrishna Centre.

10 Anonymous (1912) *The Life of the Swami Vivekananda by his Eastern and Western Disciples.* Almora, Uttar Pradesh: Advaita Ashrama.

11 Anonymous (1961) *Indian University Students in Britain.* (PEP Report No. 456.) London: Political and Economic Planning.

12 Anonymous (1964) Integrating the Immigrant into the Community. In *The Immigrant in Bradford.* Bradford: Council of Social Service Inc.

13 Anonymous (1972) Asian Minorities in East Africa and Britain. *New Community* **1**: 406–16.

14 Anthony, D. Needleman, J., and Robbins, T. (n.d.) *Conversion, Coercion and Commitment in New Religious Movements.* New York: Crossroads Books (in press).

15 Anthony, D. and Robbins, T. (1974) The Meher Baba Movement: its Effect on Post-Adolescent Youthful Alienation. In I. Zaretsky and M. Leone (eds) *Religious Movements in Contemporary America.* Princeton, N.J.: Princeton University Press.

16 — (1978) The Effect of Detente on the Rise of New Religions. In J. Needleman and G. Baker (eds), *Understanding New Religions.* New York: Seabury.

17 Anthony, D., Robbins, T., Curtis, T., and Doucas, M. (1977) Patients and Pilgrims: Changing Attitudes toward Psychotherapy of Converts to Eastern Mysticism. *American Behavioural Scientist* **20**(6): 861–66.

18 Anwar, M. (1974) Pakistanis and Indians in the 1971 Census: Some Ambiguities. *New Community* **3**: 394–96.

19 — (1974–75) Asian Participation in the October 1974 General Election. *New Community* **4**: 376–83.

20 — (1976) *Between Two Cultures: a Study of Relationships between Generations in the Asian Community in Britain.* London: Commission for Racial Equality.

21 — (1976) Young Asians: Between Two Cultures. *New Society*, 16 December, 563–65.

22 Anzar, N. (1974) *The Beloved: the Life and Work of Meher Baba.* North Myrtle Beach, S. Ca.: Sheriar Press.

23 Aroa, V.K. (1968) *The Social and Political Philosophy of Swami Vivekananda.* Calcutta: Punthi Pusthak.

24 Aseshananda, Swami (1982) *Glimpses of a Great Soul: a Portrait of Swami Saradananda.* Hollywood, Calif.: Vedanta Press.

25 Aslam, M.(1979) The Practice of Asian Medicine in the United Kingdom. PhD. thesis, University of Nottingham.

26 Aslam, M. and Healy, H. (1979) Asian Medicine. *Update* **27**: 1043–054.

27 Athalye, D.V. (1979) *Swami Vivekenanda: a Study.* New Delhi: Ashish Publishing House.

28 Aurobindo, Sri (1978) *Sri Aurobindo, Inde Nouvelle et Libre.* Pondichéry: Éditions Auropress.

29 Aurora, G.S. (1965) Process of Social Adjustment of Indian Immigrants in Britain. *Sociological Bulletin* **14**(2): 39–42.

30 — (1967) *The New Frontiersmen: A Sociological Study of Indian Immigrants in the UK.* Bombay: Popular Prakashan.

31 Babb, L.A. (1975) *The Divine Hierarchy: Popular Hinduism in Central India.* New York: Columbia University Press.

32 Bahree, P. (1982) *India, Pakistan and Bangladesh, a Handbook for Teachers.* London: Extramural Division, School of Oriental and African Studies.

33 — (1982) *The Hindu World.* London: Macdonald.

34 Bainbridge, W.S. and Jackson, D.H. (1981) The Rise and Decline of Transcendental Meditation. In B. Wilson (ed), *The Social Impact of New Religious Movements.* New York: The Rose of Sharon Press.

35 Bainbridge, W.S. and Stark, R. (1981) The 'Consciousness Reformation' Reconsidered. *Journal for the Scientific Study of Religion* **20**(1): 1–16.

36 Baker, G. (1979) *New Religious Movements in America.* New York: Rockefeller Foundation.

37 Balasingham, C. (1974) *Sai Baba and the Hindu Theory of Evolution.* Delhi: Macmillan.

38 Ballard, C. (1977–78) Arranged Marriages in the British Context. *New Community,* **6**: 181–96.

39 — (1979) Conflict, Continuity and Change: Second-generation South Asians. In V.S. Khan (ed.) *Minority Families in Britain.* London: Macmillan.

40 Ballard, R. (1982) South Asian Families. In R.N. Rapoport, M.P. Fogarty and R. Rapoport (eds) *Families in Britain.* London: Routledge & Kegan Paul.

41 Ballard, R. and Vellins, S. (1985) South Asian Entrants to British Universities: A Comparative Note. *New Community* **12**: 260–65.

42 Bamford, F.N. (1971) Immigrant Mother and her Child. *British Medical Journal* **1**: 276–80.

43 Barcon, D. J. (1984) An Anthropological Study of the Hare Krishnas. MA thesis, California State University.

44 Barot, R. (1972–73) A Swaminarayan Sect as a Community. *New Community* **2**: 34–7.

45 — (1974) Varna, Nāt-Jāt and Atak among Kampala Hindus. *New Community* 3: 59–66.

46 — (1980) The Social Organization of a Swaminarayan Sect in Britain. PhD thesis, University of London (SOAS).

47 Barz, R. (1976) *The Bhakti Sect of Vallabhācārya*. Faridabad: Thomson Press.

48 Bath, K.S. (1972) The Distribution and Spiritual Patterns of Punjabi Populations in Wolverhampton. MA thesis, University of Wales (Aberystwyth).

49 Bedfordshire Education Service (n.d.) *Divali Backgrounds*. ('Something to Celebrate' Project). Bedford: Resources Unit, Bedfordshire Education Service.

50 Bell, R. T. (1968) *The Indian Background*. In R. Oakley (ed) *Immigrant Child at Home and at School*. London: Oxford University Press for the Institute of Race Relations.

51 Bellah, R. (1970) *Beyond Belief: Essays on Religion in a Post-Traditional World*. New York: Harper and Row.

52 Bellah, R. and Glock, C. (1976) *The New Religious Consciousness*. Berkeley and Los Angeles: University of California Press.

53 Bennett, P.J. (1983) Temple Organization and Worship among the Puṣṭimārgīya-Vaiṣṇavas of Ujjain. PhD thesis, University of London (SOAS).

54 Benson, H. and Wallace, R.K. (1972) Decreased Drug Abuse with Transcendental Meditation: a Study of 1862 Subjects. In C.J.D. Zarafonetis (ed) *Proceedings of the International Symposium on Drug Abuse*. Philadelphia: Lea & Febiger.

55 Berger, P. and Luckmann, T. (1963) Sociology of Religion and Sociology of Knowledge. *Sociology and Social Research* 47: 417–27.

56 Berkshire Education Authority (1982) *Religious Heritage and Personal Quest*. Guidelines for Religious Education. Reading: Berkshire Education Authority.

57 Bharati, A. (1961) *The Ochre Robe*. London: Allen & Unwin.

58 — (1970) The Hindu Renaissance and its Apologetic Patterns. *Journal of Asian Studies* 29: 267–87.

59 — (1973) Hindus Ignorant of Hinduism: Phoney Swamis Abroad. *Illustrated Weekly of India*, 18 March.

60 — (1976) Ritualistic Tolerance and Ideological Rigour: the Paradigm of the Expatriate Hindus in East Africa. *Contributions to Indian Sociology* 10(2) (N.S.): 341–65.

61 Bhatt, G.H. (1953) The School of Vallabha. In H. Bhattacharya (ed.) *The Cultural Heritage of India*. Vol. 3. Calcutta: Ramakrishna Mission.

62 — (1980) *Sri Vallabhacharya and his Doctrines*. Delhi: Butula.

63 Bhattacharya, J.N. (1896) *Hindu Castes and Sects: An Exposition of the Hindu Caste System and the Bearing of the Sects Towards Each Other and Other Religious Systems*. Calcutta: Thacker, Spink.

64 Bhatti, F.M. (1976–77) Language Difficulties and Social Isolation: the Case of South Asian Women in Britain. *New Community* **5**: 115–17.

65 Bhavyananda, Swami (1972) *Meditation*. London: Ramakrishna Vedanta Centre.

66 Bhopal, R.J. (1986) The Inter-relationship of Folk, Traditional and Western Medicine within an Asian Community in Britain. *Social Science and Medicine* **22**(1): 99–106.

67 Billion, A. (1979) *Kundalini: Secret of the Ancient Yogis*. West Nyack N.Y.: Parker.

68 Bloomfield, H.H., Cain, M.P., Jaffe, T.T., and Kory, R.B. (1976) *TM: How Meditation Can Reduce Stress*. London: Allen & Unwin.

69 Bodewitz, H.W. (1976) *The Daily Evening and Morning Offering (Agni-hotra) according to the Brahmanas*. Leiden: E.J. Brill.

70 Bon, B.H. (1973) *Sri Caitanya*. New Delhi: Oxford and IBH.

71 Booth, J. (1977) Indian Girls. *Libertarian Education*. **23**: 4–7.

72 Bose, N. (1963) *Social Thinking of Vivekenanda*. Lucknow: Bina Bose.

73 Bowen, D. (1981) *Hinduism in England*. Bradford: Bradford College.

74 — (1981) The Hindu Community in Bradford. In D. Bowen (ed.) *Hinduism in England*. Bradford: Bradford College.

75 — (1984) Hinduism: a Teacher's Approach. *British Journal of Religious Education* **6** (3): 126–32.

76 — (1985) Hindus in Britain. In M. Hayward (ed.), *Understanding the Hindu Tradition: Papers of the 3rd York Shap Conference*. York: York Religious Education Centre.

77 — (1985) The Sri Sathya Sai Community in Bradford: its Origin and Development, Religious Beliefs and Practices. PhD thesis, Leeds University.

78 — (1986) *The Sathya Sai Baba Community in Bradford*. Leeds: the University (Community Religions Project).

79 Bradford, K. (1975) Marriage by Proxy. *New Community* **4**: 254–55.

80 Brah, A. (1977–78) South Asian Teenagers in Southall: their Perceptions of Marriage, Family and Ethnic Identity. *New Community* **6**: 197–206.

81 Brahmananda, Swami (1974–75) How the Teachings of Lord Caitanya Came to the Western World. *Back to Godhead* **66**:7–10; **68**:6–11; **10**(1):9–15.

82 Bramacari, P. (1924–34). *Śrīśrīcaitanya Caritāvalī [The Life of Chitanya]* 5 vols. Gorakhpur: Gita Press.

83 Brear, A.D. (1984) An Approach to the Complexities of the Hindu Tradition. *British Journal of Religious Education* **6**(3): 107–15.

84 Brent, P. (1973) *Godmen of India*. Harmondsworth: Penguin.

85 Brewin, C. (1980) Explaining the Lower Rates of Psychiatric Treatment among Asian Immigrants to the United Kingdom: a Preliminary Study. *Social Psychiatry* **15**: 17–19.

86 Bridger, P. (1975) *A Hindu Family in Britain*. (Originally published 1969.) Oxford: Religious Education Press.

87 Briggs, G.W. (1920) *The Chamars*. Calcutta: Association Press.

88 Briggs, H.C. (1849) *The Cities of Gujarashtra: their Topography and History Illustrated in a Journal of a Recent Tour*. Bombay: The Times Press.

89 Bristow, M. (1976–77) Britain's Response to the Uganda Asian Crisis: Government Myths versus Political and Resettlement Realities. *New Community* 5: 265–79.

90 — (1979) Ugandan Asians: Racial Disadvantage and Housing Markets in Manchester and Birmingham. *New Community* 7: 203–16.

91 Bristow, M. and Adams, B.N. (1977–78) Ugandan Asians and the Housing Market in Britain. *New Community* 6: 65–77.

92 Bristow, M., Adams, B. N., and Pereira, C. (1975) Ugandan Asians in Britain, Canada, and India: Some Characteristics and Resources. *New Community* 4: 155–66.

93 Bromley, D.G. and Richardson, J.T. (n.d.) *The Brainwashing/Deprogramming Controversy: Sociological, Psychological, Legal, and Historical Perspectives*. New York and Toronto: Edwin Mellon (in press).

94 Bromley, D.G. and Shupe, A.D. (1982) *Strange Gods: the Great American Cult Scare*. Boston: Beacon.

95 Bromley, P.M. (1981) *Family Law*. 6th edn. London: Butterworth.

96 Brook, M. (1980) The 'Mother-tongue' Issue in Britain: Cultural Diversity or Control? *British Journal of the Sociology of Education* 1(3): 237–55.

97 Brooke, T. (1979) *Sai Baba, Lord of the Air*. New Delhi: Vikas.

98 Brooks, D. and Singh, K. (1978). *Aspirations versus Opportunities: Asian and White School Leavers in the Midlands*. London: Walsall/Leicester CRCs and the Commission for Racial Equality.

99 — (1978–79) Ethnic Commitment versus Structural Reality: South Asian Immigrant Workers in Britain. *New Community* 7: 19–30.

100 — (1979) Pivots and Presents: Asian Brokers in British Foundries. In S. Wallman (ed.) *Ethnicity at Work*. London: Macmillan.

101 Brown, P.A. (1976) Differential Utilization of the Health Care Delivery System by Members of Ethnic Minorities. *Journal of Sociology and Social Welfare* 3: 516–23.

102 Bühler, G. (1975). *The Laws of Manu*. Delhi: Motilal.

103 Burghart, R. (1983) Renunciation in the Religious Traditions of South Asia. *Man* 18 (N.S.): 635–53.

104 — (1984) Regional Circles and the Central Overseer of the Vaishnavite Sect in the Kingdom of Nepal. In K. Ballhatchet and D. Taylor (eds) *Changing South Asia: Religion and Society*. Hong Kong: Asian Research Service.

105 Burke, A.W. (1976) Attempted Suicide among Asian Immigrants in Birmingham. *British Journal of Psychiatry* 128: 528–33.

106 Burke, M.L. (1958) *Swami Vivekananda in America: New Discoveries*. Calcutta: Advaita Ashrama.

107 Burr, A. (1984) *I Am Not My Body: a Study of the International Hare Krishna Sect*. Delhi: Vikas.

108 Butler, D.G. (1975) *Many Lights*. London: Geoffrey Chapman.

109 — (1980) *Life Among Hindus* (Friends and Neighbours Series). London: Edward Arnold.

110 Butterworth, E. and Kinnibrugh, D. (1970) *The Social Background of Immigrant Children from India, Pakistan and Cyprus*. London: Books for School, Ltd., for the Schools Council.

111 Cameron, C. (1973) *Who Is Guru Maharaj Ji?* New York: Bantam Books.

112 Campbell, A. (1977) *The Mechanics of Enlightenment: an Examination of the Teaching of Maharishi Mahesh Yogi*. London: Gollancz.

113 Candlin, S. (1969–70) *A Survey of the Utilization of the Health and Welfare Services by Asian Immigrants during Pregnancy in Lancaster 1968–1969*. (Health Visitors' Course 1969–1979 Project.) Boston: Boston Institute of Technology.

114 Carey, S.F. (1980) A Sociological Study of the Ramakrishna Mission in Great Britain. PhD thesis, University of Newcastle upon Tyne.

115 — (1982–83) The Hare Krishna Movement and Hindus in Britain. *New Community* **10**: 477–86.

116 Cater, J.C. and Jones, T.P. (1978) Asians in Bradford. *New Society*, 13 April: 81–2.

117 Caturvedi, P. (1951) *Uttarī Bhārat kī Sant-paramparā. (Sant Sects of Northern India) Prayāg: Bhāratī Bhaṇḍār.*

118 Chakraborty, T.S. (1963) *Patriot-saint Vivekananda*. Allahabad: Ramakrishna Mission Sevashram.

119 Chamupati, P. (n.d.) *The Ten Principles of the Arya Samaja*. Madras: Pandit K. Jnani.

120 Chandra, F.A. (1981) The Essentials of Hinduism. In D. Bowen (ed.) *Hinduism in Britain*. Bradford: Bradford College.

121 Chansarkar, B.A. (1973) A Note on the Maratha Community in Britain. *New Community*, **2**: 302–05.

122 Chaudhuri, N. (1980) *That Compassionate Touch of Ma Anandamayee*. Delhi: Motilal Banarsidass.

123 Chavda, D.C. (1983) *Directory 1983*. Bradford: Kshatriya Sudharak Mandal.

124 Cheetham, C.J. (1977) *Some Hindu and Muslim Attitudes towards Western Education*. MEd thesis, University of Birmingham.

125 Claxton, G. (1981) *Wholly Human: Western and Eastern Visions of the Self and its Perfection*. London: Routledge & Kegan Paul.

126 Clothey, F.W. (1978) *The Many Faces of Murukan*. The Hague: Mouton.

127 Clothey, F.W. and Long, J. B. (1983) *Experiencing Siva: Encounters with a Hindu Deity*. New Delhi: Manohar.

128 Cochrane, R. (1979) Psychological and Behavioural Disturbance in West Indians, Indians and Pakistanis in Britain. *British Journal of Psychiatry* **134**: 201–10.

129 Cochrane, R. and Stopes-Roe, M. (1977) Psychological and Social

Adjustment of Asian Immigrants to Britain. *Social Psychiatry* 12: 195–207.

130 Coedès, G. (1968) *The Indianized States of Southeast Asia.* Honolulu: East–West Center.

131 Cohen, G. (1984–85) Ethnicity in a Middle-class London Suburb. *New Community* 12: 89–100.

132 Cole, W. O. (1972) *Religion in the Multi-Faith School.* Yorkshire: Committee for Community Relations (2nd rev. edn, Amersham: Hulton, 1983).

133 — (1981) *Five Religions in the Twentieth Century.* Amersham: Hulton (2nd rev. edn, 1985).

134 — (1985) The Hindu Religious Tradition and Religious Education. In M. Hayward, (ed.), *Understanding the Hindu Tradition: Papers of the 3rd York Shap Conference.* York: York Religious Education Centre.

135 Collet, S.D. (1871) *Keshub Chunder Sen's English Visit.* London: Strahan & Co.

136 Community Relations Council, Coventry (1974) *Ethnic Minorities in Coventry.* Coventry: Community Relations Council.

137 Coney, J. (1985) Recent Changes in Rajneeshism. *Religion Today* 2(2): 8–9.

138 Coonan, J.L. (1960) Asian Overseas Students in England. *Asia* 12: 684–90.

139 Cox, H. (1979) *Turning East: The Promise and Peril of the New Orientalism.* London: Allen Lane.

140 Craske, M. (1980) *The Dance of Love: My Life with Meher Baba.* North Myrtle Beach, S. Ca.: Sheriar Press.

141 Crishna, S. (1975) *Girls of Asian Origin in Britain.* London: YMCA.

142 Dahya, B. (1974) The Nature of Pakistani Ethnicity in Industrial Cities in Britain. In A. Cohen (ed.) *Urban Ethnicity.* London: Tavistock.

143 — (1981–82) Gender Roles and Ethnic Relations. *New Community* 9: 111–12.

144 Damrell, J.D. (1977) *Seeking Spiritual Meaning: The World of Vedanta.* London & Beverley Hills: Sage.

145 Daner, F. (1975) Conversion to Krishna Consciousness: the Transformation from Hippie to Religious Ascetic. In R. Wallis, (ed.), *Sectarianism.* London: Peter Owen.

146 — (1976) *The American Children of Krishna.* New York: Holt, Rinehart, & Winston.

147 Das, T. (1949) *Social Philosophy of Swami Vivekananda.* Calcutta: Co-operative Book Depot.

148 Das, V. (1977) *Structure and Cognition: Aspects of Hindu Caste and Ritual.* Oxford: Oxford University Press.

149 — (1983) Language of Sacrifice. *Man* 18 (N.S.): 445–62.

150 Datta, B. (1954) *Svami Vivekananda: Patriot-Prophet.* Calcutta: Nababharat.

151 Dave, H.T. (1974) *Life and Philosophy of Shree Swaminarayan 1781–1830.* London: Allen & Unwin.

152 — (1977) *Shree Swaminarayan's Vachanamritam.* Bombay: Bharatiya Vidya Bhavan.

153 David, K. (1977) Hierarchy and Equivalence in Jaffna, North Sri Lanka. In K. David (ed.), *The New Winds*. The Hague: Mouton.

154 Davids, L. (1964) The East Indian Family Overseas. *Social and Economic Studies* **13**: 383–96.

155 Davies, R. (1981) *Holy Books* (The Religious Dimension Series). London: Longman.

156 De, S.K. (1961) *Early History of the Vaiṣṇava Faith and Movement in Bengal*. 2nd edn. Calcutta: K.L. Mukhopadhyay.

157 Deakin, N. (1964–65) Residential Segregation in Britain: a Comparative Note. *Race*, **6**: 18–26.

158 Derrett, J.D.M. (1970) *A Critique of Modern Hindu Law*. Bombay: N.M. Tripathi.

159 — (1978) *The Death of a Marriage Law: Epitaph for the Rishis*. New Delhi: Vikas.

160 — (1979) Unity in Diversity: the Hindu Experience. *Bharata Manisha* **5**: 21–36.

161 Desai, R. (1963) *Indian Immigrants in Britain*. London: Oxford University Press.

162 Devi, I. (1979) *Sai Baba and Sai Yoga*. Delhi: Macmillan.

163 Dhavamony, M. (1971) *Love of God according to Śaiva Siddhanta*. Oxford: Clarendon Press.

164 Dhingra, B. (1981) *Visages de Ma Anandamayi*. Paris: Les Éditions du Cerf.

165 Dimock, E. (1968) *In Praise of Krishna*. London: Jonathan Cape.

166 Dines, M. (1973) Cool Reception. *New Community* **2**: 380–83.

167 Diwakar R.R. (1956) *Paramahansa Sri Ramakrishna*. Bombay: Bharatiya Vidya Bhavan.

168 Downton, J.V. (1979) *Sacred Journeys: the Conversion of Young Americans to Divine Light Mission*. New York: Columbia University Press.

169 Driver, G. and Ballard, R. (1979) Comparing Performance in Multiracial Schools: South Asian Pupils at 16-plus. *New Community* **7**: 143–53.

170 D'Souza, A.A. (1972) The Indian Family in the 70s: An Integrated Family Policy. *Social Action* Jan–March: 1–15.

171 Dumont, L. (1970) *Homo Hierarchicus: the Caste System and Its Implications*. London: Weidenfeld & Nicholson (paperback edn. Paladin 1972).

172 Dunuwila, R.A. (1985) *Saiva Siddhanta Theology*. Delhi: Motilal Banarsidass.

173 Durham Report (1970) *The Fourth R – The Durham Report on Religious Education*. London: National Society and SPCK.

174 Eck, D. (1979) Krishna Consciousness in Historical Perspective. *Back to Godhead* **14** (10): 26–9.

175 Ellwood, R.S. (1973) *Religious and Spiritual Groups in Modern America*. Englewood Cliffs, N.J.: Prentice-Hall.

176 — (1973) The International Society for Krishna Consciousness. In R. Ellwood (ed.) *Religious and Spiritual Groups in Modern America*. Englewood Cliffs, N.J.: Prentice-Hall.

177 — (1979) *Alternative Altars: Unconventional and Eastern Spirituality in America*. Chicago: Chicago University Press.

178 Emmett, P. (1984) Creating a Favourable Climate for the Teaching of Hinduism. *British Journal of Religious Education* 6(3): 137–40; 160.

179 Ewan, J. (1977) *Understanding Your Hindu Neighbour*. London: Lutterworth Press.

180 Farquhar, J.N. (1919) *Modern Religious Movements in India*. London: Macmillan.

181 Fenton, M. (1977) *Asian Households in Owner-occupation: a Study of the Pattern, Costs and Experiences of Households in Greater Manchester*. (Working Papers on Ethnic Relations, No. 2.) Bristol: SSRC Research Unit on Ethnic Relations.

182 Forem, J. (1975) *Transcendental Meditation, Maharishi Mahesh Yogi and the Science of Creative Intelligence*. London: Allen & Unwin.

183 Forester, T. (1978) Asians in Business. *New Society*, 23 February.

184 Fornaro, R. (1969) Sivananda and the Divine Life Society: a Paradigm of the 'Secularism', 'Puritanism', and 'Cultural Dissimulation' of a Neo-Hindu Religious Society. PhD thesis, Syracuse University.

185 Francis, E.K. (1976) *Interethnic Relations*. New York: Elsevier.

186 French, H.W. (1974) *The Swan's Wide Waters: Ramakrishna and Western Culture*. London: Kennikat Press.

187 Gambhirananda, Swami (1955) *Life of Sri Ramakrishna compiled from Various Authentic Sources*. Calcutta: Advaita Ashrama.

188 — (1957) *History of the Ramakrishna Math and Mission*. Calcutta: Advaita Ashrama.

189 — (1967) *The Apostles of Ramakrishna*. Calcutta: Advaita Ashrama.

190 Ganapati, R. (1981) *Baba Sathya Sai: his Early Life and Subsequent Life through his Devotees' Lives*. (Adapted in English from the Tamil book *Svami* by H. Ramamoorthy and R. Ganapati.) Madras: Satya Jyoti.

191 Ganguli, M. (1907) *Swami Vivekananda: a Study*. Calcutta: Lalchand Dutta.

192 Gates, B.E. (1975) The Politics of Religious Education. In M. Taylor, (ed.) *Progress and Problems in Moral Education*. Slough: NFER.

193 — (1976) Religion in the Developing World of Children and Young People. PhD thesis, University of Lancaster.

194 — (1977) Religion in the Child's Own Core Curriculum. *Learning for Living*, Autumn.

195 — (1980) Children's Understanding of Death. In J. Prickett (ed.) *Death*. London: Lutterworth.

196 — (1982) Children Prospecting for Commitment. In R. Jackson (ed.) *Approaching World Religions*. London: John Murray.

197 Gelberg, S.J. (1983) *Hare Krishna, Hare Krishna: Five Distinguished Scholars on the Krishna Movement in the West*. New York: Grove Press.

198 Ghanananda, Swami (1970) *Sri Ramakrishna and his Unique Message*. London: Ramakrishna Vedanta Centre.

199 Ghurye, G.S. (1964) *Indian Sadhus* (2nd edn.) Bombay: Popular Prakashan.

200 Gidwani, N.N. and Navalani, K. (1974) *A Guide to Reference Materials on India.* Jaipur: Saraswati.

201 Gnanasoorian, K. (1980) *A Date with Destiny: an Introduction to Hindu Saiva Bhakti and Saiva Siddhanta.* London: Institute for International Tamil Renaissance.

202 Gokak, V.K. (1973) *A Value Orientation to our System of Education.* New Delhi: Gulab Singh.

203 — (1975) *Bhagavan Sri Sathya Sai Baba: The Man and the Avatar: An Interpretation.* New Delhi: Abhinav.

204 — (1975) *The Golden Book of Sri Sathya Sai Lyrics.* Kadugodi: Sri Sathya Sai Education and Publication Foundation.

205 — (1979) *In Defence of Jesus Christ and Other Avatars.* New Delhi: Gulab Singh.

206 — (1980) The Sathya Sai Theory of Education. In *Golden Age.* Prasanthi Nilayam: Sri Sathya Sai Books and Publications.

207 Goswami, Satsvarupa Das (1980–82) *Srila Prabhupada-lilamrta.* A biography in 4 vols of Srila Prabhupad. Los Angeles: Bhaktivedanta Trust.

208 Gould, C., Routh, C., and Smith, S. (1985) Hinduism: Books and Audio-Visual Materials. In *Living Faiths: Six Religions in Britain Today.* Reading: Berkshire Library and Arts Dept, Education Library Service.

209 Gregory, R.G. (1971) *India and East Africa: a History of Race Relations within the British Empire 1890–1939.* Oxford: Clarendon Press.

210 Griffith, J.A.G. (1960) *Coloured Immigrants in Britain.* London: Oxford University Press.

211 Grimmitt, M. (1981) When is 'Commitment' a Problem in R.E.? *British Journal of Educational Studies* **29**: 1.

212 — (1982) World Religions and Personal Development. In R. Jackson (ed.) *Approaching World Religions.* London: John Murray.

213 Gumperz, J. (1982) Interethnic Communication. In *Discourse Strategies.* Cambridge: Cambridge University Press.

214 Gupta, Krishna Prakash (1974) Religious Evolution and Social Change in India: a Study of the Ramakrishna Mission Movement. *Contributions to Indian Sociology* **8** (N.S.): 25–50.

215 Gupte, S.V. (1976) *Hindu Law of Marriage* (2nd edn). Bombay: N.M. Tripathi.

216 Gyan, S.C. (1980) *Sivananda and His Ashram.* Madras: Christian Literature Society.

217 Hahlo, K.G. (1980) Profile of a Gujarati Community in Bolton. *New Community* **8**: 295–307.

218 Hall, J.R. (1978) *The Ways Out: Utopian Communal Groups in an Age of Babylon.* London: Routledge & Kegan Paul.

219 Hailsham of Marylebone, Lord (1976) *Halsbury's Laws of England* (4th edn) London: Butterworth.

220 Hardy, F. (1984) How Indian are the New Indian Religions in the West? *Religion Today* 1(2/3): 15–18.

221 Harper, M.H. (1972) *Gurus, Swamis and Avataras: Spiritual Masters and their American Disciples.* Philadelphia: Westminster.

222 Hasan, K. (1967) *The Cultural Frontier of Health in Village India.* Bombay: Manaktalas.

223 Hay, D. and Morisy, A. (1978) Reports of Ecstatic, Paranormal and Religious Experience in Great Britain and the USA: A Comparison of Trends. *Journal for the Scientific Study of Religion* 17(3).

224 Hedayetullah, M. (1977) *Kabir: the Apostle of Hindu-Muslim Unity.* Delhi: Motilal Banarsidass.

225 Hemingway, P.D. (1976). *The Transcendental Meditation Primer.* New York: Dell.

226 Henley, A. (1979) *Asian Patients in Hospital and at Home.* London: King Edward's Hospital Fund.

227 Herbert, J. (1938) *Swami Vivekananda: Bibliographie.* Paris: Advien Maisonneuve.

228 Hick, J. (1973) *God and the Universe of Faiths.* London: Macmillan.

229 Hill, C. (1971) Immigrant Sect Development in Britain: a Case of Status Deprivation. *Social Compass* 18(2): 231–36.

230 Hill, M. (1972) *A Sociological Yearbook of Religion in Britain.* Vol.5. London: SCM Press.

231 Hilliard, F.H. (1961) *Teaching Children about World Religion.* London: Harrap.

232 Hinnells, J.R. (1970) *Comparative Religion in Education.* Newcastle: Oriel Press.

233 Hinnells, J.R. and Sharpe, E.J. (1972) *Hinduism.* Newcastle: Oriel Press.

234 Hiro, D. (1969) *The Indian Family in Britain.* London: Community Relations Council.

235 Hirst, P. (1965) Morals, Religion and the Maintained School. *British Journal of Educational Studies* 14: 5–18.

236 — (1972) Christian Education: A Contradiction in Terms? *Learning for Living* 11(4): 6–11.

237 — (1973) Religion: a Form of Knowledge? A Reply. *Learning for Living* 12(4): 8–10.

238 Holland, B. (1979) *Popular Hinduism and Hindu Mythology: An Annotated Bibliography.* Westport, Conn.: Greenwood.

239 Holm, J. (1984) Growing Up in Hinduism. *British Journal of Religious Education.* 6(3): 116–20.

240 Holroyde, P., Iqbal, M., and Vohra, D.K. (1971) *East Comes West: a Background to Some Asian Faiths.* London: Community Relations Commission.

241 Homans, H.Y. (1980) Pregnant in Britain: a Sociological Approach to Asian and British Women's Experience. PhD thesis, University of Warwick.

242 Hooker, M.B. (1975) *Legal Pluralism.* Oxford: Clarendon Press.

243 Hope, E., Kennedy, M., and de Winter, A. (1976) Homeworkers in North

London. In D.L. Barker and S. Allen (eds) *Dependence and Exploitation in Work and Marriage*. London and New York: Longman.

244 Hopkins, T. (1981) A Vital Transition. *Back to Godhead* 16(8): 21–8.

245 — (1983) Interview with Thomas J. Hopkins. In S.J. Gelberg (ed.) *Hare Krishna, Hare Krishna*. New York: Grove.

246 Hummel, R. (1983) Asiatic Religions in Europe. In J. Coleman and G. Baum (eds) *Concilium: New Religious Movements*. Edinburgh: T. & T. Clark.

247 Hunt, S. (1976) The Food Habits of Asian Immigrants. In *Getting the Most Out of Food*. London: Van den Berghs & Jurgens.

248 Iliffe, L. (1978) Estimated Fertility Rates of Asian and West Indian Immigrant Women in Britain 1969–1974. *Journal of Biosocial Science* 10: 189–97.

249 Inden, R. and Nicholas, R. (1977) *Kinship in Bengali Culture*. Chicago: University of Chicago Press.

250 Indian Council of Social Science Research (1970) *Doctorates in Social Sciences Awarded by Indian Universities 1969*. New Delhi: ICSSR.

251 International Society for Krishna Consciousness (1975) *The Krishna Consciousness Movement is Authorized*. New York: Bhaktivedanta Book Trust.

252 Isherwood, C. (1948) *Vedanta for the Western World*. London: Unwin Books.

253 — (1959) *Ramakrishna and his Disciples*. New York: Simon & Schuster.

254 Iyengar, B.K.S. (1976) *Light on Yoga*. London: Allen & Unwin.

255 Iyengar, K.R. Srinivasa (1945) *Sri Aurobindo*. Calcutta: Arya.

256 Jackson, R. (1976) Holi in North India and in an English City: Some Adaptations and Anomalies. *New Community* 5(3): 203–10.

257 — (1976) *Perspectives on World Religions*. London: School of Oriental & African Studies.

258 — (1981) The Place of Hinduism in Religious Education. In D. Bowen (ed.), *Hinduism in England*. Bradford: Bradford College.

259 — (1981) The Shree Krishna Temple and the Gujarati Hindu Community in Coventry. In D. Bowen (ed.) *Hinduism in England*. Bradford: Bradford College.

260 — (1982) *Approaching World Religions*. London: John Murray.

261 — (1984) The Concerns of Religious Education and the Characterization of Hinduism. *British Journal of Religious Education* 6(3): 141–46.

262 — (1985) Hinduism in Britain: Religious Nurture and Religious Education. *British Journal of Religious Education*, 7(2): 68–75.

263 — (1985) The Hindu Religious Tradition and Religious Education. In M. Hayward (ed.) *Understanding the Hindu Tradition: Papers of the 3rd York Shap Conference*. York: York Religious Education Centre.

264 Jackson, R. and Nesbitt, E. (1986) Sketches of Hindu Nurture. *World Religions in Education*. Shap Working Party Mailing.

265 Jahoda, G., Thomas, S., and Bhatt, S. (1972) Ethnic Identity and Preference among Asian Immigrant Children in Glasgow: a Replicated Study. *European Journal of Social Psychology*. 2: 19–32.

266 James, A. (1974) *Sikh Children in Britain*. London: Oxford University Press.

267 Jayawardena, C. (1973) Migrants, Networks and Identities. *New Community*, **2**: 353–57.

268 John, D. (1969) *Indian Workers' Associations in Britain*. London: Oxford University Press.

269 Johnson, G. (1973) An Alternative Community in Microcosm: the Evolution of Commitment to a Vedic Sect. PhD thesis, Harvard University.

270 — (1976) The Hare Krishnas in San Francisco. In R. Bellah and C. Glock (eds) *The New Religious Consciousness*. Berkeley and Los Angeles: University of California Press.

271 Jones, K.W. (1976) *Arya Dharma: Hindu Consciousness in Nineteenth Century Punjab*. Berkeley and Los Angeles: University of California Press.

272 Jones, P.N. (1976) Colored Minorities in Birmingham, England. *Association of American Geographers Annals* **66** (March): 89–103.

273 Jones, P.R. and Shah, S. (1980) Arranged Marriages: a Sample Survey of the Asian Case. *New Community* **8**: 339–43.

274 Jordens, J.T.F. (1978) *Dayanand Sarasvati: His Life and Ideas*. Delhi: Oxford University Press.

275 — (1981) *Swami Shraddhananda: His Life and Causes*. Delhi: Oxford University Press.

276 Judah, J.S. (1967) *The History and Philosophy of the Metaphysical Movements in America*. Philadelphia: Westminster.

277 — (1974a) *Hare Krishna and the Counter Culture*. New York: Wiley.

278 — (1974b) The Hare Krishna Movement. In I. Zaretsky and M.P. Leone (eds) *Religious Movements in Contemporary America*. Princeton: Princeton University Press.

279 Jupp, T. and Hodlin, S. (1970) Language: Asians in the Factory. *Race Today* **2**: 124–26.

280 Jussawalla, A. (1965) Indifference. In H. Tajfel and J.L. Dawson (eds) *Disappointed Guests*. London: Oxford University Press.

281 Kalsa, S.S. (1979) *Daughters of Tradition*. Birmingham: Third World Publications.

282 Kane, P.V. (1953–73) *History of Dharmasastra*. 5 vols. Poona: Bhandarkar Oriental Research Institute.

283 Kanellakos, D.P. and Ferguson, P. (1974) *The Psychobiology of Transcendental Meditation* (An Annotated Bibliography). Reading, Penn.: W.A. Benjamin.

284 Kanitkar, H. (1964) Indian Students and Professionals in Britain – a Research Note. *Institute of Race Relations Newsletter* May: 27–8.

285 — (1969) The Indian Regional Association Abroad – its Chief Functions. *Keralam* (London) **1**(2): 21–3.

286 — (1972a) An Indian Elite in Britain. *New Community* **1**(5): 378–83.

287 — (1972b) The Social Organization of Indian Students in the London Area. PhD thesis. University of London (SOAS).

288 — (1978) Social Aspects of Hinduism. In R. Jackson (ed.) *Perspectives on World Religions*. London: School of Oriental & African Studies.

289 — (1981) Caste in Contemporary Hindu Society. In D. Bowen (ed.) *Hinduism in England*. Bradford: Bradford College.

290 Kanitkar, H. and Jackson, R. (1982) *Hindus in Britain*. London: School of Oriental & African Studies.

291 Kanitkar, V.P. (Hemant) (1979) A School for Hindus? *New Community* 7: 178–83.

292 —(1984) *Hindu Festivals and Sacraments*. New Barnet: V.P. Kanitkar.

293 — (1985) *Hinduism*. Hove: Wayland.

294 Kanu, V. (1981) *Sai Baba: God Incarnate*. London: Sawbridge Enterprises.

295 Kapadia, K.M. (1966) *Marriage and Family in India* (3rd edn) Calcutta: Oxford University Press.

296 Kapur, O.B.L. (1977) *The Philosophy and Religion of Sri Caitanya: the Philosophical Background of the Hare Krishna Movement*. New Delhi: Munshiram Manoharlal.

297 Karanjia, R.K. (1977) *Kundalini Yoga*. New Delhi: Arnold-Heinemann.

298 Karn, V. (1968–69) Property Values amongst Indians and Pakistanis in a Yorkshire Town. *Race* 10: 269–84.

299 Kasturi, N. (1961–80) *Sathyam, Sivam, Sundaram: the Life of Bhagavan Sri Sathya Sai Baba*. 4 parts. Prasanthi Nilayam: Sri Sathya Sai Books and Publications.

300 — (n.d.) *Sathya Sai Speaks*. Vol. 8. Bombay: Sri Sathya Sai Education Foundation.

301 Keay, F.E. (1931) *Kabir and his Followers*. Calcutta: Association Press.

302 Kennedy, M.T. (1925) *The Chaitanya Movement: a Study of the Vaishnavism of Bengal*. New York: Oxford University Press.

303 Khera, A.K. (1981) The Status of Women in Hindu Society. In D. Bowen (ed.), *Hinduism in England*. Bradford: Bradford College.

304 Killingley, D. (1980) *A Handbook of Hinduism*. Newcastle: Newcastle upon Tyne Education Committee.

305 — (1984) *A Handbook of Hinduism for Teachers*. Newcastle: Grevatt & Grevatt.

306 — (1984) Hinduism, Tolerance and Community Education. *British Journal of Religious Education* 6(3): 147–51, 160.

307 King, J.R. (1977) Immigrants in Leeds: An Investigation into their Socioeconomic Characteristics, Spatial Distribution, Fertility Trends and Population Growth. PhD thesis, University of Leeds.

308 King, U. (1978) Indian Spirituality, Western Materialism: An Image and its Function in the Reinterpretation of Modern Hinduism. *Social Action* 28(1): 62–86.

309 — (1981) Hinduism in a Western Context. In D. Bowen (ed.) *Hinduism in England*. Bradford: Bradford College.

310 — (1983) Forschungsbereit über den Hinduismus in England. *Zeitschrift für Missionswissenschaft und Religionswissenschaft* 67(3): 220–36.

311 King, W.L. (1970) Eastern Religions: A New Interest and Influence. *Annals of the American Association of Political and Social Science* **387**: 66–76.

312 Knott, K. (1977) A Study of Hinduism in Leeds: Evening Arti in the Mandir. MA thesis, University of Leeds.

313 — (1982) From Vasna to Leeds: the Changing Complexion of Popular Hinduism. *Resource* **5**(1).

314 — (1982) Hinduism in Leeds: a Study of Religious Practice in the Indian Hindu Community and Hindu-related Groups. PhD thesis, University of Leeds.

315 — (1986) *Hinduism in Leeds*. Leeds: The University (Community Religions Project).

316 — (1986) *My Sweet Lord: the Hare Krishna Movement*. Wellingborough: Aquarian Press.

317 Knott, K. and Toon, R. (1982) Muslims, Sikhs and Hindus in the UK: Problems in the Estimation of Religious Statistics (Religious Research Paper No. 6). Leeds: The University (Dept of Sociology).

318 Kohler, D. (1973) Public Opinion and the Ugandan Asians. *New Community* **2**: 194–97.

319 Kopf, D. (1969) *British Orientalism and the Bengal Renaissance: the Dynamics of Indian Modernization 1773–1835*. Berkeley and Los Angeles: University of California Press.

320 — (1979) *The Brahmo Samaj and the Shaping of the Modern Indian Mind*. Princeton: Princeton University Press.

321 Kramer, J. (1974) Profiles: the Ugandan Asians. *The New Yorker*, 8 April.

322 Kuepper, W.G., Lackey, G.L., and Swinnerton, E.N. (1976) Ugandan Asian Refugees: Resettlement Centre to Community. *Community Development Journal* **11** (October): 199–208.

323 Kumar, Surendra (1973) Manchester Reception. *New Community* **2**: 386–88.

324 Laing, R. and Mason, P. (1982) *The Embodiment of Love*. London: Sawbridge Enterprises.

325 Lapping, A. (1969) Our Brown Doctors. *New Society* **14**: 161–62.

326 Law, N.N. (1949) *Sri Krsna and Sri Caitanya*. London: Luzac.

327 Lee, R.M. (1982) Sai Baba: Salvation and Syncretism. *Contributions to Indian Sociology* **16**(1): 125–40.

328 Leeds Hindu Temple (n.d.) *Hinduism – Sanatana Dharma*. Leeds: Hindu Temple.

329 Lemaitre, S. (1984) *Ramakrishna and the Vitality of Hinduism*. Woodstock, N.Y.: Overlook Press.

330 Levine, F. (1974) *The Strange World of the Hare Krishnas*. Greenwich: Fawcett.

331 Levine, N. and Nayar, T. (1974–75) Modes of Adaptation by Asian Immigrants in Slough. *New Community* **4**: 356–65.

332 Linguistic Minorities Project (1985) *The Other Languages of England*. London: Routledge & Kegan Paul.

333 Lipski, A. (1977) *Life and Teachings of Sri Anandamayi Ma*. Delhi: Motilal Banarsidass.

334 Littlewood, R. and Lipsedge, M. (1982) *Aliens and Alienists: Ethnic Minorities and Psychiatry*. Harmondsworth: Penguin.

335 Lomas, G.B.G. (1973) *Census 1971: the Coloured Population of Great Britain, Preliminary Report*. London: Runnymede Trust.

336 — (1977) Analysis of Census Data on Housing. *New Community* 6(1): 8–18.

337 Louden, D. (1977–78) Self-esteem and Locus of Control: Some Findings on Immigrant Adolescents in Britain. *New Community* 6: 218–34.

338 Lutyens, M. (1975) *Krishnamurti: the Years of Awakening*. London: John Murray.

339 Lyon, M.H. (1972–73) Ethnicity in Britain: the Gujarati Tradition. *New Community* 2: 1–11.

340 Mack, J. (1979) The Muslims Get a School of their Own. *New Society* 28 June, 762–65.

341 Mackie, L. (1979) Inquiry urged on Organization's Extremist Links. *The Guardian, 28 September*.

342 Madan, R. (1979) *Coloured Minorities in Great Britain: a Comprehensive Bibliography, 1970–1977*. London: Aldwych.

343 Maharishi Mahesh Yogi (1962) *The Divine Plan: Enjoy Your Own Inner Divine Nature*. Los Angeles: SRM Foundation.

344 Majumdar, A.K. (1969) *Caitanya: His Life and Doctrine*. Bombay: Bharatiya Vidya Bhavan.

345 Majumdar, R.C. (1963) *Swami Vivekananda Centenary Memorial Volume*. Calcutta: Swami Vivekananda Centenary.

346 — (1965) *Swami Vivekananda: a Historical Review*. Calcutta: General Printers and Publishers.

347 Mallison, F. (1974) La Secte Krishnaite des Svami-narayani au Gujarat. *Journal Asiatique* **262** (3–4): 437–71.

348 Mandelbaum, D. (1966) Transcendental and Pragmatic Aspects of Religion. *American Anthropologist* 68: 1174–191.

349 Mangalvadi, V. (1977) *The World of Gurus*. New Delhi: Vikas.

350 Mangat, J.S. (1969) *A History of the Asians in East Africa c. 1886 to 1946*. Oxford: Clarendon Press.

351 Marfatia, M. (1967) *The Philosophy of Vallabhacarya*. Delhi: Munshiram Manoharlal.

352 Marsh, P. (1966) *The Anatomy of a Strike: Unions, Employers and Punjabi Workers in a Southall Factory*. London: Institute of Race Relations.

353 Marshall, P.J. (1970) *The British Discovery of Hinduism in the Eighteenth Century*. Cambridge: Cambridge University Press.

354 Marvell, J. (1973) The Religious Beliefs and Moral Values of Immigrant Children. MEd. thesis, University of Leicester.

355 — (1974) Moral Socialization in a Multi-Racial Community. *Journal of Moral Education* 3(3): 249–57.

356 — (1975) The Formation of Religious Belief in a Multi-Racial Community. *Learning for Living* 15(1): 17–23.

357 — (1976) Phenomenology and the Future of Religious Education. *Learning for Living* 16(1): 4–8.

358 Mayer, A.C. (1960) *Caste and Kinship in Central India.* London: Routledge & Kegan Paul. (Republished in 1966.)

359 Mazoomdar, P.C. (1887) *The Life and Teachings of Keshub Chunder Sen.* Calcutta: Baptist Mission Press.

360 McCart, M. (1973) Wandsworth: Unsettled Ugandan Refugees. *New Community* 2: 383–86.

361 McGrath, M. (1976–77) The Economic Position of Immigrants in Batley. *New Community* 5: 239–49.

362 Meher Baba (1971) *Beams from Meher Baba on the Spiritual Path.* New York: Harper & Row.

363 Menen, A. (1974) *The New Mystics and the True Indian Tradition.* London: Thames & Hudson.

364 Menski, W. F. (1977) Verteilungs- und Funktionsmerkmale des Asiatischen Einzelhandels in Englischen Industriestädten dargestellt am Beispiel von Leicester. MA thesis, University of Kiel.

365 — (1984) Role and Ritual in the Hindu Marriage. PhD thesis, University of London (SOAS).

366 Messer, J. (1976) Who is Guru Maharaj-ji? In R. Bellah and C. Glock (eds) *The New Religious Consciousness.* Berkeley and Los Angeles: University of California Press.

367 Michaelson, M. (1979) The Relevance of Caste among East African Gujaratis in Britain. *New Community* 7(3): 350–60.

368 — (1983) Caste, Kinship and Marriage: a Study of Two Gujarati Trading Castes in England. PhD thesis, University of London (SOAS).

369 Milne, H. (1986) *The God that Failed.* London: Caliban Publications.

370 Minor, R.N. (1978) *Sri Aurobindo: the Perfect and the Good.* Calcutta: Minerva Associates.

371 Minority Group Support Service, Coventry (n.d.) *How a Hindu Prays.* Coventry: Coventry Education Authority.

372 Mital, P.D. (1962) *Caitanya Mat aur Braj Sāhitya (The Doctrine of Caitanya and the Braj Literature)* Mathurā: Sāhitya Saṁsthān.

373 — (1968) *Braj ke Dharma-sampradāyoṁ kā Itihās (The History of the Religious Traditions of Braj).* Delhi: National Publishing House.

374 Mitter, S. (1985) *Hindu Festivals.* Hove: Wayland.

375 Monier-Williams, M. (1882) The Vaishnavite Religion with Special Reference to the Sikshapatri of the Modern Sect called Swaminarayan. *Journal of the Royal Asiatic Society* 14 (N.S.): 289–316.

376 — (1899) *A Sanskrit-English Dictionary.* Oxford: Clarendon Press.

377 Moody, J.F. (1978) Ethics and the Counter Culture: An Analysis of the Ethics of Hare Krishna. PhD thesis, Claremont Graduate School.

378 Morgan, K.W. (1953) *The Religion of the Hindus.* New York: Ronald.

379 Morris, H.S. (1968) *The Indians of Uganda*. London: Weidenfeld & Nicolson.

380 Morrish, I. (1971) *The Background of Immigrant Children*. London: Allen & Unwin.

381 Mukherjee, H. and Mukherjee, U. (1964) *Sri Aurobindo and the New Thought in Indian Politics*. Calcutta: Firma K.L. Mukhopadhyay.

382 Mukherji, A. (1982) *Kundalini: the Arousal of the Inner Energy*. Delhi: Calrion Books.

383 Muktananda Paramahamsa, Swami (1974) *Satsang with Baba: Questions and Answers Between Swami Muktananda and his Devotees*. 5 vols. Ganeshpuri: Shree Gurudev Ashram.

384 Mulji, K. (1865) *History of the Sect of Maharajas, or Vallabhacharyas in Western India*. London: Trubner.

385 Mullan, B. (1983) *Life as Laughter: Following Bhagwan Shree Rajneesh*. London: Routledge & Kegan Paul.

386 Mullins, D. (1979) Asian Retailing in Croydon. *New Community* 7: 403–05.

387 Murari, T. (1972) Portrait of an Asian Identity. *Twentieth Century* **179** (1048): 22–3.

388 Murphet, H. (1973) *Sai Baba: Man of Miracles*. London: Muller.

389 — (1979) *Sai Baba Avatar: a New Journey into Power and Glory*. London: Muller.

390 — (1982) *Sai Baba: Invitation to Glory*. Delhi: Macmillan India.

391 Nagra, J.S. (1979) Asian Supplementary Schools and the Attitudes of Asian Children and Parents towards the Teaching of the Mother Tongue. MEd. thesis, University of Birmingham.

392 Nath, J. (1970) Some Aspects of the Life of Indians and Pakistanis in Newcastle with special Reference to Women. MA thesis, University of Durham.

393 Needleman, J. (1970) *The New Religions*. New York: Doubleday.

394 — (1971) Winds from the East: Youth and Counter-Cults. *Commonweal* **44** (30 April).

395 Needleman, J. and Baker, G. (1978) *Understanding the New Religions*. New York: Seabury Press.

396 New York University (1979–80) Alternative Religions: Government Control and the First Amendment. *New York University Review of Law and Social Change* (Special Issue) **9**(1).

397 Nidich, S., Seeman, W., and Dreskin, T. (1974) Influence of Transcendental Meditation: a Replication. *Journal of Counseling Psychology*.

398 Nidich, S., Seeman, W., and Seibert, M. (1974) Influence of Transcendental Meditation on State Anxiety. *Journal of Consulting and Clinical Psychology*.

399 Nikhilananda, Swami (1962) *Holy Mother: Being the Life of Sri Sarada Devi Wife of Sri Ramakrishna and Helpmate in his Mission*. London: Allen & Unwin.

400 Nivedita, Sister (1910) *The Master as I Saw Him: Being Pages from the Life of Swami Vivekananda*. London: Longmans, Green.

401 Nowikowski, S. and Ward, R. (1978–79) Middle Class or British? An Analysis of South Asians in Suburbia. *New Community* 7: 1–10.

402 O'Connell, J. (1973) The Word 'Hindu' in Gaudiya Vaisnava Texts. *Journal of the American Oriental Society* 93: 340–44.

403 O'Keefe, B. (1980) Hindu Family Life in East London. PhD thesis, University of London (LSE).

404 O'Neil, L.T. (1979) *Towards the Life Divine: Sri Aurobindo's Vision*. New Delhi: Manohar.

405 Orme-Johnson, D.W. (1973) Autonomic Stability and Transcendental Meditation. *Psychosomatic Medicine* 35(4): 341–49.

406 Orme-Johnson, D.W., Domash, L.H., and Farrow, J.T. (1974) *Scientific Research on Transcendental Meditation: Collected Papers*. Los Angeles: MIU Press.

407 Osborne, A. (1975) *The Incredible Sai Baba*. London: Rider.

408 Pancholi, N. (1982) Hinduism. In W. Owen Cole, (ed) *Comparative Religions*. Poole: Blandford.

409 Pandey, D. (1972) *The Arya Samaj and Indian Nationalism (1875–1920)*. New Delhi: S. Chand.

410 Pandey, R.B. (1976) *Hindu Samskaras: A Socio-Religious Study of Hindu Sacraments*. Delhi: Motilal Barnarsidass.

411 Paranjoti, V. (1954) *Saiva Siddhanta*. London: Luzac.

412 Parekh, M.C. (1980) *Shri Swaminarayan* (3rd edn). Bombay: Bharatiya Vidya Bhavan.

413 Parrinder, G. (1970) *Avatar and Incarnation*. New York: Barnes & Noble.

414 — (1971). Teaching about Indian Religions. *Learning for Living* 10(5): 5–9.

415 Patel, N. (1976) Hinduism outside India: Selective Retention in Gujarati Families. In G.R. Gupta (ed.) *Family and Social Change in Modern India*. New Delhi: Vikas.

416 Patel, Narsi (1972) A Passage from India. *Society* (New Brunswick, N.J.) 9 (April): 25–63.

417 — (1972) Family Dispersal among Indian Immigrants. *International Journal of Sociology of the Family* (Mysore) 2: 168–78.

418 Pearl, D. (1972–73) Immigrant Marriages: Some Legal Problems. *New Community*, 2: 67–73.

419 — (1974–75) Legal Decisions affecting Immigrants. *New Community*, 4: 250–53; 384–87; 445–51.

420 — (1976–77) Legal Decisions affecting Immigrants and Sex Equality. *New Community* 5: 142–46; 259–64.

421 — (1977–78) Legal Decisions affecting Immigrants and Discrimination. *New Community* 6: 287–90.

422 — 1978–79. Legal Decisions Relating to Ethnic Minorities and Discrimination. *New Community* 7: 104–10; 272–77.

423 — (1981–82) Legal Decisions affecting Ethnic Minorities and Discrimination. *New Community* 9: 106–10.

424 Phizacklea, A.M. and Miles, R. (1977–78) The Strike at Grunwick. *New Community* 6: 268–78.

425 Piet, J.H. (1952) *The Logical Presentation of the Saiva Siddhanta Philosophy*. Madras: Christian Literature Society of India.

426 Pocock, D.F. (1957) The Bases of Faction in Gujerat. *British Journal of Sociology* 8: 295–306.

427 — (1972) *Kanbi and Patidar*. Oxford: Clarendon Press.

428 — (1973) *Mind, Body and Wealth*. Oxford: Basil Blackwell.

429 — (1976) Preservation of the Religious Life: Hindu Immigrants in England. *Contributions to Indian Sociology* 10(2) (N.S.): 342–65.

430 Ponniah, V. (1952) *The Saiva Siddhanta Theory of Knowledge*. Annamalainagar: Annamalai University.

431 Prabhavananda, Swami (1961) *The Eternal Companion: Spiritual Teaching of Swami Brahmananda*. Madras: Sri Ramakrishna Math.

432 — (1968) *Religion in Practice*. London: Allen & Unwin.

433 Prabhupada, Swami Bhaktivedanta (1972) *Bhagavad Gita as It Is*. New York: Macmillan.

434 — (1972) *The Perfection of Yoga*. New York: Bhaktivedanta Book Trust.

435 — (1977) *The Science of Self-Realization*. London: Bhaktivedanta Book Trust.

436 Prasad, Ram Chandra (1978) *Rajneesh: The Mystic of Feeling*. Delhi: Motilal Banarsidass.

437 Price, M. (1977) Divine Light in a Festive Mood. *New Society* 40(766): 500–01.

438 Prickett, J. (1978) *Initiation Rites*. London: Lutterworth.

439 — (1980) *Death*. London: Lutterworth.

440 — (1985) *Marriage and the Family*. London: Lutterworth.

441 Purdom, C.B. (1964) *The God-Man*. London: Allen & Unwin.

442 Pye, E.M. (1979) On Comparing Buddhism and Christianity. *Studies* 5: 1–20.

443 Rai, L.L. (1967) *A History of the Arya Samaj*. Bombay: Orient Longmans.

444 Rai Chaudhuri, S.K. (1966) *Swami Vivekananda, the Man and His Mission*. Calcutta: Scientific Book Agency.

445 Rajdev, S.M. (1966) *Bhakta Shri Jalaram*. Rajkot: the author.

446 Rajghatta, C. (1985) Is Sai Baba on His Way Out? *Sunday* (Madras): 8–14 September.

447 Ram, S. (1984) *A Geographical Analysis of Indians in Bradford: Spatial Distribution and Temporal Trends, 1971–1981* (Working Paper No. 384). Leeds: University of Leeds.

448 Ramachandran, A. (1979) *Hanuman*. London: A & C Black.

449 Ramamoorthy, H. and Ganapati, R. (1981) *Baba: Sathya Sai*. Madras: Satya Jyoti.

450 Ramanujan, A.K. (1973) *Speaking of Siva*. Harmondsworth: Penguin.

451 Rampton, M.B.H. (1981) The English of UK Ethnic Minority School-children of South Asian Extraction. MA thesis, University of London (Institute of Education).

452 Rankin, J. (1984) Teaching Hinduism: Some Key Ideas. *British Journal of Religious Education* **6**(3): 133–36, 160.

453 Rao, D.P.S. (1972) *Five Contemporary Gurus in the Shirdi (Sai Baba) Tradition*. Bangalore: Christian Institute for the Study of Religion and Society.

454 Rao, V.K.R.V. (1979) *Swami Vivekananda: the Prophet of Vedantic Socialism*. New Delhi: Ministry of Information and Broadcasting.

455 Ravindra (1978) *The White Lotus: at the Feet of the Mother*. New Delhi: S. Chand.

456 Ray, S. (1985) *Saraswati Puja*. Exeter: Religious and Moral Education Press.

457 Rayapati, J.P. (1973) *Early American Interest in Vedanta*. London: Asia Publishing House.

458 Redfield, R. (1956) *Peasant Society and Culture*. Chicago: University of Chicago Press.

459 Renzio, T.D. (1969) *The Flower Children*. London: Solstice.

460 Resource Centre for Multiracial Education, Peterborough (1981) *Divali and Other Aspects of Hinduism* (3rd edn). Peterborough: Resource Centre for Multiracial Education.

461 Rex, J. (1982) West Indian and Asian Youth. In E. Cashmore and B. Troyna (eds) *Black Youth in Crisis*. London: Allen & Unwin.

462 Richardson, H. (1977) *Deprogramming: Documenting the Issue*. New York and Toronto: American Civil Liberties Union and the Toronto School of Theology.

463 — (1980) *New Religions and Mental Health*. New York and Toronto: Edwin Mellon.

464 Richardson, J. T. (1978) *Conversion Careers: In and Out of the New Religions*. Beverly Hills: Sage.

465 — (1982) *The Deprogramming Controversy: Sociological, Psychological, Legal and Historical Perspectives*. New York: Edwin Mellon.

466 Richmond, A.H. (1975–76) Black and Asian Immigrants in Britain and Canada: Some Comparisons. *New Community* **4**: 501–16.

467 Ries, J.P. (1975) 'God is Not Dead, He Has Simply Changed Clothes ...' A Study of the International Society for Krishna Consciousness. PhD thesis, University of Wisconsin.

468 Robbins, T., and Anthony, D. (1972) Getting Straight with Meher Baba: A Study of Drug-Rehabilitation, Mysticism and Post-adolescent Role Conflict. *Journal for the Scientific Study of Religion*, **11** (June): 122–40.

469 — (1978) New Religious Movements and the Social System: Integration, Disintegration, or Transformation. *The Annual Review of the Social Sciences of Religion*. The Hague.

470 — (1981) *In Gods We Trust: New Patterns of Religious Pluralism in America*. New Brunswick (N.J.) and London: Transaction Books.

471 — (1982) Deprogramming, Brainwashing, and the Medicalization of Deviant Religious Groups. *Social Problems* **29**(3): 283–97.

472 Robbins, T., Anthony, D., and Richardson, J. (1978) Theory and Research on Today's New Religions. *Sociological Analysis*, **39**(2): 95–122.

473 Robinson, V. (1979) Contrasts between Asian and White Housing Choice. *New Community*, **7**: 195–202.

474 — (1979) Choice and Constraint in Asian Housing in Blackburn. *New Community* **7**: 390–96.

475 — (1980) Correlates of Asian Immigration: 1959–1974. *New Community* **8**: 115–22.

476 — (1986) *Transients, Settlers and Refugees: Asians in Britain*. Oxford: Clarendon Press.

477 Rochford, E.B. (1982) Recruitment Strategies, Ideology and Organization in the Hare Krishna Movement. *Social Problems* **29**(4): 399–410.

478 — (1985) *Hare Krishna in America*. New Brunswick, N.J.: Rutgers University Press.

479 Rogaly, J. (1977) *Grunwick*. Harmondsworth: Penguin.

480 Rolls, E. (1977) Religious Education in a Pluralist Society: A Basic Course in Hinduism. *Character Potential* **8**(2): 86–91.

481 Ronalds, C., Vaughan, J.P., and Sprackling, P. (1977) Asian Mothers' Use of General Practitioner and Maternal/Child Welfare Services. *Journal of the Royal College of General Practitioners* pp. 281–83.

482 Rose, E.J.B. (1969) *Colour and Citizenship*. London: Oxford University Press.

483 Rose, E.J.B. and Deakin, N. (1969) The Sending Societies: the Migrations from India and Pakistan; Adaptation or Withdrawal: Indians. In *Colour and Citizenship: A Report on British Race Relations*. London: Oxford University Press.

484 Roy, B.K. (1970) *Socio-political Views of Vivekananda*. New Delhi: People's Publishing House.

485 Ruhela, S.P. and Robinson, D. (1976) *Sai Baba and his Message: a Challenge to Behavioural Sciences*. Delhi: Vikas.

486 Sahukar, M. (1973) *Sai Baba: The Saint of Shirdi*. Bombay: Somaiya.

487 Saifullah-Khan, V. (1975) Asian Women in Britain: Strategies of Adjustment of Indian and Pakistani Migrants. In A. De Souza (ed.) *Women in Contemporary India*. Delhi: Manohar.

488 — (1977) *Bilingualism and Linguistic Minorities in Britain*. London: Runnymede Trust.

489 — (1979) Work and Network: South Asian Women in South London. In S. Wallman (ed.) *Ethnicity at Work*. London: Macmillan.

490 — Ethnic Identity among South Asians in the UK. In M. Gaborieau and A. Thorner (eds) *Asie du Sud: Traditions et Changements*. Paris: Éditions du CNRS.

491 — (1979) *Minority Families in Britain*. London: Macmillan.

492 — (1980) The 'Mother-Tongue' of Linguistic Minorities in Multicultural England. *Journal of Multilingual and Multicultural Development* **1**(1): 71–88.

493 — (1982) The Role of the Culture of Dominance in Structuring the Experience of Ethnic Minorities. In C. Husband (ed.) *'Race' in Britain: Continuity and Change*. London: Hutchinson.

494 Saliba, J.A. (1980) The Guru: Perceptions of American Devotees of the Divine Light Mission. *Horizons* 7(1): 69–81.

495 Sandweiss, S.H. (1975) *Sai Baba: The Holy Man and the Psychiatrist*. San Diego: Birth Day Publishing.

496 Saran, A.K. (1969) Religion and Society: the Hindu View. *International Yearbook for the Sociology of Religion* 5: 42–67.

497 Sarkar, P.R. (1973) *Baba's Grace: Discourses of Shri Shri Anandamurti*. Los Altos Hills, Calif.: Ananda Marg.

498 Sastri, S. (1911) *History of the Brahmo Samaj*. 2 vols. Calcutta: R. Chatterji.

499 Saunders, N. (1975) *Alternative England and Wales*. London: Nic Saunders.

500 Schofield, D. and Channan, O.N. (1974) Oaths of Hindu, Sikh and Muslim Witnesses. *New Community* 3: 409–11.

501 Schomerus, H.W. (1912) *Der Caiva-Siddhanta: eine Mystik Indiens*. Leipzig: J.C. Hinrichs'sche Buchhandlung. (Partial English translation in *Saiva Siddhanta*, 1966, 1:2,3,4; 1967, 2:1/2; 1974, 9:3/4; 1975, 10:1/2; 1976, 11:2,3; 1977, 12:1; 1978, 13:1/2; 1979, 14:1,3.

502 Schools Council (1971) *Religious Education in Secondary Schools* (Schools Council Working Paper No. 36). London: Evans/Methuen.

503 — (1978) *The Hindu Way* ('Journeys into Religion' series, Schools Council Religious Education in Secondary Schools Project). St Albans: Hart-Davis Educational.

504 Schubring, W. (1962) Sahajananda und die Svami-Narayaniyas, eine Reformierte Brahmanische Gemeinde. In *Nachrichten der Akademie der Wissenschaften in Göttingen, Philologische-Historische Klasse*. Göttingen: Vandenhoeck und Ruprecht.

505 Schulman, A. (1971) *Baba*. New York: Viking Press.

506 Schwartz, B.M. (1967) *Caste in Overseas Indian Communities*. San Francisco: Chandler.

507 Scott D. (1976) Kabir: Maverick and Mystic. PhD thesis, University of Wisconsin (Madison).

508 Sen, P.K. (1933) *Biography of a New Faith*. Calcutta: Thacker, Spink.

509 Shah, I.H. (1980) Sri Sathya Sai Seva Organization: Aims and Accomplishments. In *Golden Age 1980*. Prasanthi Nilayam: Sri Sathya Sai Books and Publications.

510 Shapiro, R. (1978) Mind Control or Intensity of Faith: the Constitutional Protection of Religious Beliefs. *Harvard Civil Rights – Civil Liberties Law Review* 13 (3): 751–97.

511 Sharma, A. (1974) The Hare Krishna Movement: A Study. *Visvabharati Quarterly*, 40(2): 154–78.

512 Sharma, D. (1984) *Hindu Belief and Practice*. London: Edward Arnold.

513 Sharma, S.M. (1980) Perception of Political Institutions among Asian and English Adolescents in Britain. *New Community* **8**: 240–47.

514 Sharma, U. (1971) *Rampal and his Family*. London: Collins.

515 Sharpe E.J. (1971) *Thinking about Hinduism*. London: Lutterworth.

516 — (1975) *Comparative Religion: A History*. London: Duckworth.

517 — (1975) The Phenomenology of Religion. *Learning for Living* **15**(1).

518 Shringy, R.K. (1977) *Philosophy of J. Krishnamurti*. New Delhi: Munshiram Manoharlal.

519 Shupe, A. D. and Bromley, D. (1980) *The New Vigilantes: Anti-Cultists, Deprogrammers, and the New Religions*. Beverly Hills: Sage.

520 Shupe, A. D., Spielman, R., and Stigall, S. (1977) Deprogramming: the New Exorcism. *American Behavioural Scientist* **20**(6): 941–56.

521 Sinclair-Stevenson, M. (1920) *The Rites of the Twice-Born*. London: Oxford University Press. (Reprinted 1971, Oriental Books Reprint Co., New Delhi.)

522 Singer, M. (1959) The Great Tradition in a Metropolitan Center: Madras. In M. Singer (ed.) *Traditional India: Structure and Change*. New York: American Folklore Society.

523 — (1968) The Radha-Krishna Bhajans of Madras City. In M. Singer (ed.) *Krishna: Myths, Rites and Attitudes*. Chicago: Chicago University Press.

524 Singer, P. (1970) *Sadhus and Charisma*. Bombay: Asia Publishing House.

525 Singh, A.K. (1963) *Indian Students in Britain*. London: Asia Publishing House.

526 Singh, Arjan (1979) *Dayanand Saraswati: Founder of Arya Samaj*. New Delhi: Ess Ess Publications.

527 Singh, T.B. (1976) *Satya Sai Baba: the Godman of India*. Delhi: Hind Pocket Books.

528 Sinha, Jadunath (1976). *The Philosophy and Religion of Chaitanya and His Followers*. Calcutta: Sinha.

529 Sivananda Radha, Swami (1978) *Kundalini: Yoga for the West*. Spokane, Wash.: Timeless Books.

530 Smart, N. (1964) *The Teacher and Christian Belief*. London: James Clarke.

531 — (1967) A New Look at Religious Studies: the Lancaster Idea. *Learning for Living*, September.

532 — (1968) *Secular Education and the Logic of Religion*. London: Faber & Faber.

533 — (1969) *Doctrine and Argument in Indian Philosophy*. London: Allen & Unwin.

534 — (1971) *The Religious Experience of Mankind*. London: Fontana.

535 — (1973) *The Science of Religion and the Sociology of Knowledge*. Princeton: Princeton University Press.

536 — (1982) Asian Cultures and the Impact of the West. In E. Barker (ed.) *New Religious Movements: a Perspective for Understanding Society*. New York: Edwin Mellon.

537 Smith, D.J. (1976) *The Facts of Racial Disadvantage: a National Survey*. London: Political and Economic Planning.

538 Smith, W. C. (1964) *The Meaning and End of Religion*. New York: Mentor Books.

539 Solanki, R. (1975–76) A View of the Asian Press in Britain. *New Community* 4: 471–72.

540 Sopher, D.E. (1967) *Geography of Religions*. Englewood Cliffs, N.J.: Prentice Hall.

541 Spittles, B. (1974) Bhushra's Life. *New Society* **498**: 30 May.

542 Swallow, D.A. (1976) Living Saints and their Devotees: A Study of Guru Cults in Urban Orissa. PhD thesis, University of Cambridge.

543 — (1982) Ashes and Powers: Myth, Rite and Miracle in an Indian Godman's Cult. *Modern Asian Studies* **16**(1): 123–58.

544 Sykes, D.E. (1973) Transcendental Meditation as applied to Criminal Justice Reform, Drug Rehabilitation and Society in General. *University of Maryland Law Forum* **3**(2): 37–53.

545 Tambs-Lyche, H. (1975) A Comparison of Gujarati Communities in London and the Midlands. *New Community* 4: 349–55.

546 — (1980b) Gujarati Communities in Norway and Britain: Some Comparative Notes. *New Community* 8: 288–94.

547 — (1980a) *London Patidars*. London: Routledge & Kegan Paul.

548 Tapasyananda, Swami (1969) *Sri Sarada Devi: the Holy Mother*. Mylapore (Madras): Sri Ramakrishna Math.

549 Tart, C.T. (1969) *Altered States of Consciousness*. New York: John Wiley.

550 Taylor, D. (1984) The Sai Baba Movement and Multi-ethnic Education in Britain. *Religion Today* 1 (2/3): 13–14.

551 — (1986) The Sai Baba Movement in Britain: Aims and Methods. In P. Clarke (ed.) *The New Evangelists*. London: Ethnographica Publishers.

552 Taylor, J.H. (1972–73) High Unemployment and Coloured Leavers: the Tyneside Pattern. *New Community* 2: 85–9.

553 — (1976) *The Half-Way Generation*. Newcastle: NFER.

554 Teifion, M. B. (1982) A Way to God: Hindu Beliefs in Leicester and Leicestershire. MPhil thesis, University of Leicester.

555 Thakur, M. and Williams, R. (1975–76) Hopeful Travellers: a Study of Asian Graduates working in Britain. *New Community* 4: 476–92.

556 Thakur, Bhaktivinoda (1946) *Sri Chaitanya Mahaprabhu: His Life and Precepts* (7th edn). Calcutta: Gaudiya Mission.

557 Thomas, W. (1930) *Hinduism Invades America*. New York: Beacon.

558 Thompson, J. and Heelas, P. (1986) *The Way of the Heart: The Rajneesh Movement*. Wellingborough; Aquarian.

559 Thoothi, N.A. (1935) *The Vaishnavas of Gujarat*. London and Bombay: Longmans.

560 Tinker, H. (1974) *A New System of Slavery: the Export of Indian Labour Overseas, 1830–1920*. London: Oxford University Press.

561 — (1976) *Separate and Unequal: India and the Indians in the British Commonwealth, 1920–1950*. London: C. Hurst.

562 — (1977) *The Banyan Tree: Overseas Emigrants from India, Pakistan and Bangladesh*. London: Oxford University Press.

563 Tirtha, B.P. (1947) *Sri Chaitanya Mahaprabhu*. Calcutta: Gaudiya Mission.

564 Turnbull, D. (1985) A Critique of Materials Used to Present Hinduism in English Schools. MLitt. thesis, University of Oxford.

565 Turner, V. (1974) *Dramas, Fields and Metaphors*. Ithaca: Cornell University Press.

566 Underhill, M.M. (1921) *The Hindu Religious Year*. Calcutta: Association Press.

567 Vable, D. (1983) *The Arya Samaj: Hindu without Hinduism*. New Delhi: Vikas.

568 Van Den Berghs and Jurgens Ltd (1976) *Asians in Britain*. London: Nutrition Publication.

569 Vaudeville, C. (1974) *Kabir*. Oxford: Clarendon Press.

570 Visram, R. (1986) *Ayahs, Lascars and Princes: the Story of Indians in Britain 1700–1947*. London: Pluto.

571 Vivekananda, Swami (1964) *The Complete Works of Swami Vivekananda*. 8 vols. Calcutta: Advaita Ashrama.

572 Waardenburg, J. (1973) *Classical Approaches to the Study of Religion*. 2 vols. The Hague: Mouton.

573 — (1978) *Reflections on the Study of Religion*. The Hague: Mouton.

574 Wach, J. (1944) *Sociology of Religion*. Chicago: Chicago University Press.

575 Wallace, R.K. (1970) Physiological Effects of Transcendental Meditation. *Science* **167** (March 27): 1751–754.

576 Wallace, R.K. and Benson, H. (1972) The Physiology of Meditation. *Scientific American* **226**(2): 84–90.

577 Wallis, R. (1975) *Sectarianism: Analyses of Religious and Non-religious Sects*. London: Peter Owen.

578 — (1976) *The Road to Total Freedom: a Sociological Analysis of Scientology*. New York: Columbia University Press.

579 — (1979) *Salvation and Protest: Studies of Social and Religious Movements*. London: Frances Pinter.

580 Ward, R.H. (1973) What Future for the Ugandan Asians? *New Community* **2**: 372–78.

581 Ward, R.H., Nowikowski, S., and Fenton, M. (1978) Settlement in the Suburbs: an Analysis of Asians in Manchester. *International Journal of Contemporary Sociology*.

582 Watson, J.L. (1977) *Between Two Cultures*. Oxford: Basil Blackwell.

583 Weber, M. (1958) *The Religion of India*. New York: The Free Press; London: Collier-Macmillan.

584 — (1968) *Economy and Society*. (Edited by G. Roth and C. Wittich.) Vol. 1. New York: Bedminster Press.

585 Weeraperuma, S. (1965) Colour and Equality. In H. Tajfel and J. Dawson (eds) *Disappointed Guests*. London: Oxford University Press.

586 Weightman, S.C.R. (1978) Hinduism and Religious Education. In R. Jackson (ed.) *Perspectives on World Religions*. London: School of Oriental & African Studies.

587 — (1984) Hinduism, Scholarship and the Teacher. *British Journal of Religious Education* **6**(3): 121–25.

588 Weir, S. (1973) Ugandan Asians: One Year Later. *New Community* **2**: 379–80.

589 West London Institute of Higher Education (n.d.) *A Hindu Family in Southall.* London: West London Institute of Higher Education.

590 Westcott, G.W. (1907) *Kabir and the Kabir Panth.* Cawnpore: Christ Church Mission Press.

591 White, C.S.J. (1972) Sai Baba Movement: Approaches to the Study of Indian Saints. *Journal of Asian Studies* **31**: 863–84.

592 White, J. (1972) *The Highest State of Consciousness.* New York: Doubleday.

593 White, J.W. (1979) *Kundalini, Evolution and Enlightenment.* New York: Anchor Books.

594 Whitworth, J. and Shiels, M. (1982) From Across the Black Water, Two Varieties of Hinduism – the Hare Krishnas and the Ramakrishna Vedanta Society. In E. Barker (ed.) *New Religious Movements.* New York: Edwin Mellon.

595 Wilding, J. (1981) *Ethnic Minority Languages in the Classroom? A Survey of Asian Parents in Leicester.* Leicester: Council for Community Relations.

596 Wilkinson, T. (1974) Uganda Asians in Leicester: Initial Resettlement. *New Community* **3**: 147–49.

597 Williams, R.B. (1982) Holy Man as Religious Specialist. *Encounter* **43**(1): 61–97.

598 — (1984) *A New Face of Hinduism: the Swaminarayan Religion.* Cambridge: University Press.

599 Wilson, A. (1978) *Finding a Voice: Asian Women in Britain.* London: Virago.

600 Wilson, B. (1970) *Religious Sects: A Sociological Study.* London: Weidenfeld & Nicolson.

601 — (1973, 1975) *Magic and the Millenium.* London: Heinemann/ St Albans: Granada.

602 — (1976) *Contemporary Transformations of Religion.* London: Oxford University Press.

603 — (1978) *Sects and Society.* Westport, Conn.: Greenwood.

604 — (1981) *The Social Impact of New Religious Movements.* New York: Rose of Sharon.

605 Winchester, S.W.C. (1974–75) Immigrant Areas in Coventry 1971. *New Community* **4**(1): 97–104.

606 Winslow, J.C. (1958) *The Christian Approach to the Hindu.* London: Edinburgh House.

607 Woodlum, E. (1977) The Development of the Transcendental Meditation Movement. *The Zetetic,* 1/2 (Spring/Summer): 38–48.

608 Wright, P.L. (1968) *The Coloured Worker in British Industry: with Special Reference to the Midlands and North of England.* London: Oxford University Press.

609 Yajnik, J.A. (1972) *The Philosophy of Swaminarayan.* Ahmedabad: L.D. Institute of Indology.

610 Yale, J. (1961) *A Yankee and the Swamis.* London: Allen & Unwin.

611 Yogananda, P. (1973) *Autobiography of a Yogi.* Los Angeles: Self-realization Fellowship.

612 Yogeshananda, Swami (1973) *The Way of the Hindu.* Amersham: Hulton.

613 York Shap (1985) *Understanding the Hindu Tradition: Papers of the 3rd York Shap Conference.* York: York Religious Education Centre.

614 Young, R.F. (1981) *Resistant Hinduism: Sanskrit Sources on Anti-Christian Apologetics in Early Nineteenth Century India.* (Publications of the De Nobili Research Library No. 8.) Leiden: E.J. Brill.

615 Zarwan, J. (1977) Indian Businessmen in Kenya during the Twentieth Century. PhD thesis, Yale University.

616 Zeretsky, I. and Leone, M.P. (1974) *Religious Movements in Contemporary America.* Princeton: Princeton University Press.

CLASSIFICATION BY SUBJECT

The task of compiling a bibliography on Hinduism in Great Britain is fraught with problems. Religion pervades so many aspects of a Hindu's life – diet, health, family, economic achievement – that it is impossible to draw a line between what is and what is not religious. To this confusion, a further complication is added. Hinduism is commonly understood to be the religion of Hindu people; that is, people of South Asian origin. Yet there are modern Hindus who claim not to believe in religion and who accordingly distance themselves from Hinduism. And there are some people (e.g. English and Welsh) who are not Hindu by birth but who become 'Hindu' in the sense that they convert to a Hindu religious tradition. Thus there are Hindus who are not Hindu; and there are non-Hindus who are. Hinduism seems to defeat the aim of the bibliographer to operate in world of clear, unambiguous categories.

Given these problems, it seemed sensible to consider the bibliography as emerging out of two different, but related, interests: first, the literature on Hindu peoples in Britain; and second, Hindu religious traditions in Britain. I have accordingly divided this classification into these two broad, and partially overlapping, categories.

The first section comprises the literature on Hindu peoples; that is, Hindu peoples of South Asian origin who – in some sense of the term – consider themselves to be Hindu. Thus the literature on Muslims, Sikhs, Jains, and Christians has been excluded. This material has then been grouped into appropriate sub-sections: caste, education, ethnicity, family, etc. Religion, in the sense of formal religious institutions (e.g. temple worship, religious sects, and festivals), is one of the sub-sections. The other sub-sections, to a greater or lesser extent, have bearing on the topic of religion.

The second section comprises the literature on Hindu religious traditions, or what some sociologists call 'new religious movements'. In compiling this section, entries were restricted to those religious traditions which actually operate in Great Britain for which information is available. Thus important Hindu religious traditions, such as the Ramanandis, have been excluded because they have no following in this country; and other traditions, such as the Brahma Kumaris, have not been included, for I have been unable to find published information on them. Since all the Hindu religious traditions in Britain are organized internationally and based in India, there seemed no sense in limiting the entries in this section to the research carried out in Britain. Hence I have supplemented the entries with some information on these traditions in India as well as in other countries overseas. It must be mentioned that several of these religious organizations run their own publishing houses. Some also have their own research institutes wherein devotees prove the scientific or rational basis of the sectarian leader's spiritual methods. To include all this sort of literature – promotional, 'scientific', and otherwise – would have required, in turn, a book-length bibliography. I have shied away from such an undertaking.

HINDUS IN BRITAIN

For further information on Hindus and Hinduism in Britain the reader may find the following bibliographies of use: 200, 238, 342.

Name index

Abji Bapa 72; cult 70–1
Abramson, H.J. 158
Aggarwal, M. 220
Agni 5, 165–66, 169
Akhandadhidasa 90–1, 99
Amba Mata 25, 39–40; *see also* Mata
Amin, Idi 8
Avyaktananda, Swami 6

Babb, L.A. 174–75
Bahree, P. 222n
Baldeva Singh, Raja 5
Ballard, C. 64, 180, 196
Barot, R. vii, 12, 35, 67–80
Bart, R. 68
Berger, P. 32
Bhagavan Goswami Maharaja 88
Bhagavantham, Dr 130
Bhaktisiddhanta Saraswati 83–4
Bhaktivedanta Swami Prabhupada 82–8
Bhaktivinoda Thakur 83
Bharati, A. 140
Bhattacharya, J.N. 69
Bodewitz, H.W. 166
Bowen, D. vii, 9, 12, 15–31, 232, 248
Brah, A. 180
Bridger, P. 212
Briggs, H.C. 68
Bromley, P.M. 180, 190–91, 193

Burghart, R. vii, 1–14, 85, 118, 224–51
Butler, D.G. 211, 222n

Carey, S.F. vii, 6, 13, 81–99, 134–56, 228, 234, 240–41, 248
Chaitanya, Sri 83
Channan, O.N. 231
Chatterjee family 97–8
Chavda, D.C. 22
Clothey, F.W. 118n
Coedès, G. 3
Cole, W.O. 209, 211, 217
Cox, H. 137

Dahya, B. 16, 18
Daner, F. 82
Das, V. 51, 152
David, K. 118n
Davies, R. 211
Dayanand, Swami 5
Derrett, J.D.M. 182
Desai, R. 7, 9, 26, 30n, 208
de Silva, P.R. *see* Subramanium, Guru
Dimock, E. 84
Dumont, L. 78–9
Dvarakanath Tagore 5

Ewan, J. 222n

Subject index